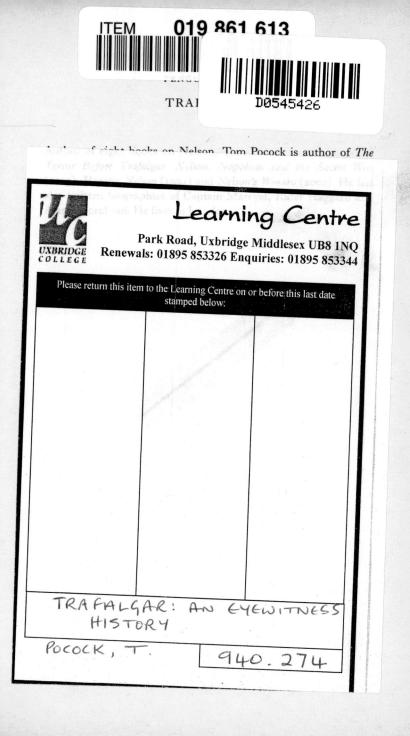

ITEM **019 861 613**

D0545426

TRA

Author of eight books on Nelson, Tom Pocock is author of *The
Terror Before Trafalgar, Nelson, Napoleon and the Secret War*,
Horatio Nelson (1994) and *Nelson's Women* (2003). He had
written biographies of Captain Marryat, Rider Haggard and
Lord Exmouth. He lives in London.

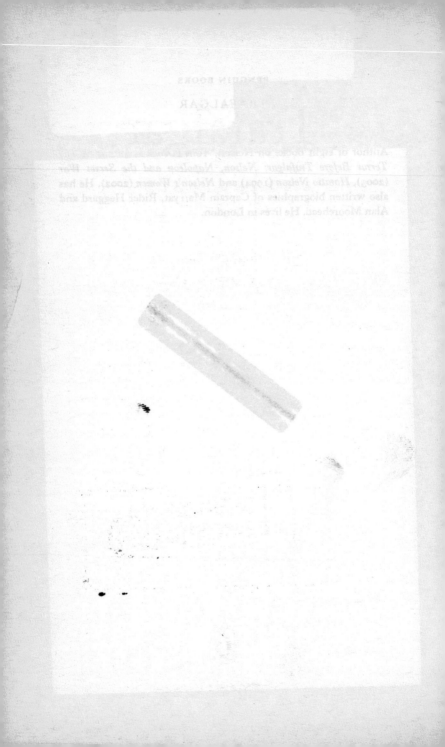

Trafalgar

AN EYEWITNESS HISTORY

Edited and Introduced by
TOM POCOCK

PENGUIN BOOKS

PENGUIN BOOKS

Published by the Penguin Group
Penguin Books Ltd, 80 Strand, London WC2R ORL, England
Penguin Group (USA), Inc., 375 Hudson Street, New York, New York 10014, USA
Penguin Group (Canada), 90 Eglinton Avenue East, Suite 700, Toronto, Ontario, Canada M4P 2Y3
(a division of Pearson Penguin Canada Inc.)
Penguin Ireland, 25 St Stephen's Green, Dublin 2, Ireland
(a division of Penguin Books Ltd)
Penguin Group (Australia), 250 Camberwell Road,
Camberwell, Victoria 3124, Australia (a division of Pearson Australia Group Pty Ltd)
Penguin Books India Pvt Ltd, 11 Community Centre,
Panchsheel Park, New Delhi – 110 017, India
Penguin Group (NZ), cnr Airborne and Rosedale Roads, Albany,
Auckland 1310, New Zealand (a division of Pearson New Zealand Ltd)
Penguin Books (South Africa) (Pty) Ltd, 24 Sturdee Avenue,
Rosebank 2196, Johannesburg, South Africa

Penguin Books Ltd, Registered Offices: 80 Strand, London WC2R ORL, England

www.penguin.com

First published by The Folio Society 2005
Published in Penguin Books 2005
1

Selection and editorial matter copyright © Tom Pocock, 2005
All rights reserved

Map and Plans drawn by Reginald Piggott

The moral right of the author has been asserted

Printed in England by Clays Ltd, St Ives plc

CONTENTS

Introduction

The Battle of Trafalgar on 21 October 1805 was more than a decisive naval engagement. It did, of course, have a profound effect on the course of the war with Napoleonic France, militarily, economically and politically. But it also changed the way that the British saw themselves and their place in the world. Its direct effects lasted for a century but its echoes continue to resound.

At the time, Lord Nelson's victory at Trafalgar was seen, first and foremost, as the final defeat of Napoleon's hopes of invading the British Isles. Napoleon himself had been directly involved in such plans since 1798 – before his expedition to Egypt – and by 1805 had assembled hundreds of landing-craft along the coast of northern France and the Low Countries. When the battle was fought, it was known that the *Grande Armée* had struck camp along the Channel coast and was marching east. However this was not the end of the threat. The emperor urgently needed to crush his Austrian and Russian enemies before their armies could combine, and he did so that year at Ulm and Austerlitz. But he had not abandoned his plan to invade Britain: 'I shall stop the Russians and Austrians from uniting. I shall beat them before they can meet. Then, the Continent pacified, I shall come back to the camp on the ocean and start work all over again.' He would soon have built more than enough battleships to replace those he had lost at Trafalgar. But he knew that for all his brilliant success on land and for all his public bluster, he could never again face the British at sea.

With the command of the sea – the narrow seas around Europe and the broad oceans beyond – that Nelson won in October 1805, he gave his country complete freedom for its global trade, a freedom now denied to the French Empire and which was not to be challenged until the rise of an aggressive Germany and the First World War. Only the British could now expect to trade unopposed with the West and East Indies, the Americas, India and the Far East. Understanding this, Napoleon was impelled to expand the land frontiers of his empire. This led to British fears that he might seek to dominate, and even annex, the vast, ramshackle Ottoman Empire in the Middle East, which he could reach overland. It was also a factor in his decision to invade Russia. That was to be his undoing, as it was for Hitler more than a century later.

Seen from the twenty-first century, naval warfare in the time of sail requires a major effort of the imagination. Accustomed to weapons of mass destruction, satellite surveillance and communication, and nuclear-powered submarines, we find it difficult to envisage those fleets of wooden battleships driven by great spreads of canvas and dependent upon the vagaries of the wind. Nelson's flagship, the *Victory*, preserved in dock at Portsmouth, can only hint at the spectacle once presented by a fleet at sea.

The sailing warship, powered by wind and human muscle, was the ultimate development of technology before the coming of steam and iron. A first-rate ship of the line, a battleship, mounting a hundred two- to three-ton guns, would be built of some three thousand tons of timber and propelled by nearly ten tons of sails covering more than two acres, controlled by a thousand wooden pulley blocks in the rigging. Each ship was manned by more than eight hundred men, and would embark provisions to maintain them at sea for four months.

Before Trafalgar, the fleet that Nelson had led across the Atlantic and back in pursuit of the French was at sea for two years. Seamen were rarely allowed ashore for fear that they might desert. They became, in effect, creatures of the sea, strong as leopards and agile as monkeys from their constant duties high on the masts, yards and rigging, making, or taking in, sail. Many were volunteers, who joined to escape privation ashore or in the hope of prize-money; others were simply rounded up by press-gangs at British seaports in a crude form of conscription; some had even been released from prison to serve at sea.

To train and discipline such men to work their ships

and fight the enemy was the task of the officers, who led regulated careers, wore standard uniforms* and hoped to make a fortune from the prize-money that was earned by captures at sea. By the time of Trafalgar, this was a popular career for the younger sons of the aristocracy, the middle classes, and those who had risen by merit from the lower deck.

Most of the captains of Nelson's ships at Trafalgar had been at sea since the age of twelve or thirteen. Their education had mainly been in seamanship, navigation and gunnery but they sometimes had, like their contemporaries ashore, a smattering of the Classics and were taught to write in copperplate style so that their logs would be legible. They were physically tough, most of them unsophisticated men inspired by a simple patriotism; and they were unashamedly emotional. It has been said that never before 1805 had the Royal Navy been at so high a pitch of skill, health and morale.

Nelson himself possessed the qualities he tried to inspire. The son of a gentle, well-educated, middle-class clergyman in rural Norfolk and of a forthright mother related to the landowning aristocracy, he had gone to sea at twelve in 1771. As a young captain, he had made his name on an expedition against the Spanish in Nicaragua and in the Caribbean. Returning home, he had then been unemployed on half pay in the village of his birth, Burnham Thorpe, where he lived with the wife he had married in the West Indies, Fanny Nisbet. There he read not only the newspapers in the hope of reports that war might again be imminent – with the prospect of a naval mobilisation that might give him employment – but also books of seafaring and travel, as well as the plays of Shakespeare, which would inspire some of his most memorable sayings.

Recalled to duty for the war against Revolutionary France at the beginning of 1793, Nelson quickly made up for his wasted years, distinguishing himself in action afloat and ashore in the Mediterranean. When the British were

---

* Seamen wore practical clothing, usually made of wool, sailcloth and waxed canvas, although rich captains sometimes paid for their boats' crews to wear smart uniforms of their design.

driven from that sea in 1797, he achieved his first fame at the Battle of Cape St Vincent in the Atlantic: without orders, he steered his ship into the heart of the enemy fleet and captured two enemy ships. Promoted rear-admiral, he survived the defeat that followed his victory, when his attack on Tenerife failed miserably and he lost his right arm in storming ashore. But he had been seen to lead from the front, taking personal risks which were usually regarded as unnecessary for an officer of his rank.

So, to his surprise and delight, it was the one-armed Nelson who, in 1798, was chosen to lead the British back into the Mediterranean. It was he who searched for the French fleet when General Bonaparte (as he still was) disappeared from Toulon that summer with a huge convoy of troopships and nobody knew where he had gone. He found them off the coast of Egypt and, although the French army had already been landed, he destroyed the escorting fleet in Aboukir Bay on 1 August. French plans to occupy and colonise Egypt, and eventually march on India, had been thwarted.

Now followed the most controversial period of Nelson's life. In Naples to refit his flagship, the *Vanguard*, and to recover from a wound, he fell in love with Emma Hamilton, wife of the British minister to the kingdom of the Two Sicilies (southern Italy and Sicily), Sir William Hamilton. The scandal tarnished Nelson's reputation, as did his disregarding of orders he considered unwise and his part in the ruthless suppression of the republican rising in Naples.

Nelson returned to England in November 1800. Following the Hamilton affair, and his final break with his wife, he was ostracised at court and by polite society. However, as his legend spread, he came to be loved by the mass of the population as much as by the men he commanded. This was not only because he was seen to share their hardships and dangers, and had shown extraordinary courage in action, but because he appeared as vulnerable to temptation as the next man.

Nelson was socially insecure but he was also ambitious. His success rested not only upon his brilliance as a tactician at sea but on his skill as a communicator and administrator. He was able to make fast friends of his captains, even after only one or two meetings. Often those who had never met him regarded him as a friend; only five of his twenty-seven captains at Trafalgar had served with him before but they all dined with him in his flagship before the battle and thereafter saw their relationship with him as having been close. One of these, Edward Codrington, said that, above all, they all wanted to please Nelson; twenty-six of these captains repainted their ships' hulls before the battle in Nelson's favourite colours – yellow and black bands – so that when the gun-ports were open the 'Nelson's chequer' effect was produced.

When, just before the battle, Nelson made his famous signal, 'England expects that every man will do his duty,' the remarkable thing was not so much the message itself but that, by using the new signal code invented by Commodore Sir Home Popham, he seemed to have spoken personally to the whole fleet. Signals had previously been used to order practical manoeuvres, give warnings and orders to open or cease fire; this was the first time they had been used to speak person to person.

As a naval administrator Nelson paid more attention than other admirals to the welfare of his men, including the supply of fresh food, notably fruit and vegetables to guard them against scurvy and other illnesses prevalent at sea. It was obviously impossible for an admiral to monitor the personal problems of the thousands of men in his ships, but by the example of his concern for welfare in the *Victory* and amongst the captains he knew, he hoped to spread such attitudes to his officers. Stories of Nelson's humanity were well known by the ratings. While he would stand on the quarterdeck throughout an action, he expected that, before his ship opened fire, his men would lie down between their guns to minimise casualties.

Nelson's fame and popularity were undimmed by what was seen as an unnecessary victory over the Danes at Copenhagen in 1801 and a clear defeat off Boulogne in the same year. When the Peace of Amiens collapsed and war was renewed in May 1803, the government unhesitatingly chose Nelson as the new commander-in-chief in the Mediterranean. He had set new standards for the Royal Navy in leadership and in fighting: from now on the enemy had not only to be defeated but annihilated.

The importance of the Mediterranean, for both sides, was that the main French naval base was at Toulon, which, with Brest, would be the principal springboard for any future offensive by sea, whether to the Middle East, the West Indies or the British Isles. It was the threat of invasion that concentrated British minds most. British strategy aimed to prevent the combining of the French fleets into a force which could cover a cross-Channel invasion. The enemy fleets had to be blockaded in their ports – Brest, Rochefort and Toulon and, once Spain had entered the war in December 1804, Spanish ports as well. But this was not the final answer. There was always the chance that they could escape: an offshore gale that would carry them out of port would also drive the blockaders off-station, so opening a passage to the seas.

If the enemy were intercepted at sea, success would depend upon two factors. First, the use of tactics to outwit the enemy so as to reduce and eliminate any advantage in numbers he might have, perhaps by overwhelming one part of his fleet before the remainder could come to his aid. Second, by making the fullest use of the superior skills of British sailors in working and fighting their ships, acquired from long experience at sea.

Fundamentally, there was little to choose between the ships of the opposing fleets; indeed, those built by France and its ally Spain were sometimes superior to the weather-worn ships of the British. There was no lack of courage among French and Spanish crews, as was to be demonstrated at Trafalgar. Experience was what counted. To the British, accustomed to long months at sea, the handling of sails and the fighting of guns in a pitching and rolling ship had become routine. This was not so for the French and Spanish, cooped up in port for so long. Moreover, the British were led by officers bred to the life and glorying in a tradition of success. The French officer corps had been broken up by the Revolution and had yet to recover.

At the beginning of 1805, the French had fifty-six ships of the line ready for sea and were building another fifteen, against eighty-three British ships with another twenty to thirty in reserve or refitting. But when the Spanish fleet was added to the French the combined fleets comprised more than one hundred battleships. So the opposing fleets could expect to meet on broadly equal terms. And that is what happened in October 1805.

Reports of Trafalgar reached Paris about ten days after the battle and were forwarded to Napoleon in central Europe. It is tempting to imagine that they might have arrived even sooner because of a grim event in Paris. Exactly one week after the battle, a British naval officer, Captain John Wright, who had been an intelligence agent operating with the French royalists inside France, was murdered in the Temple prison. Could this have been revenge for Trafalgar? Was it possible for the news to have reached Paris from Cadiz in a week? Probably this will never be known.

The news reached Napoleon in Moravia while he was on the march towards Austerlitz. When the despatch was handed to him at dinner, he was said to have shown no emotion and remarked that it would not change his 'plans for cruising'. Either he did not comprehend the consequences, or was in denial of them. But he did impose a tight censorship of the press until one newspaper, the *Journal du Commerce*, printed a report of 'a most bloody action' off Cadiz in which 'both fleets fought with the greatest determination' and which had been followed by a violent storm that 'dispersed the ships'. Spanish newspapers were under no such inhibition, presenting the catastrophe as an honourable, indeed glorious, defeat. The truth was kept from the French people until after the announcement of Napoleon's great victory at Austerlitz on 2 December.

In May 1806, when the emperor had returned to Paris, he received the two French captains who had most distinguished themselves at Trafalgar – Lucas of the *Redoutable* and Infernet of the *Intrépide* – and decorated them with the Légion d'honneur. That, however, was the only glory he could snatch from the disaster.

In the English-speaking world, the memory of Nelson, his achievement and his death at the hour of victory was kept alive by what amounted to a commemorative industry. It began with paintings and prints, continued with monuments and memorials, plaster busts and Staffordshire pottery figures. There was an outpouring of verse, songs and theatrical tableaux and, eventually, plays and films. Towns, rivers and mountains around the world were named after Nelson. His achievements were spelled out in hundreds of books, beginning with the commissioning in 1806 of a major biography by the Reverend James Stanier Clarke and John McArthur – who knew many of Nelson's friends through their writing for the *Naval Chronicle* – and reaching a zenith in the bicentennial year 2005. Not only do the wardrooms of the Royal Navy continue to hold Trafalgar Night dinners and toast 'The Immortal Memory of Lord Nelson', but there are also innumerable groups, formal and informal, and two societies devoted to the commemoration and study of Nelson.

The decisive outcome at Trafalgar has inevitably been a subject for revisionist historians. It has even been said that Trafalgar was of little real importance because the result of any such encounter was a foregone conclusion. This might not have been entirely so in other circumstances: had Nelson himself been absent, or had his former rival been present, the able French admiral Louis-René Latouche-Tréville, who had defeated him off Boulogne and commanded what was to be the opposing fleet until his sudden death in 1804. The importance of the battle is that it *was* fought and won.

A more absurd canard, often repeated, is that Nelson was seeking his own death in battle that day because he foresaw the breakdown of his relationship with Emma Hamilton and the probability of his own blindness, for the sight of his undamaged eye – his right eye had been almost blinded in 1794 during the campaign in Corsica – was deteriorating. This notion is refuted by the amount of written evidence to the contrary. Nelson was still in love with Emma, adored their child, Horatia, and longed to see them both again. He had certainly felt premonitions of death in battle, or from disease, for he was a lifelong hypochondriac and pessimist. Thoughts of suicide, however, would never have entered his head.

The most significant results of the victory were long-term. Nelson himself gave the British a hero, a figurehead, such as they had lacked, to counter the baleful appeal of Napoleon himself. His extraordinary life ended not only in high style but in what has been described as 'the poetry of Trafalgar'. His serenity during the last days of his life and the sublime words of his prayer before battle seemed to assume almost religious undertones: the saviour sacrificing himself for his people. Indeed, Lord Byron described Nelson as 'Britannia's god of war', and his image, as no other, has remained at the heart of the British ethos.

The victory itself, the culmination of what had become accustomed success at sea, if not on land, gave the British, now secure on their island, an unshakeable self-confidence. Later in the nineteenth century, this sometimes led to over-confidence and the Royal Navy, upon which all depended, became inclined to rest on its laurels. The two great challenges by Germany in the twentieth century brought Britain close to defeat, but it could be argued that this self-confidence, although often unjustified, was the most significant single factor in carrying the nation through to eventual victory. After Trafalgar, every British admiral would be judged by what were seen to be the standards of Nelson.

Trafalgar itself continues to be subjected to as close scrutiny as the character and actions of Nelson himself. The tactics he employed in his final battle have been analysed by a wide range of investigators, ranging from the report in 1913 of *The Committee Appointed by the Admiralty to Examine and Consider the Evidence Relating to the Tactics Employed by Nelson at the Battle of Trafalgar, Presented to Parliament by Command of His Majesty* to the thesis *Admiral Nelson's Tactics at the Battle of Trafalgar*, written for the University of Edinburgh in 2004 by a German academic Dr Marianne Czisnik, which pays particular attention to Nelson's feint attack on the enemy van. The battle has been the subject of lectures, debates and seminars in the bicentennial year as well as television and radio programmes for mass audiences.

Perhaps 2005 is an appropriate time to look back at this pivotal event. With Britain now a racially and religiously mixed nation and on the brink of drawing even closer to integration with its old enemies on the Continent in some form of United Europe, the event of October 1805 can be seen with more detachment; with admiration for past skill and courage, with nostalgia for perceived lost glories, or simply with wonder. Certainly it cannot be ignored, or forgotten.

TOM POCOCK

2005

Editorial Note

This book tells the story of the Battle of Trafalgar and the two-year naval campaign that preceded it primarily through the words of those who took part. Many of the accounts are taken from letters home, others from despatches, reports, logs, journals and even recorded conversations. They frequently cover a longer period of time than the day of the battle itself, ranging from the two years of the entire campaign through the month of the final deployments to the week of the engagement and the storm that followed. In order to provide a generally chronological narrative, such texts have often had to be divided into separate sections rather than reproduced in their entirety.

By their very nature, the extracts included in this book do not attempt to provide a systematic or objective account of any individual's role in the campaign nor a comprehensive overview of all the key incidents in the battle. They have been selected for their value in illuminating the reactions and behaviour of those – on both sides and from most ranks – involved in the battle as much as for their record of the most significant episodes in the engagement. All are linked together by editorial commentary which aims to set their contemporary viewpoints in the context of the people involved, the politics of the time, the tactical and strategic decisions taken, and, indeed, in the sweep of history.

Many subsequent accounts of Trafalgar have suffered from the inherent confusion which the participants must have felt after Nelson's and Collingwood's divisions broke the enemy line. As has already been noted (p. xvi), the essence of Nelson's plan was to create a 'pell-mell battle' of individual, close-quarter engagements, in which superior British gunnery would prove decisive. This is what happened and, as the two British columns and the van, centre and rear divisions of the Franco-Spanish combined fleet became inextricably intermingled, it can be difficult to keep hold of the thread. To prevent readers from losing their bearings entirely, the narrative follows the attack of Collingwood's column, then presents that by Nelson's, even though they overlapped in time; and thereafter treats the 'pell-mell battle' as such without attempting to follow throughout the erratic course of every individual ship. The final positions of the two fleets, when night fell and the hurricane began to blow out of the Atlantic, wiped the tactical slate clean. The outcome was clear to all.

With the extracts selected for this book coming from such a variety of printed and manuscript sources, a certain degree of standardisation is necessary in order for readers not to be unduly distracted by often markedly different stylistic preferences. To this end, such things as typographical conventions, spellings, capitalisation, the styling of ships' names and (to a lesser extent) punctuation have been gently harmonised. However, in those instances where the departure from current usage seems particularly characteristic, then the original forms have been left unchanged. On the few occasions where, for clarity's sake, it has been necessary to make minor excisions (usually of brief cross-references to something described elsewhere in a source), this has been done silently. Significant cuts within extracts, though, have been marked with ellipses. Other substantive emendations or editorial interpolations within quoted matter have been placed inside square brackets. All footnotes are editorial, and have been confined to elucidating otherwise obscure remarks within the eyewitness accounts.

Neptuno 80
Scipion 74
Intrépide 74
Formidable 80
Mont-Blanc 74
Duguay-Trouin 74
Rayo 100
San Francisco de Asis 74
San Augustin 74
Héros 74
Santissima Trinidad 140
Bucentaure 80
Redoutable 74
San Justo 74
Neptune 84
San Leandro 64
Indomptable 80
Santa Ana 112
Fougueux 74
Monarca 74
Pluton 74
Algésiras 74
Bahama 74
Aigle 74
Swiftsure 74
Argonaute 74
Argonauta 80
San Ildefonso 74
Achille 74
Principe de Asturias 112
Berwick 74
San Juan Nepomuceno 74

Montañes 74

Africa 64

N

Wind direction

Euryalus 36
Neptune 98
Victory 100
Téméraire 98
Leviathan 74
Britannia 100
Ajax 74
Conqueror 74
Agamemnon 64
Orion 74
Royal Sovereign 100
74 Belleisle
Prince 98
74 Mars
80 Tonnant
Minotaur 74
Bellerophon 74
Spartiate 74
Achilles 74
Colossus 74
Thunderer 74
Dreadnought 98
Revenge 74
Defence 74
Defiance 74
Swiftsure 74
Polyphemus 64

The Victory Cutting the Line
12.45 p.m.

San Augustin
Héros
Conqueror
Leviathan
Santissima Trinidad
Britannia
Neptune
Bucentaure
Ajax
Téméraire
Neptune
Victory
Redoutable
Orion
San Justo
San Leandro

Santa Ana
Royal Sovereign
Indomptable
Mars
Belleisle
Fougueux

TRAFALGAR
Position of the Fleets
12 noon

British ships
French ships
Spanish ships
74 Number of guns

CHAPTER I

Prelude

In May 1803, the gardens of Merton Place, an elegant country house in Surrey to the south-west of London, were at their best. Indeed, all that Merton had promised to its owner, Vice-Admiral Viscount Nelson, seemed about to be fulfilled. Although it had been his home for nearly eighteen months, only now did he feel himself sole master of his long-imagined retreat. Sir William Hamilton, the husband of his lover, had died in April; although this would not enable him to marry Emma – his wife Fanny was still alive and divorce was out of the question – he would be able to flout convention and live there with her. Also, their two-year-old child Horatia could at last be removed from the care of her nurse in London, and be brought to live with them, albeit as Nelson's ward, or god-daughter. At Marylebone parish church, she was christened Horatia Nelson Thompson, so maintaining the public fiction of her origins.

Yet now Nelson had to leave what he called 'Paradise Merton' and return to sea. For there were even greater holds on his loyalty: his professional ambition and sense of duty. Renewed war with France had seemed increasingly inevitable since the beginning of the year and memories of the lull in the fighting – the Peace of Amiens with its social jollities and the fashion for trips to Paris – were already fading. Napoleon Bonaparte, First Consul and dictator of France, had broken the spirit of the truce: he had refused to evacuate Holland, had annexed Piedmont, Parma and Elba, and had put down a Swiss revolt against French domination, while accusing the British of treachery for failing to hand over Malta to his Russian allies. When war came, the British would have to defend themselves by containing the French fleet in their Atlantic and Mediterranean ports.

Nelson had, nearly five years earlier, destroyed Bonaparte's fleet at the Battle of the Nile in Aboukir Bay and made the Mediterranean his own. Aware that he would have to secure the Mediterranean again, he had, at the beginning of the year, when attending the House of Lords, sent a note to the Prime Minister,

Henry Addington, saying simply, 'Whenever it is necessary, I am your admiral.' Britain despatched an ultimatum to France: if she would evacuate Holland and agree to the British occupation of Malta for another ten years, peace could continue. There was no agreement. On 16 May, Nelson was appointed commander-in-chief in the Mediterranean. Two days later Britain declared war on France, and Nelson hoisted his flag in the *Victory*, a stately three-decked battleship, at Spithead off Portsmouth. The *Victory* was not only the most famous ship of the line in the Royal Navy but she had often served as a flagship and had been fitted as such. She might be old, laid down in 1759, ten months after Nelson's birth, but she was a fast sailer and mounted a hundred guns, or more, as a first-rate line of battle ship.

Nelson's yearning for Emma, Horatia and Merton was set aside. Next day, the admiral wrote to Lord St Vincent, the First Lord of the Admiralty: 'You may rely, my dear lord, that nothing shall be left undone by me, by a vigorous and active exertion of the force under my command, to bring about a happy peace. If the devil stands at the door, the *Victory* shall sail tomorrow forenoon.' On 20 May it was reported: 'This morning, about ten o'clock, his Lordship went off in a heavy shower and sailed with a northerly wind' to take up his command. For Nelson, it was a climactic moment.

The admiral's orders were to make for Ushant and there to rendezvous with Admiral Sir William Cornwallis – his friend 'Billy Blue' – whose fleet was blockading the French naval base of Brest. Should Cornwallis need reinforcements, the Admiralty had instructed Nelson to transfer to the *Amphion*, a fine frigate commanded by another old friend Captain Thomas Hardy, and leave the *Victory* off Brest. Arriving off Ushant, Nelson found no sign of Cornwallis's fleet, which had been blown off-station by a gale. 'It blows strong,' he wrote. 'What a wind we are losing! If I cannot find the admiral by six o'clock, we must all go into the *Amphion* and leave the *Victory* to my great mortification. So much for the wisdom of my superiors.' The deadline past, Nelson and his staff were rowed across to the frigate in a rough sea. John Scott, the admiral's Secretary, explained in a letter to Lady Hamilton:

Lord Nelson is in excellent good health and spirits. We

were hopeful when we left Spithead to have fallen in with Admiral Cornwallis off Brest, and that he would have allowed the *Victory* to have gone on with us, but we were much disappointed at not finding the commander-in-chief, particularly as his Lordship considered it proper to leave the *Victory* to *add* to the *show* off Brest, and proceed in this ship [the *Amphion*]. This change gave a good deal of trouble, besides the many inconveniencies which must be submitted to before the *Victory* may join. His Lordship left his steward with *all* his stock, etc., a few trunks of linen excepted, on board that ship, so that until we get her, we shall not be able to commence regular *house*keeping, but I beg to assure your Ladyship, the moment that is the case, the most strict regard shall be paid to everything that concerns his Lordship's interests.

Nelson made the best of it, writing to Emma Hamilton, 'Our wind has been foul, blowing fresh and a nasty sea . . . Your dear picture and Horatia's are hung up and it revives me even to look upon them.'

At Gibraltar, Nelson went ashore to tell the governor that war had been declared and to ask for news from within the Mediterranean. His principal task was the same as Cornwallis's: to blockade the French fleet in port. The foundation of British naval strategy was to prevent the French squadrons from leaving their Mediterranean and Atlantic bases and forming a fleet that could dominate the English Channel and cover the invasion of England by Napoleon's *Grande Armée*, then massing along the Continental shores of the Channel and North Sea. In the Mediterranean, the main French base was at Toulon, and this became the focus of Nelson's attention. He was also determined to prevent French expeditions again sailing for Egypt or against his old friends the Bourbon King Ferdinand and Queen Maria Carolina of the Two Sicilies and their twin capitals of Naples and Palermo.

Before forming his fleet off Toulon, Nelson decided to sail in the *Amphion* round the western basin of the Mediterranean and assess the strategic and political scene. He was depressed by what he found, particularly by the state of the Bourbon's kingdom, which he himself had saved from French occupation four years earlier and which was now maintaining an uneasy neutrality. After calling at Messina, he noted in a memorandum:

The state of Sicily is almost as bad as a civilised country can be. There are no troops fit to be called such, with a scarcity of corn never known, and of course bread so dear that the lower class of people are discontented. The nobles are oppressors, and the middle rank wish for a change; and although they would prefer us to the French, yet I believe they would receive the French, rather than not change from the oppression of the nobles. The citadel of Messina is strong and in good order, but with a few miserable troops badly paid, if paid at all; therefore, what could be expected from them? A French frigate has been there lately . . . they have good eyes, and many at Messina are seduced by them; and if the Neapolitan troops at Malta were removed there, I fear we should find more enemies and the French more friends . . .

The lower class of boat-people came on board with fruit, etc. – their expressions were strong, and ought to be received with caution, yet with their hearts in their hands, you may gather sentiments to form a pretty accurate opinion. '*Viva il rè! Viva Inglesé!* When will the English come back to Messina?' On asking them if they had any Jacobins in the city, 'Yes, the gentry who wear their hats so – on one side the head' – *vide* Bond Street loungers.

The *Amphion* continued on to Naples, where the king and queen were in residence. Here, five years before, Nelson had fallen in love with Emma Hamilton and now he allowed himself a moment of nostalgia, writing to her, 'Close to Capri, the view of Vesuvius calls so many circumstances to my mind that it almost overpowers my feelings.' He called on the royal family briefly to assure them that a British ship of the line would be stationed in the Bay of Naples in case another French invasion forced them to flee once more to Palermo. Sailing on towards Toulon, Nelson arrived there on 8 July to take command of his fleet, comprising nine ships of the line and three frigates. Soon afterwards, he was joined by his flagship, the *Victory*, which

Cornwallis had released from duty off Brest.

Here, too, there was an echo of the Hamiltons; in this case, Sir William's love of antiquity. Nelson wrote to Henry Addington, the Prime Minister, of a recent capture at sea:

There has been taken in the *Arab*, French corvette, 26 cases of statues, busts, etc., etc., from Athens for the French government. I have taken upon me to order them to be sent to England assigned to Sir Joseph Banks as President of the Royal Society for, if our government choose to buy these articles of antiquity, I think it but proper that it should have the offer. They would sell well in this country. Lord Elgin, I am told, offered £6,000 for a part of them. Of course, the captors think them of great value, but the more valuable, the more desirable for our country to obtain.

Nelson's task was, of course, 'to keep the French fleet in check' and, as he said, 'if they put to sea, to have force enough to *annihilate* them'. As he began the tedious duties of blockade, he explained his unorthodox technique in letters to friends: 'My system is the very contrary to blockading. Every opportunity has been offered the enemy to put to sea, for it is there we hope to realise . . . the expectation of our country'; and 'There seems an idea that I am blocking up the French fleet in Toulon. Nothing could be more untrue. I have never blockaded them a moment. All my wish and the anxious wish of this fleet is to have them out.' His zeal was given an edge by the fact that the seven French battleships and five frigates ready for sea at Toulon were commanded by Vice-Admiral Louis-René Latouche-Tréville, who had decisively defeated his attack on Boulogne two years before. Personal antagonism had been maintained between the two: Latouche sent a few heavy ships to sea to drive off the watching British frigates, then slipped back into Toulon.

As summer turned to autumn, seasonal gales blew in the Gulf of Lyons and sea-keeping changed from cruising in sunshine to riding out storms. Stationing frigates within sight of Toulon and his main fleet below the horizon, Nelson needed a base for replenishment and the repair of storm-damage, and for the rest and recuperation of his men. Corsica was occupied by the French and Malta and Gibraltar were too far away. Nelson, who also worried about his own health, wrote to his agent and confidant, Alexander Davison:

My crazy fleet are getting in a very indifferent state, and others will soon follow. The finest ships in the service will soon be destroyed. I know well enough that if I was to go into Malta, I should save the ships during this bad season; but if I am to watch the French, I must be at sea, and if at sea, must have bad weather; and if the ships are not fit to stand bad weather, they are useless. I do not say much, but I do not believe that Lord St Vincent would have kept the sea with such ships. But my time of service is nearly over. A natural anxiety, of course, must attend my station; but my dear friend, my eyesight fails me most dreadfully. I firmly believe that, in a very few years, I shall be stone blind. It is this only, of all my maladies, that makes me unhappy; but God's will be done. If I am successful against the French, I shall ask my retreat; and if I am not, I hope I shall never live to see it; for no personal exertion on my part shall be spared.

In the end, Nelson chose an anchorage among the barren Maddalena Islands, off the northern tip of Sardinia, named Agincourt Sound; there his ships could shelter from the worst of the gales, while remaining ready to return to their stations south of Toulon when warned by the watching, storm-beaten frigates that the French were out. But, for most of the time, the fleet was at sea, and Nelson paid particular attention to the health of his men, writing in March 1804 to an old friend from the Caribbean, Dr Benjamin Moseley, who now cared for old soldiers at Chelsea Hospital:

The great thing is health, and you will agree with me, that it is easier for an officer to keep men healthy than for a surgeon to cure them, situated as this fleet has been, without a real friendly port where we could get all the things so necessary for us. Yet I have, by changing the cruising ground, not allowing the sameness of prospect to satiate the mind, sometimes looking at Toulon, Ville Franche; sometimes

Barcelona, Rosas; running round Minorca, Majorca, Sardinia, and Corsica, and two or three times anchoring for a few days sending a ship to this place for *onions*, which I find the best thing which can be given to seamen, having always good mutton for the sick; cattle, when we can get it, and plenty of fresh water. In the winter, giving half the allowance of grog instead of all wine. These things are for the commander-in-chief to look to; and shut very nearly out from Spain, and only getting refreshments by stealth from other places, my task has been an arduous one. Cornwallis has great merit for his persevering cruise, but he has everything sent him – we have nothing – we seem forgot by the great folks at home. But our men's minds are always kept up with the daily hope of meeting the enemy. I send you as a curiosity, an account of our deaths and sent to the hospital out of 6,000 men. The fleet put to sea, May 18th, 1803, and is still at sea, not a ship has been refitted or recruited, except what we have done at sea.

You will readily believe that all this must have shook me. My sight is getting very bad, but *I must not* be sick till after the French fleet is taken; after which, I shall soon hope to take you by the hand.

As health improved, life on board the big ships settled into what was, for the officers, a comfortable routine, as Dr Gillespie, a surgeon in the *Victory*, recorded:

At six o'clock my servant brings a light and informs me of the hour, wind, weather and course of the ship, when I immediately dress and generally repair to the deck. Breakfast is announced in the admiral's cabin, where Lord Nelson, Rear-Admiral Murray (the captain of the fleet), Captain Hardy, commander of the *Victory*, the chaplain, secretary, one or two officers of the ship and your humble servant assemble and breakfast on tea, hot rolls, toast, cold tongue, etc., which when finished we repair upon deck to enjoy the majestic sight of the rising sun (scarcely ever obscured in this fine climate) surmounting the smooth and placid waves of the Mediterranean, which supports the lofty and tremendous bulwarks of Britain, following in regular train their admiral in the *Victory*.

Between the hours of seven and two, there is plenty of time for business, study, writing and exercise. At two o'clock a band of music plays till within a quarter of three, when the drum beats the tune called 'The Roast Beef of Old England', to announce the admiral's dinner, which is served up exactly at three o'clock and which generally consists of three courses and a dessert of the choicest fruit, together with three or four of the best wines, champagne and claret not excepted. If a person does not feel himself perfectly at ease, it must be his fault, such is the urbanity and hospitality which reign here . . .

Coffee and liqueurs close the dinner about half-past four or five o'clock, after which the company generally walk the deck, where the band of music plays for nearly an hour. At six o'clock, tea is announced, when the company again assemble in the admiral's cabin, where tea is served up before seven o'clock and, as we are inclined, the party continue to converse with his Lordship, who at this time generally unbends himself, though he is at all times free from stiffness and pomp as a regard to proper dignity will admit, and is very communicative. At eight o'clock a rummer of punch with cake or biscuit is served up, soon after which we wish the admiral a good night (who is generally in bed before nine o'clock). Such is the journal of a day at sea in fine, or at least moderate, weather, in which this floating castle goes through the water with the greatest imaginable steadiness.

Nelson himself had his own daily round:

My routine goes on so regular that one day, except the motion of the ship, is the same as the other. We rise at five, walk the deck till near seven . . . breakfast at seven precisely . . . Dine at three, in fine weather always some of the captains; in general, twelve at table . . . after coffee and tea, no more eating. At a quarter- or half-past eight, give the necessary orders for the night, go to bed, sleep and dream of what is nearest my heart.

The Reverend Alexander Scott, the chaplain of the flagship,* described Nelson's eating habits, which had become frugal since an attack of gout: 'the liver and wing of a fowl and a small plate of macaroni in general composing his meal, during which he occasionally took a glass of champagne. He never exceeded four glasses of wine after dinner and seldom drank three; and even those were diluted with Bristol or common water.' Nelson never went ashore, 'generally walking on deck six or seven hours in the day'. This was in fine weather but the western basin of the Mediterranean was notorious for its storms. At sea, Nelson was unsparing of himself, as Scott recorded:

He possessed such a wonderful activity of mind as even prevented him from taking ordinary repose, seldom enjoying two hours of uninterrupted sleep; and, on several occasions, he did not quit the deck the whole night. At these times, he took no pains to protect himself from the wet, or night air, wearing only a thin greatcoat; and he has frequently, after having his clothes wet through with rain, refused to have them changed, saying that the leather waistcoat which he wore over his flannel one, would secure him from complaint. He seldom wore boots and was consequently very liable to have his feet wet. When this occurred he has often been known to go down to his cabin, throw off his clothes and walk on the carpet in his stockings for the purpose of drying the feet of them. He chose to adopt this uncomfortable expedient rather than give his servants the trouble of assisting him to put on fresh stockings, which, from his having only one hand, he could not himself conveniently effect.

In June 1804, Nelson thought the decisive moment had finally come. He was cruising off Toulon with five sail of the line, while his second-in-command, Rear-Admiral Sir Richard Bickerton, lay sixty miles further out with the rest of the fleet. Two British frigates had given chase to two French ships when they sighted, emerging from the outer harbour of Toulon, eight ships of the line, including Latouche-Tréville's flagship, and six

* A linguist, Scott was also the admiral's interpreter, translator and, in effect, his intelligence officer.

frigates. Nelson formed line of battle but the French, having rescued their two frigates, which appears to have been their sole aim, turned back for Toulon. To Nelson, it seemed 'merely a gasconnade' and another example of what he joked about: 'My friend sometimes plays bo-peep in and out of Toulon, like a mouse at the edge of her hole.' Some weeks later, however, he saw in a Continental newspaper Latouche's report to Paris in which he claimed to have driven the British away from Toulon and pursued them until nightfall. Nelson was incensed, writing to his brother, 'You will have seen Monsieur La Touche's letter of how he chased me and how I *ran*. I keep it and, by God, if I take him, he shall *eat* it!'

This proved a false hope. On 18 August, Latouche, whose health had never recovered from fever contracted during an expedition to the Caribbean to suppress a revolt in Ste Domingue two years earlier, died suddenly on board his flagship. Although he and Nelson had become almost personal rivals, they had been worthy of one another. Many French officers recognised what they had lost, one writing:

After his arrival at Toulon, de Latouche had infected his squadron with his own ardour. We were moored in the outer roads, and two of our vessels in turn were ceaselessly on watch at the entrance of the channel, in order to reply to the insults of the English. As soon as the latter approached, as they were wont to do without suffering any damage, the scouts slipped their cables and within eight minutes were under sail and chasing the enemy. If the latter were supported, additional vessels of ours went to sea. It was continual manoeuvres, followed by engagements which trained our crews and commanders. The admiral, established on the top of Cape Sepet, dominating the Toulon approaches, observed everything both inside and outside, preparing for Nelson worthy adversaries. Unfortunately the bad luck which at that time dogged the affairs of the navy prevented the accomplishment of these great aims; the admiral's health, worn down by bad climates, deteriorated daily, and we had the pain of losing this leader who incarnated so many hopes. He died the 18 August, 1804, during a sortie, on board his vessel *Bucentaure*. His squadron buried him at the top of Cape Sepet, his habitual observation point, and erected a monument in the form of a pyramid, which future generations of sailors will contemplate with respect.

In my career I had already seen many officers, but never met a real leader who could give, like the leader we had just lost, an impression of superior will capable of transforming men and dominating events. Nothing less than a leader of this stamp would have been enough to confront the English squadron, which had been brought to a high degree of perfection by continuous practice at sea and a long sequence of successes. The famous Nelson who commanded it is in my opinion one of the most accomplished seamen who ever lived; a man of rare intelligence, valiant, of indomitable energy, and in addition an implacable enemy of our nation. He made war on us less from duty than from hatred, and drew from this feeling an ardour and an energy which he knew how to share with each of his sailors.

Latouche's command passed to another former officer of the royalist navy, Vice-Admiral Pierre de Villeneuve, who had been one of the few to escape from Nelson's destruction of the French fleet at the Battle of the Nile in 1798. His appointment coincided with a reassessment of grand strategy in Paris by the First Consul and his Minister of Marine, Rear-Admiral Denis Decrès.

The aim was still the invasion of England. This would require control of the English Channel for days, if not weeks, but it was heavily defended by the Royal Navy. Covering the narrows and the southern North Sea, Admiral Lord Keith commanded more than twenty sail of the line; while off Brest and Ushant lay Admiral Sir William Cornwallis with more than thirty battleships, some deployed in detached squadrons cruising off the more southerly Atlantic ports. Then there was Nelson off Toulon with about a dozen sail of the line and the same number of frigates. In addition there were dozens of frigates, brigs and, in the Channel, gunboats.

The French, in port, could muster about the same force, although numbers fluctuated on both sides as ships were sent for refitting, or, in the case of the British, replenishment. In

Brest, Vice-Admiral Honoré Ganteaume commanded more than twenty sail of the line; at least half a dozen, under Rear-Admiral Burgues Missiessy, lay at Rochefort; more ships were scattered around the Spanish coasts, for Spain allowed the French shelter in their ports; and, at Toulon, Villeneuve had about a dozen ships of the line ready for sea.

Then, in the autumn of 1804, the naval balance tilted in favour of the French. Spain, hoping to remain neutral, had been bullied into an alliance with France under which the choice was either to pay huge subsidies to the French or to declare war on Britain. She chose the former option but the British regarded this as almost as belligerent as the latter. In October, British frigates intercepted a Spanish squadron loaded with treasure from South America. When the Spanish refused to surrender, the British opened fire: one ship blew up and the other three were captured. Spanish pride allowed only one response, and on 12 October Spain declared war on Britain. This had the immediate effect of adding a potential reinforcement of some thirty serviceable Spanish ships of the line to the French fleets.

However, the French command was aware that, ship for ship, they were no match for the British, who spent most of their time at sea, gaining experience in working their ships and training in gunnery, while they themselves lay blockaded in harbour. Consequently, they would have to muster overwhelming strength to seize command of the Channel and the only way to achieve this would be to lure the main British fleets away. Their aim was for the French squadrons to break out of Rochefort and Toulon and make for the Caribbean, enticing the British after them, while Ganteaume slipped out of Brest to land an army in Ireland. After attacking the British West Indian islands, the Caribbean force would then double back, making for the Channel to escort the *Grande Armée* across it. Orders for these operations were sent out at the end of 1804.

Accordingly, on 11 January 1805, under cover of a snowstorm, Rear-Admiral Missiessy led five sail of the line and three frigates, with 3,500 soldiers embarked, out of Rochefort and into the Atlantic. His destination was unknown to the British but it seemed as likely that he was heading for the Mediterranean as for the Caribbean. A week after Missiessy's escape, Villeneuve left Toulon with eleven sail of the line and seven frigates. He was immediately sighted by Nelson's watching frigates, which made all sail for Sardinia. Then, as a later account put it:

On January 19th, 1805, Nelson was at anchor in Agincourt Roads, when two of his frigates, the *Active* and *Seahorse*, appeared at the entrance of the Straits of Bonifacio, under a press of sail, with the long expected signal, 'The enemy is at sea.' It was at three o'clock in the afternoon when they anchored near the *Victory*, and at half-past four the English fleet was under sail. It becomes dark there about five o'clock at that time of the year: the wind was blowing strong from the westward, and the fleet could not work to windward against it, so that it was necessary to go through one of the eastern passages which open into the Tuscan sea. Though it was now completely dark, Nelson took the lead in the *Victory*, and resolved to conduct his eleven ships of the line between the rocks of Biscia and the north-east extremity of Sardinia. This passage, whose breadth does not exceed a quarter of a mile, has never since been attempted by any fleet. The English squadron cleared it; formed in a single line ahead; each ship showing a light astern, to guide the one which followed.

Nelson was leading a line of eleven battleships, a force equal to Villeneuve's, but he did not know where to go. Again he suspected another Napoleonic lurch to the east and set sail for Alexandria. But he found no sign of the French and returned to the western Mediterranean. There, on 19 February, he heard that the gale that had carried Villeneuve out to sea had so damaged his ships that he had had to put back and was again at anchor in the calm, sheltered water at Toulon.

Despite a winter at sea, or in the bleak Sardinian anchorage, the health and morale of Nelson's fleet remained good. Dr Gillespie wrote from the flagship to his sister:

As a proof of the state of health enjoyed by the seamen, I may instance the company of this ship, which, consisting of 840 men, contains only one man confined to his bed from sickness, and the other ships (twelve of the line), of from eighty-four to seventy-four guns, are in a similar situation as to health, although the most of them have been stationed off Toulon for upwards of twenty months, during which time very few of the men or officers (in which number is Lord Nelson) have had a foot on shore. You will perceive from this account, my dear sister, that the duties of my office are not likely at present to prove very laborious, and my duty as Inspector of the Naval Hospitals will occasion me to visit, as may be found necessary, Malta, Sicily, Gibraltar, and perhaps Naples, so that from all appearances and my experience hitherto I have no reason to be displeased with the comforts, duties, or emoluments of the office I at present fill, my salary being £465 per annum, and being situated so as to live in a princely style, free from any expense. This exemption from expense arises from my having the honour of forming one of the suite and family of Lord Nelson, whose noble frankness of manner, freedom from vain formality and pomp (so necessary to the decoration of empty little great men), can only be equalled by the unexampled glory of his naval career and the watchful and persevering diligence with which he commands this fleet. On my coming on board I found that the recommendations which my former services in the navy had procured for me from several friends, had conciliated towards me the good opinion of his Lordship and his officers, and I immediately became one of the family.

Meanwhile, in the Caribbean, Missiessy had been raiding British islands with some success until, in March, he heard from Paris that Villeneuve had failed to break out of Toulon and that therefore he must return. This attempt to exercise global strategy had failed.

CHAPTER 2

Chase

In December 1804, the First Consul of France had been crowned emperor. At a flamboyant ceremony in the cathedral of Notre Dame, he himself had taken the crown from the hands of the Pope, whom he had bullied into participating, and placed it on his own head. Intent on founding a new royal dynasty not only for France but for Europe, Napoleon began to present his relations with the thrones and principalities of Europe and to create a new aristocracy out of his marshals and political favourites. It was time to stamp his will upon his new world with an invasion of the British Isles that would add them to his empire. His planned strategy still seemed sound, lessons had been learned from the abortive attempt in January, and he now decided that the grand design should be carried out on an even larger scale. However, the current deployments were not quite as seen from Paris. The orders for Missiessy to return to France had been countermanded and he had been instructed to remain in the Caribbean until joined by the other squadrons from Europe; but these instructions never reached him and he was on his way back across the Atlantic when, early in March 1805, Napoleon's new directives were sent to Brest and Toulon.

This time, Ganteaume was to break out of Brest with twenty-one sail of the line, collect four French and nine Spanish battleships from Ferrol, then cross the Atlantic to join Missiessy at Martinique. Villeneuve was to follow from Toulon with eleven ships of the line and a dozen Spanish ships from Cartagena and Cadiz. Then the combined fleet of some fifty ships of the line would be led by Villeneuve back across the Atlantic – leaving, it was hoped, the pursuing British searching for them among the sugar islands – to seize command of the English Channel so that the invasion could begin. But, unknown to the French admirals at Brest and Toulon, Missiessy would not be in the Caribbean to meet them. He had sailed back across the Atlantic as ordered and would be in Rochefort by the time the main fleets could reach the Caribbean.

On 27 March, Ganteaume's fleet weighed anchor and left the great harbour of Brest, waiting in Berthaume Bay for a wind to carry them west. When the twenty-one battleships had cleared the harbour mouth, the horizon had been empty, but later that day it was crowded with the distant sails of seventeen British ships of the line – with doubtless more just out of sight – ready for the climactic battle they had awaited so long. On board one of them, the *Mars*, Captain George Duff wrote to his wife in England:

The French fleet have got out of Brest harbour, and are anchored in Berthaume Bay. We were within four or five miles of them, our inshore ships just out of gunshot. We are all clear for action, but it depends entirely upon them to come to it, or not. If they do, I trust we shall be victorious, and have a lasting peace. They are at present four sail of the line more than us; but if we do our duty, I think we shall give a very good account of them. Should I unfortunately fall, I hope that our friends will take care of you and our dear little ones. I have done all, my dearest Sophia, to make you and them comfortable, that our small funds would allow; but I am sorry to say, they are very small indeed.

Ganteaume, however, decided that he could not risk fighting his way through the British blockade, but two days later Villeneuve escaped from Toulon with eleven ships of the line. It was a repeat of his last attempt except that, this time, there was a strong breeze from the north-east, exactly right for the run south-west to the Straits of Gibraltar. Only two British frigates were off Toulon, while Nelson and his twelve sail of the line cruised off Majorca. The news reached Nelson on 4 April but there was no hint as to Villeneuve's destination. So, again fearing an attack on Naples, Sicily or Alexandria, Nelson steered for Palermo as a central position from which to meet any threat within the Mediterranean. But the danger was elsewhere: on the 18th, Nelson heard that ten days earlier the French fleet had passed Gibraltar westward-bound. The enemy was in the Atlantic, but where was he going now? It seemed probable that Villeneuve would head north to collect the squadrons from the Spanish and French ports on the Atlantic coast and then make for the English Channel to cover an invasion. Nelson crowded sail in pursuit, passing Gibraltar himself and, off Cape Trafalgar, hailed a Portuguese warship to learn that the French had been sighted steering west into the Atlantic. That could only mean an attack in the West Indies. Nelson sailed in pursuit.

Villeneuve, believing Nelson to have gone to Alexandria, had sailed confidently westward, failing to stop at Cartagena to collect the Spanish ships lying there, but calling at Cadiz to summon Admiral Don Frederico Gravina to follow him with as many of his fifteen battleships as were ready for sea. So began the long chase, with Nelson knowing that he was a week behind his quarry. A young officer aboard the 74-gun *Intrépide*, Lieutenant the Marquis Gicquel des Touches, recorded the mood in the French fleet:

. . . we left on 29 March for the West Indies, thereby beginning that interminable voyage in which, badly commanded, held back by the slower ships, we crossed the seas, haunted by the spectre of Nelson . . .

However, fortune at first seemed to favour us. Nelson, learning that the French squadron had left Toulon, hurried into pursuit. Misled by certain signs, and by skilfully managed rumours, he went as far as Egypt in search of it. Meanwhile we quietly effected our union with the Spanish squadron at Cadiz on 8 April. We then made sail directly for Martinique, where we arrived on 12 May . . .

The boredom of this crossing and the hesitations of the command had led to a certain lassitude, one consequence of which was that my brother Oliver, then a midshipman on the *Fougueux*, resigned on arrival at Martinique. I tried to dissuade him, but he said he was tired of that idle life, and would fight the English on his own account and in his own way. He had made the acquaintance of some Saint Malo sailors who with their privateers were waging ceaseless war against the English in the Gulf of Mexico, ravaging the coasts and taking merchant ships.

French spirits, however, recovered when Villeneuve ordered that their first objective was to recapture Diamond Rock. This sheer, almost unclimbable crag rearing out of the sea a mile off the harbour of Fort de France in Martinique had been seized by the British a year and a half before and had defied all attempts to retake it. Manned by a lieutenant and a hundred seamen, it had been cheekily named 'His Majesty's Sloop *Diamond Rock*' and the heavy and long-barrelled guns, which had been hoisted up the cliffs, had an extreme range of two miles. Villeneuve was so furious when one of his ships passed within its reach and was hit by 24-pound shot that he detached a squadron to bombard it. But, as the French soon found, 'The enemy, having concealed themselves in caves, the balls were unable to annoy them.' Although troops were landed on a little beach, they came under heavy fire and, lacking scaling ladders, could not attempt an assault. Four days later, with the British running short of ammunition, an earthquake tremor cracked the water cistern, which began to leak, and French sailors used ropes to reach the cave where British provisions were stored. At long last, the British surrendered.

Meanwhile Nelson's pursuit of Villeneuve was hampered by the slow sailing of one of his ships, the *Superb*, commanded by his friend Captain Richard Keats. With the characteristic generosity that endeared him to his captains, Nelson wrote to Keats in mid-Atlantic, sending his letter across by boat:

My dear Keats,

I am fearful that you may think that the *Superb* does not go so fast as I could wish. However that may be (for if we all went ten knots, I should not think it fast enough), yet I would have you be assured that I know and feel that the *Superb* does all which is possible for a ship to accomplish; and I desire that you will not fret upon the occasion . . . I think we have been from Cape St Vincent very fortunate, and shall be in the West Indies time enough to secure Jamaica, which I think is their object.

For the British, Villeneuve's destination was still a mystery. Nelson decided to make straight for Barbados in the hope of hearing definite news. On 4 July, he anchored in Carlisle Bay and was immediately given conflicting reports. The senior naval officer in the Caribbean thought the French must have made for Jamaica to the north-west and he had already sent reinforcements there, while two generals opted for Trinidad to the south-east. Nelson himself expected (rightly) that Villeneuve had first gone to the French island of Martinique, which he would now have left. Finally, with reinforcements already sent to Jamaica, he reluctantly accepted the generals' view that he himself should make for Trinidad. He wrote to Emma Hamilton: 'I find myself within six days of the enemy and I have every reason to hope that the 6th June will immortalise your own Nelson . . . Pray for my success and my laurels I shall lay with pleasure at your feet and a sweet kiss will be ample reward for all your faithful Nelson's hard fag.'

But when he arrived off Trinidad the calm blue bays were empty and he realised that he had been misled: 'Ah, my Emma, June 6th would have been a great day for me . . . I have ever found that if I was left and acted as my poor noodle told me was right I should seldom err.'

While at Martinique, Villeneuve had been reinforced by one French and six Spanish battleships, which had followed from Cadiz. His orders were to wait there forty days until Ganteaume arrived from Brest; then the combined fleets were to sweep back across the Atlantic to seize and hold the English Channel so that Napoleon's invasion could begin. While waiting, Villeneuve was expected to ravage the rich British sugar islands. His first target was Antigua and, lying in the roadstead off the capital, St John's, he found a British convoy of sugar-ships. Mrs Jane Kerby, an Englishwoman who was staying there, wrote home:

You will have heard, no doubt, how the combined fleet escaped by magic; how in reality (for I counted them myself) they rode triumphant on our element for some weeks; how the gallant hero of the Nile followed them; how he, misled, could not catch them; and how they, afraid of him, gave up the attack on the little England of the archipelago [Antigua], whose bulwarks are rock instead of oak; how they tried to look warlike and form a line of battle but they could not; but how, alas!, they scampered after our sugar, took fourteen ships full of that and various good things going to our friends; and how to our great joy they burnt this treasure . . . by the manoeuvres of a [British] sloop of war, who, afraid of being taken, threw out signals as for approaching friends and they, *toujours Nelson en tête*, saw his ghost and destroyed their prizes in the most premature and shameful hurry. I cannot attempt to describe our terrors, movings, removings, packings and unpackings. I consider myself now quite as a heroine, having commanded myself . . . Since Lord Nelson left us, which was on the 12th or 14th June (the French fleet having been with us on the 8th), we have been quiet.

While off Antigua, Villeneuve heard for the first time that Nelson had arrived in the Caribbean with more than a dozen battleships and was in hot pursuit. He conferred with Admiral Gravina and decided that, rather than face Nelson, they would follow the emperor's broad strategy and return to Europe. So, on 11 June, after only twenty-seven days in the Caribbean instead of the prescribed forty, and a week after Nelson's arrival, the combined fleet sailed back across the Atlantic. Nelson soon heard that the enemy had gone and assumed that they were making for Cadiz, or the Mediterranean. He sent a letter to the Admiralty by a fast brig, reporting his plans, at the same time writing to a friend in London, saying, 'I have only a moment to say I am going towards the Mediterranean after Gravina and Villeneuve and hope to catch them.' Two days after Villeneuve had sailed, Nelson followed. A week later, scanning the sea ahead, he noted, 'Saw three planks, which I think came from the French fleet. Very miserable, which is very foolish.'

'Out of humour', as he put it, Nelson could only guess at whether Villeneuve was heading for the Mediterranean, the Spanish ports or the English Channel. His frustration was compounded by the wind, which often dropped so that his ships heaved slowly over the swell at walking-pace. When it was calm and boats could be launched, he tried to cheer himself by inviting his captains across from their ships to dine, on one occasion writing to Captain William Hargood of the *Belleisle*: 'As the day is very fine, I was in hopes that you would have come on board and dined. From winds, and the expectation of winds, I have been afraid to ask my friends to dinner; but I need not, I hope, assure you how glad I am always to see you.' But invitations would quickly be cancelled if Nelson saw high, wispy clouds or the twitch of a sail that might indicate a coming breeze.

He expressed his mood in letters to the Admiralty and friends at home. Although he knew that by the time any letter arrived the chase might well have reached its conclusion, Nelson wrote to his friend the Duke of Clarence, the king's son and the future King William IV, who had served with him at sea:

Your Royal Highness will easily conceive the misery I am feeling at having missed the French fleet; and entirely owing to false information sent from St Lucia . . . But for that false information, I should have been off Port Royal [Fort de France in Martinique] as they were putting to sea; and our battle, most probably, would have been fought on the spot where the brave Rodney beat de Grasse.* I am rather inclined to believe they are pushing for Europe to get out of our way: the moment my mind is made up, I shall stand for the Straits' Mouth [Gibraltar].

With no news of the enemy at the Azores, Nelson sailed on to Gibraltar, where he anchored on 20 July. At last, he wrote, 'Went on shore for the first time since June 16th, 1803, and from having my foot out of the *Victory*, two years wanting two days.' To Emma, he wrote, 'After two years' hard fag it has been mortifying not being able to get at the enemy . . . John Bull may be angry but he never had an officer who served him more faithfully.' But John Bull was not angry and Nelson was cheered by a letter from an old friend, Hercules Ross, a former West Indian sugar planter, who recognised the epic scale of the long chase:

I have both by night and day accompanied your Lordship across the Atlantic and as far to the westward as the scene of our earlier days, and imagination has often carried me aloft to look for the flying enemy. Though disappointed, thank God, my noble friend has returned in health. But there still remains some great action to be achieved by him worthy of his fame.

---

* The Battle of the Saints in 1782, when Rodney broke the French line.

CHAPTER 3

Interlude

The news that Villeneuve was returning from the Caribbean and probably making for the English Channel reached the Admiralty late on the night of 8 July 1805. Next morning, Lord Barham, the elderly First Lord, was told and at once sent orders to Cornwallis that the squadron commanded by Vice-Admiral Sir Robert Calder off Cape Finisterre, the north-westerly point of Spain, must be reinforced urgently, while he himself with the Channel fleet barred the Bay of Biscay between Finisterre and Ushant. On 22 July, Calder's fourteen ships of the line were cruising some one hundred miles off Finisterre when out of the morning fog emerged the enemy. It was indeed Villeneuve with his twenty sail of the line and seven frigates. The British formed line of battle and action began. Calder was brave and as ambitious but he lacked initiative and dash; otherwise the outcome would surely have been different.

Lieutenant des Touches of the *Intrépide* imagined that the combined fleet had evaded the British in the thick weather when, as he recorded:

We encountered off Cape Finisterre an English squadron, commanded by Admiral Calder and consisting of 15 ships, of which four were three-deckers. On July 22, in mist, we came upon this squadron about 20 leagues from Ferrol. Neither admiral seemed in a hurry to get to grips, but a fight was inevitable, although it had no decisive result. The persistent mist was a great hindrance. I was at my action station on the forecastle, from which I transmitted to the senior officers such indications as might help them manoeuvre the ship. We supported with our gunfire as long as possible two Spanish ships, the *Firme* and the *San Rafael*, which, having been dismasted, drifted into the English squadron and were taken. Our mizen-mast threatened to fall, and we had to leave the battlefield so as not to share the same fate. Admiral Villeneuve did nothing to rescue the imperilled ships and this uncertain battle, known as the Battle of Cape Finisterre, turned to our disadvantage, because in spite of our enormous numerical superiority we caused no damage to the English . . .

Admiral Calder made no attempt to exploit the timidity of his opponent.

Although Villeneuve escaped with relatively minor loss, he knew that the emperor's grand design of dominating the Channel and invading England had, for the time being, failed. Calder, despite being seen by the British as a failure, had in fact won a strategic victory. Villeneuve was now caught in the net of British fleets and squadrons: Cornwallis with twenty battleships off Brest; Calder off Ferrol with fourteen; Vice-Admiral Sir Cuthbert Collingwood off Cadiz with four; and Nelson off Cape St Vincent and heading north with eleven. Yet even though the French and Spanish could command a stronger battle-fleet – seventy sail of the line against some fifty British – Villeneuve knew that he was trapped and that the only option was to make for a secure port. Cadiz was the obvious choice, but Nelson would be there before him. The only option was Ferrol in northwestern Spain, where he arrived at the end of July.

Nelson meanwhile received orders to leave most of his squadron with Cornwallis and return to Portsmouth in the *Victory*, accompanied by Captain Keats's slow-sailing *Superb*. But before he reached Spithead, he heard details not only of Calder's action but of the disappointment with which the outcome had been received in London. On 16 August, Nelson wrote to his friend Captain Tom Fremantle of the *Neptune* in the knowledge that his views would be circulated amongst his other captains:

I was in truth bewildered by the account of Sir Robert Calder's victory and the joy of the event; together with hearing that John Bull was not content, which I am sorry for. Who can, my dear Fremantle, command all the success which our country may wish? We have fought together and therefore well know what it is. I have had the best disposed fleet of friends, but who can say what will be the event of a battle? And it most sincerely grieves me that in any of the papers it should be insinuated that Lord Nelson could have done better. I should have fought the enemy, so did my friend Calder; but who can say that he will be more successful than another? I only wish to stand on my own merits and not by comparison, one way or the other, upon the conduct of a brother officer. You will forgive this dissertation but I feel upon the occasion . . . I beg my best respects to Mrs Fremantle and with the most sincere wishes that you may have the *Neptune* close alongside a French three-decker.

The *Victory* anchored at Spithead on 18 August. After calling on the admiral commanding at Portsmouth, Nelson hired a fast chaise and set out on the London road, planning to call at his home on the way to the Admiralty. Travelling through the night, he arrived at Merton Place before the household was awake. His welcome was ecstatic. 'What a day of rejoicing at Merton!' exclaimed Emma Hamilton, 'How happy he is to see us all!' Their daughter Horatia was now a lively child of four and his pleasure in her, her mother and the house itself, which Emma had fashioned as a shrine to his fame, was unbounded.

After more than two years at sea, Nelson had noticeably aged and weathered. A Danish visitor, calling at Merton, observed:

Lord Nelson was of middle stature, a thin body and apparently of delicate constitution. The lines of the face were hard but the penetration of his eye threw a light upon his countenance, which tempered its severity and rendered his harsh features in some measure agreeable . . . Lord Nelson had not the least pride of rank; he combined with that degree of dignity, which a man of quality should have, the most engaging address in his air and appearance.

Another guest, Lionel Goldsmid, the young son of Nelson's Jewish friend and neighbour, the financier Benjamin Goldsmid, also failed to be awed by his famous host:

That odd fellow Lord Nelson . . . what a funny-looking fellow he was, he was dressed in a naval coat, white naval breeches with naval buttons at knees, silk stockings, invariably hanging on as if not pulled up, too large and shoes rather high in the quarters, large with buckles. He was kind in the extreme and we all loved him.

Next morning, Nelson and Emma travelled to London, where he had official appointments over the coming days. While waiting in Downing Street for a meeting with Lord Castlereagh, the Secretary of State for War and the Colonies, he shared a waiting-room with a young army officer, whom he did not recognise as Major-General Sir Arthur Wellesley – the future Duke of Wellington – lately returned from his success in India. The general later recalled that he had met

a gentleman, whom from his likeness to his pictures and the loss of an arm, I immediately recognised as Lord Nelson. He could not know who I was, but he entered at once into conversation with me, if I can call it conversation, for it was almost all on his side and all about himself and, in reality, a style so vain and so silly as to surprise and almost disgust me.

I suppose something that I happened to say may have made him guess that I was *somebody* and he went out of the room for a moment, I have no doubt to ask the office-keeper who I was, for when he came back he was altogether a different man, both in manner and matter . . . All that I had thought a charlatan style had vanished and he talked of the state of the country and of the aspect and probabilities of affairs on the Continent with a good sense and a knowledge of subjects both at home and abroad that surprised me equally and more agreeably than the first part of our interview had done; in fact, he talked like an officer and a statesman.

The Secretary of State kept us long waiting and, certainly, for the last half or three-quarters of an hour, I don't know that I ever had a conversation that interested me more. Now, if the Secretary of State had been punctual and admitted Lord Nelson in the first quarter of an hour, I should have had the same impression of a light and trivial character that other people have had, but luckily I saw enough to be satisfied that he was really a very superior man; but certainly a more sudden or complete metamorphosis I never saw.

In his interview with William Pitt (who had become Prime Minister in May 1804), Nelson took the opportunity to stress his own lack of political ambition. During the Peace of Amiens, three years earlier, Emma had encouraged his unfocused political ambitions but he had been disillusioned by his experience as a new member of the House of Lords. Lord Sidmouth, then Prime Minister, had used his fame to help force through the unpopular terms of peace with France and Nelson had been mocked and humiliated behind his back by some of his fellow-peers. With this memory still seemingly fresh in his mind, he spoke to Pitt:

I gave some specimen of a sailor's politics by frankly telling him that, not having been bred in courts, I could not pretend to a nice discrimination between the use and abuse of parties; and therefore must not be expected to range myself under the political banners of any man in or out of place. That England's welfare was the sole object of my pursuit; and where the tendency of any measure to promote a defeat that object seemed clear, I should vote accordingly without regard to other circumstances. That in matters where my judgement wavered, or to the full extent of which I might feel unequal, I should be silent as I could not reconcile to my mind the giving of a vote without full consideration of its propriety. Mr Pitt listened to me with patience and good humour; indeed paid me some compliments and observed that he wished every officer in the service would entertain similar sentiments.

The two men also discussed naval strategy. Nelson pointed out that if the enemy could concentrate a battle-fleet of sixty or seventy sail of the line only a British fleet of comparable strength could confidently be expected to overcome them. Pitt asked, 'Now, who is to take command?' 'You cannot have a better man than the present one,' replied Nelson, 'Collingwood.' 'No,' said Pitt, 'that won't do. You must take the command.' Could Nelson be ready to leave in three days' time? He answered, 'I am ready now.'

Nelson walked between meetings in Downing Street and at the Admiralty and the Navy Office. Everywhere he was recognised not only as the nation's hero but as the admiral who would save his country from invasion. One American visitor, a professor at Yale College, saw him in the Strand:

He was walking in company with his chaplain and, as usual, followed by a crowd . . . Lord Nelson cannot appear in the streets without immediately collecting a retinue, which augments as he proceeds, and when he enters a shop the door is thronged till he comes out, when the air rings with huzzas and the dark cloud of the populace again moves on and hangs upon his skirts. He is a great favourite with all descriptions of people . . . My view of him was in profile. His features are sharp and his skin is now very much burnt from his having been long at sea; he has the balancing gait of a sailor; his person is spare and of about middle height, or rather more, and mutilated by the loss of an arm and an eye, besides many other injuries of lesser magnitude.

Nelson's old friend from the Mediterranean, Lord Minto, the former diplomat Sir Gilbert Elliot,* had the same experience:

I met Nelson today in a mob in Piccadilly and got hold of his arm, so that I was mobbed too. It is really quite affecting to see the wonder and admiration, and love and respect, of the whole world; and the genuine expression of all these sentiments at once, from gentle and simple, the moment he is seen. It is beyond anything represented in a play or a poem of fame.

Nelson retired to Surrey, for he was happiest at Merton Place. Emma had filled the house with portraits of them both, gilded mirrors and naval trophies. In the garden, an ornamental

* The first Earl of Minto (1751–1814) had, as Sir Gilbert Elliot, been British viceroy in Corsica from 1794 to 1796, when Nelson had met him. Raised to the peerage in 1798, he had been minister in Vienna the following year, then returned to London as president of the Board of Control, where he resumed his friendship with Nelson. In 1807, he was appointed governor-general of India.

canal had been named The Nile after his victory in Aboukir Bay. Relations were invited to stay and friends to dine. Among the latter were the Duke of Clarence, Sir Sidney Smith – whom Nelson had once disliked and who was now being promoted rear-admiral – and Lord Minto. Minto had in the past been critical of the lavish, even vulgar, entertainment at Merton, but he saw it differently now. On arrival, as he recalled:

[I] found Nelson just sitting down to dinner surrounded by a family party . . . Lady Hamilton at the head of the table and Mother Cadogan [Emma's mother] at the bottom. I had a hearty welcome. He looks remarkably well and full of spirits. His conversation is a cordial in these low times . . . Lady Hamilton has improved and added to the house and the place extremely well without his knowing she was about it. He found it ready done. She is a clever being after all: the passion is as hot as ever.

Captain Keats of the *Superb* described walking with Nelson in the garden while the admiral outlined to him the tactics he would employ if he should meet the enemy fleet at sea:

'No day can be long enough to arrange a couple of fleets and fight a decisive battle according to the old system. When *we* meet them, for meet them we shall, I'll tell you how I shall fight them. I shall form the fleet into three divisions in three lines. One division shall be composed of twelve or fourteen of the fastest two-decked ships, which I shall always keep to windward, or in a situation of advantage; and I shall put them under an officer who, I am sure, will employ them in the manner I wish, if possible. I consider it will always be in my power to throw them into battle in any part I may choose; but if circumstances prevent their being carried against the enemy where I desire, I shall feel certain he will employ them effectually, and perhaps in a more advantageous manner than if he could have followed my orders.

'With the remaining part of the fleet formed in two lines, I shall go at them at once, if I can, about one-third of their line from their leading ship.' He then said, 'What do

you think of it?' Such a question I felt required consideration. I paused. Seeing it, he said: 'But I'll tell you what *I*
think of it. I think it will surprise and confound the enemy.
They won't know what I am about. It will bring forward a
pell-mell battle, and that is what I want.'

Nelson wanted 'a pell-mell battle' because he was confident
in the superior fire-power and gun-drill of the British, who,
unlike the French and Spanish, had continuous experience of
working and fighting their ships on the open sea.

News from the Atlantic was anxiously awaited and on the
morning of 2 September it finally arrived. A chaise drawn by
four horses swept up the drive of Merton Place, bearing a naval
officer fresh from the sea, Captain Henry Blackwood of the
frigate *Euryalus*, with an urgent despatch for the Admiralty.
Blackwood had reached Portsmouth at dusk, so the hilltop semaphore system could not be used and he had had to hire the fast
post-chaise. Knowing that Merton was on the road from Portsmouth to London, he had decided to tell Nelson the news first:
the French and Spanish ships had left Ferrol and Corunna,
sailed south and entered Cadiz. Blackwood had found and shad-
owed them, but there was nothing more he, or Admiral Collingwood's small squadron, could do but sound the alarm. *En route*
for England he had encountered Calder's fleet – now number-
ing eighteen battleships – which immediately crowded sail to
reinforce Collingwood. Nelson guessed the reason for Blackwood's call before he could be told: 'I am sure you bring me
news of the French and Spanish fleets and that I shall have to
beat them yet.'

Nelson followed Blackwood to the Admiralty and was at once
seen by Lord Barham. The First Lord informed him that his
Mediterranean command would now include the Atlantic approaches and Cadiz, then handed him a copy of the Navy List
and invited him to choose the captains he wanted for his fleet.
'Choose yourself, my Lord,' replied Nelson, 'the same spirit
actuates the whole profession; you cannot choose wrong.'

But Nelson did single out a few of his officers, amongst them
Blackwood, his old shipmates Captain Thomas Hardy – who
would be his flag-captain in the *Victory* – and Captain Sir Edward
Berry, Captain Keats, and Sir Sidney Smith, whom he invited to

command his inshore squadron off Cadiz. Smith was a curious character; as much an intelligence officer and technical innovator as a naval officer, he was planning to pre-empt any climactic battle off Cadiz by attacking the enemy in port with the newly invented rockets and torpedoes. After his official farewells, which included a visit to the louche but cultivated Prince of Wales (whom he had once feared might have his eye on Emma Hamilton), Nelson returned to Merton for his personal leave-takings.

There were more gatherings of family and friends, all emotionally charged. 'Lady Hamilton was in tears all yesterday,' Lord Minto wrote to his wife, 'could not eat and hardly drink and near swooning, all at table'; then, of Nelson, 'He is in many points a great man, in others a baby.' The son of a parsonage, Nelson had adapted his religious beliefs to fit his circumstances. Although he could not marry Emma in his wife's lifetime, he arranged a little ceremony at which they exchanged rings and vows before a priest at a private Holy Communion.

After dinner on the night of Friday, 13 September, Nelson knelt briefly at the cot of his sleeping daughter, bade farewell to Emma, and boarded the carriage which would take him overnight to Portsmouth. When the chaise stopped at a coaching inn to change horses, Nelson noted in his diary:

Friday night at half-past ten, drove from dear, dear Merton, where I left all which I hold dear in this world, to go to serve my king and country. May the great God, whom I adore, enable me to fulfil the expectations of my country; and if it is His good pleasure that I should return, my thanks will never cease being offered up to the throne of His mercy. If it is His good Providence to cut short my days upon earth, I bow with the greatest submission, relying that He will protect those dear to me that I may leave behind. His will be done. Amen, amen, amen.

Arriving early next morning at Portsmouth, he wrote to Emma: '6 o'clock, George Inn. My dearest and most beloved of women, Nelson's Emma, I arrived here this moment . . . *Victory* is at St Helen's* and, if possible, I shall be at sea this day. God protect you and my dear Horatia.' Then he set off to walk to the

* An anchorage off the Isle of Wight.

beach and the sea. Among those watching was the tutor to Lord Egremont's sons, who had brought his charges over from Petworth to watch the great man embark. He recalled:

I got up and dressed myself immediately and went to the inn, where I found so great a crowd in the gateway that it was not without some exertion that I could gain admittance. Just as I got to the foot of the stairs, I met Lord Nelson fully dressed with three or four stars on his breast; he seemed very anxious to get on board. Soon after Lord Nelson went out into the street . . . when he was followed by a number of people, who crowded after him in all directions to gain a sight of him. I was amused by the eagerness of a common sailor I met, who was running with all his might and who, on being asked by another if he had seen him, replied, 'No, but, d—n the old b—r, I should like to see him once more' and away he posted at full speed. This I suppose to be the ultimate expression of nautical affection.

Another spectator, the American who had seen him in the Strand, remembered that

by the time he had arrived on the beach some hundreds of people had collected in his train, pressing all around and pushing to get a little before him to obtain a sight of his face. I stood on one of the batteries near which he passed and had a full view of his person. He was elegantly dressed and his blue coat splendidly illuminated with stars and ribbons. As the barge in which he embarked pushed away from the shore, the people gave him three cheers, which his Lordship returned by waving his hat.

The *Victory* sailed from Portsmouth on the morning of Sunday, 15 September 1805. Next day she was off Plymouth and on the 17th Nelson sent another farewell note to Emma, which included an oblique reference to the wife who prevented their marriage:

Victory, off Plymouth, September 17th, Nine o'clock in

the morning, Blowing fresh at WSW, dead foul wind

I sent, my own dearest Emma, a letter for you, last night, in a Torbay boat, and gave the man a guinea to put it in the post-office. We have had a nasty blowing night, and it looks very dirty. I am now signalising the ships at Plymouth to join me; but I rather doubt their ability to get to sea. However, I have got clear of Portland, and have Cawsand Bay and Torbay under the lee. I entreat, my dear Emma, that you will cheer up; and we will look forward to many, many happy years, and be surrounded by our children's children. God Almighty can, when He pleases, remove the impediment. My heart and soul is with you and Horatia.

With that, the *Victory*, joined by Blackwood's frigate, the *Euryalus*, and two ships of the line, *Ajax* and *Thunderer*, sailed. As Nelson put it: 'I shall try hard to beat out of the Channel and the first northerly wind will carry me to Cape St Vincent, where nothing be wanting on my part to realise the expectations of my friends. I will try to have a motto, at least it shall be my watchword, *Touch and Take*. I will do my best . . .'

CHAPTER 4

Action Stations

As Nelson steered south, new orders were on their way from Paris to Villeneuve at Cadiz. After Calder's inconclusive but crucial action off Finisterre and Villeneuve's retreat to the Spanish ports, Napoleon had realised that his plans to invade England had to be postponed. That suited his assessment of the changing strategic pattern.

A new threat had emerged from the alliance between Austria and Russia. They had agreed in April on a plan that had the prospect not only of active British support in the Mediterranean but, most importantly, huge financial subsidy from the government of William Pitt. Napoleon doubted whether the Austrians and Russians would be able to mount a joint offensive against France before the spring of 1806 so there was time for a quick pre-emptive strike. The *Grande Armée* could march from its camps on the Channel and North Sea coasts to central Europe. Then, as he himself put it,

I shall invade Germany with 200,000 men and shall not halt until I have reached Vienna, taken Venice and everything Austria has in Italy and driven the Bourbons from Naples. I shall stop the Austrians and Russians from uniting. I shall beat them before they can meet. Then, the Continent pacified, I shall come back to the camp on the ocean and start work all over again.

The invasion of England would be postponed by perhaps two years. Accordingly, at the end of August 1805, the *Grande Armée* had begun to strike camp and march east. For the present there was no need for Villeneuve in the Channel. Instead, he could be used to guard the southern flank in the Mediterranean to prevent the British and Russian forces there from coming to the aid of Austria. On 16 September, Napoleon's orders were sent to Cadiz:

Having resolved to make a powerful diversion by directing into the Mediterranean our naval forces concentrated at the port of Cadiz, combined with those of his Catholic Majesty, we would have you know that our intention is that you will seize the first favourable opportunity of sailing with the combined fleet and proceeding into that sea . . . You will first make for Cartagena to join the Spanish squadron which is in that port; you will then proceed to Naples and disembark on some point of the coast the troops you carry on board to join the army under the orders of General St Cyr. If you find at Naples any English or Russian ships of war, you will seize them. The fleet under your command will remain off the Neapolitan shores so long as you may judge necessary to do the utmost harm to the enemy, and to intercept an expedition which they intend to send from Malta. Our intention is that wherever you meet the enemy in inferior force you will attack them without hesitation and obtain a decision against them. It will not escape you that the success of these operations depends essentially on the promptness of your leaving Cadiz.

What Napoleon did not tell Villeneuve was that he was to be replaced by Vice-Admiral François Rosily, who would travel to Cadiz overland from Paris. It was assumed that he would arrive soon after Villeneuve had received his orders while the combined fleet was still preparing to sail. Rosily was to hand Villeneuve the letter of dismissal in person. For Villeneuve, the new orders presented a more manageable alternative than that of trying to batter his way through a succession of British fleets to the Channel; now he would have to choose his moment to slip out of Cadiz and sail sixty miles south-east to the Straits of Gibraltar; once through, wind and darkness should enable him to keep ahead of his pursuers until reaching safety in a defended port.

While Villeneuve planned his escape, Nelson was sailing south in the *Victory* with five more sail of the line to follow. Off Ushant, he passed the Channel fleet, still blocking Ganteaume in Brest. Heading for his own area of command, now extended into the Atlantic approaches to the Mediterranean, he was confident that the fleet he was to command off Cadiz would be in good order although it was a hastily assembled force and had not exercised together. His confidence was founded on his old friend Collingwood, who presently commanded the fleet and would now become his second-in-command. The two men, although opposites in character, had been close friends since they had met in the Caribbean a quarter of a century before. Collingwood, while older by a decade, had always followed one step behind Nelson in his career. A tall, austere Northumbrian, Collingwood lacked Nelson's verve – one of his captains described him as 'an old bear' – but he was a man of deep professionalism and wisdom, with a hidden sensitivity and wit which became apparent in the company of close friends and of women, particularly his adored wife and two daughters. But all were aware of his dedication. As one contemporary said:

Lord Collingwood had an intimate and exact knowledge of all the technicalities of his profession . . . He insisted on everything being done rightly, and could himself splice a rope or perform any other office of the ship with as much dexterity as a common seaman . . . He once undertook some extensive repairs of his ship whilst still at sea and within sight of the port of the enemy. He could instruct the carpenter to the minutest detail.

To another, Collingwood, despite his fifty-seven years, seemed tireless:

It was his general rule in tempestuous weather, and upon any hostile emergency that occurred, to sleep upon his sofa in a flannel gown, taking off only his epauletted coat. The writer . . . has seen him upon deck without his hat, and his grey hair floating in the wind, whilst torrents of rain poured down through the shrouds, and his eye, like the eagle's, on the watch. Personal exposure, colds, rheumatism, ague – all seemed nothing to him when his duty called.

Although Collingwood rarely entertained his captains to dinner, his second-in-command did so. But Sir Robert Calder was an unhappy man. Confident that he had fulfilled expectations in fighting and turning back Villeneuve's fleet in July, Calder was mortified to hear that his failure to follow up his initial success with pursuit and total victory had disappointed a country that now expected overwhelming, Nelsonian triumphs. He decided that there was only one way to clear his name and that was through a court martial. This he had demanded; indeed, the Admiralty's assent to it was being brought out to him by Nelson himself. However, there was widespread sympathy for Calder in the fleet off Cadiz. Captain Edward Codrington of the *Orion* noted in his diary on 10 September:

Sir Robert Calder has written to get home, and says he is too much worn to continue serving. He has sent to me to dine with him today, and I intend going if possible, although I am quite confident the admiral does not like to see any of us associating together. Sir R. is not only much worn, but much out of spirits, in consequence of public opinion bearing so hard on him; and to a hospitable man fond of society and having many of his sea friends in the same fleet, it is very cruel not to allow him any intercourse with them, when their society is of value to him. How few there are who even at the close of a long life of hard service have had during all that life an opportunity of distinguishing themselves; and how few of those who have been favoured with that opportunity and done their utmost, have escaped public reprehension! Even the unnoticed service that we are now performing, without the smallest prospect of amendment, deserves at least the thanks of those whose ease and enjoyment are thereby secured to them.

A few days later, Codrington added that he had enjoyed, in Calder's company,

as social a dinner as I was ever at; and the beautiful music his band gave us to make our wine relish, made us all regret the more the difficulty of repeating our visit. It was really to me (and I am sure it would have been to you) a most animating sight; an admiral surrounded by twenty of his captains in social intercourse, showing a strong desire to support each other cordially and manfully in the event of a battle taking place.

Yet Codrington was aware of an underlying unease. Collingwood did not inspire his fleet and Calder, however popular personally, was widely seen as a failure. Even when recording his enjoyment of the dinner party, Codrington wrote from the heart, 'For charity's sake send us Lord Nelson, oh ye men of power!'

His plea was about to be answered. On 26 September, Captain Blackwood was sent ahead of the *Victory* in his frigate *Euryalus* to warn Collingwood of the imminent arrival of the new commander-in-chief. Collingwood was also told that, when the *Victory* was sighted, no salutes were to be fired and no recognition signals made; Villeneuve must assume that this was just another first-rate of the line joining the fleet off Cadiz. Indeed, that day Villeneuve reported to Decrès in Paris, 'I have just been informed that the enemy squadron has been joined by three sail of the line – one of which is a three-decker – coming from the west.' Nelson himself wrote to Emma Hamilton: 'I joined the fleet late on the evening of the 28th September but could not communicate with them until next morning.'

Nelson immediately took over the command from Collingwood and changed the pattern of the blockade. Collingwood had kept his fleet within sight of Cadiz but Nelson decided to withdraw beyond the horizon, leaving a chain of frigates to report any moves within the harbour. Nelson's arrival sent a thrill of excitement and confidence through the fleet, especially when hoists of signal flags flew up the *Victory*'s halyards ordering his captains to report to the flagship in person. Thereafter the tight discipline that had been imposed, but not the alert efficiency, was relaxed and the mail Nelson had brought relished. Richard Anderson, the navigating master of the *Prince*, jotted in his diary, 'This is a great day. All the capts. dine with *Lord Nelson*. I get a letter and some clean shirts from my dear Mary. Hurra.'

Of the captains of the twenty-seven ships of the line now under Nelson's command, only five belonged to his own Mediterranean fleet and only eight had served with him before. So it was important to meet and instruct them all, which he did at dinner over two days in a cheering change from the austere regime of his predecessor. One of those dining on the second evening was Codrington. He wrote to his wife:

The signal has been made this morning for all of us who did not dine on board *Victory* yesterday to go there today. What our late chief will think of this I don't know; but I well know what the fleet think of the difference; and even you, our good wives, who have some causes of disapprobation, will allow the superiority of Lord Nelson in all these social arrangements which bind his captains to their admiral. The signal is made that boats may be hoisted out to buy fruit, stock, or anything from vessels coming into the fleet; this, I trust, will be a common signal hereafter, but it is the first day I have seen it made.

Nelson was delighted by these occasions, writing to a friend:

The reception I met with on joining the fleet caused the sweetest sensation in my life. The officers who came on board to welcome my return forgot my rank as commander-in-chief in the enthusiasm with which they greeted me. As soon as these emotions were past, I laid before them the plan I had previously arranged for attacking the enemy.

He had the table cleared and spread upon it a chart of the Mediterranean approaches before beginning his assessment of the opposing fleets. Within Cadiz there seemed to be at least forty French and Spanish ships of the line, but it was not possible to know exactly how many were ready for sea, or what was the condition of their crews. Would they stay in port, or attempt to escape? Nelson paid little attention to the plan put forward by Captain Sir Sidney Smith, who was joining him to command the inshore squadron, to drive the enemy out by a night attack on his anchorage with rockets and torpedoes. Despite some support for Smith from the government in London, Nelson dismissed the idea, in which, he said, he had 'little faith': 'The rockets, if the account of them is true, must annoy their fleet very much; but I depend more on hunger for driving them out and upon the gallant officers and men under my command for their destruction, than any other invention.'

He had read intelligence reports of both disease and hunger within Cadiz, brought on by poor harvests; and that, combined with the Emperor Napoleon's restless, aggressive energy, he felt confident would force them to sea. There he would fight them, and he told his captains how this would be done. In essence it was the same plan he had described to Captain Keats in the garden at Merton some weeks earlier. Assuming that he could muster some forty sail of the line against about that number of enemy, Nelson expected that the combined fleets would run for the Straits of Gibraltar and try to avoid action. He would be waiting out at sea and to windward. Turning towards them, he would attack in two divisions with a third in reserve. The windward column of sixteen battleships would be led by himself and the lee column of the same strength by Collingwood. There was the obvious risk of approaching at right angles because the enemy line could concentrate their fire on his leading ships, which could not reply until the 'pell-mell battle' was joined. Each column would be led by heavy three-deckers which would burst through the enemy line, raking the ships to either side. The outcome would be decided by the superior gunnery of the British, who were able to fire at least twice as rapidly as their enemies.

Collingwood's column was to aim for the twelfth ship from the rear while Nelson would try to break through just ahead of Villeneuve's flagship if she could be identified. While both fleets were embroiled in ship-to-ship fighting, the enemy van of about twenty ships would inevitably be so slow in turning to come to the aid of their centre and rear that, outnumbered by the British, these would probably be destroyed before they could join the action. Nelson's reserve division, composed of some of his fastest ships, could be thrown into the fight wherever required. That was the plan. As Nelson wrote to Emma,

When I came to explain to them the '*Nelson touch*', it was like an electric shock. Some shed tears, all approved – 'It was new – it was singular – it was simple!' and, from admirals downwards, it was repeated – 'It must succeed, if ever they will allow us to get at them! You are, my Lord, surrounded by friends whom you inspire with confidence.'

Nelson followed this meeting by circulating a memorandum, an *aide-mémoire* encapsulating the essentials of his battle-plan, to all who had been present. It concentrated on tactics and practicalities, of course, but added that in the confusion of battle and half-blinded by gunsmoke, signals would be difficult, if not impossible, to see. So he added, 'In case signals can neither be seen or perfectly understood, no captain can do very wrong if he places his ship alongside that of an enemy.'

His plan had to be flexible, he stressed:

Something must be left to chance, nothing is sure in a sea fight beyond all others, shot will carry away the masts and yards of friends as well as foes, but I look with confidence to a victory before the van of the enemy could succour their friends [the centre and rear] and then that the British fleet would most of them be ready to receive their twenty sail of the line, or to pursue them should they endeavour to make off.

Giving orders to admiring captains was simple but Nelson's subordinate admirals required tactful handling. Two of them, Collingwood and Calder's replacement as third-in-command, Rear-Admiral the Earl of Northesk, had also been present and the former, despite their friendship, had shown signs of unease since Nelson had arrived to replace him as commander-in-chief. This came to the surface with Collingwood's resentment at being ordered to transfer from his current, familiar flagship, the *Dreadnought* – which was heavily encrusted with barnacles and so a slow sailer – into the faster *Royal Sovereign*; at this stage in the operations he did not like having to move into a different ship with different officers. Nelson tactfully enclosed a personal note with Collingwood's copy of the memorandum:

I send you my plan of attack, as far as a man dare venture to guess at the very uncertain position the enemy may be found in: but, my dear friend, it is to place you perfectly at your ease respecting my intentions, and to give full scope to your judgement for carrying them into effect. We can, my dear Coll, have no little jealousies: we have only one great object in view – that of annihilating our enemies, and getting a glorious peace for our country. No man has more confidence in another than I have in you; and no man will render your services more justice than your very old friend, Nelson and Bronte.*

Although there was no problem with Northesk, his predecessor, Admiral Calder, was eager to return home and face the court martial he had demanded. The Admiralty had decreed that he should take passage for England in the *Dreadnought*, which was due to be refitted and have her bottom careened; otherwise it would have been proper for him to return in a frigate. But Calder's hurt pride prompted him to demand that he sail in his own flagship, the *Prince of Wales*, a battleship of 98 guns, which could hardly be spared on the eve of battle. Calder also asked that three of the captains who had been present at his action off Finisterre return as witnesses for his defence. Nelson refused to let the captains go but he did allow Calder to leave on 13 October in his flagship, as he explained in a letter to Lord Barham:

I did not fail, immediately on my arrival, to deliver your message to Sir Robert Calder; and it will give your Lordship pleasure to find, as it has me, that an inquiry is what the vice-admiral wishes . . . Sir Robert felt so much, even at the idea of being removed from his own ship which he commanded, in the face of the fleet, that I much fear I shall incur the censure of the Board of Admiralty, without your Lordship's influence with the members of it. I may be thought wrong, as an officer, to disobey the orders of the Admiralty, by not insisting on Sir Robert Calder's quitting the *Prince of Wales* for the *Dreadnought*, and for parting with a 90-gun [in fact, 98] ship, before the force arrives which their Lordships have judged necessary; but I trust that I shall be considered to have done right as a man, and to a brother officer in affliction – my heart could not stand it, and so the thing must rest.

There was another admiral still to be placated, Rear-Admiral

* Nelson had been given the title of Duke of Bronte by King Ferdinand IV of the Two Sicilies.

Thomas Louis, who had fought under Nelson at the Battle of the Nile. He was chosen for what, under most circumstances, would have been a pleasant duty: replenishment at a North African port. Amongst the comings – ships detached from the Channel fleet, or returning from England after refit – and goings – to the relief of distant squadrons and diplomatic missions – were excursions ashore to stock the ships with fresh fruit, vegetables, and meat (this usually alive, to be kept and slaughtered on board) and of course water. For officers, at least, this provided an opportunity to stretch their legs and perhaps to buy presents for sweethearts and wives. As Midshipman James Robinson of the *Mars* put it, 'We went several times to the Mediterranean, to Tetuan for water. Captain Duff bought a most elegant dress for Mrs Duff at Tangiers for which he gave 20 dollars: it was made of camel's hair. I should have liked very much to have got one for my mother but it did not suit my purse.'

But with a fleet action seeming to be imminent, this was the last order any admiral, or captain, wanted to hear. When Admiral Louis was told to take his flagship, the *Canopus*, and five other sail of the line to Gibraltar and Tetuan for replenishment, he appealed to Nelson for a postponement, protesting over dinner in the *Victory*, 'You are sending us away, my Lord. The enemy will come out and we shall have no share in the battle.' Nelson replied:

My dear Louis, I have no other means of keeping my fleet complete in provisions and water but by sending them in detachments to Gibraltar. The enemy will come out and we shall fight them; but there will be time for you to get back first. I look upon *Canopus* as my right hand and I send you first to ensure your being here to help beat them.

These were valuable ships – one mounting ninety-eight guns; another, eighty – which would be needed as much as Calder's flagship on the day of battle. Their captains were all experienced officers; one of them, Louis's flag-captain, was Captain Charles Austen, a brother of the aspiring novelist Jane Austen. Nevertheless the squadron sailed for Gibraltar on 3 October.

Meanwhile the British fleet at sea had plenty to occupy its

time. Nelson's ships were painted in his favourite colours: black and yellow stripes around the hulls – and the iron hoops around the masts also yellow – so that, when the gun-ports were open, their sides appeared chequered. Later, Lieutenant John Owen of the Royal Marines, who was serving aboard the 74 *Belleisle*, recorded:

At this time the foresight of Lord Nelson was evinced by what unpractised persons would have called a trifle, but which was in reality a circumstance of great importance to the *Belleisle*, which happened to be the only ship of the fleet which had the hoops of her lower masts painted black, while it was universally done in the French ships. The admiral, therefore, by signal, directed the *Belleisle* to paint the hoops of her masts yellow, because in action the masts would be seen through the smoke when the hull could not, and the *Belleisle* would thereby become liable to be fired into by the British ships. For a similar reason, although the admiral's flag was red, the fleet was ordered to fight under the St George's or white ensign, to mark their colours more distinctly from those of the French in the smoke, the fly of the French ensign being red.

Guns now were cleaned, swords, cutlasses and pikes sharpened, rigging and tackle checked, medical stores and surgical instruments got ready. One of the surgeon's assistants (known as a 'loblolly boy') in the *Victory* was Jack Rider. As a contemporary wrote:

It was his duty to do anything and everything that was required – from sweeping and washing the deck, and saying 'Amen' to the chaplain, down to cleaning the guns, and helping the doctor to make pills and plasters, and mix medicines. On 17 October Jack was ordered by the doctor to fetch a bottle that was standing in a particular place. Jack ran off, post haste, to the spot, where he found what appeared to be an empty bottle. Curiosity was uppermost: 'What', thought Jack, 'can there be about this empty bottle?' He examined it carefully, but couldn't comprehend the mystery, so he thought that he would call in the aid of a candle, to throw light on the subject. The bottle contained ether, and the result of the examination was that the vapour ignited, and the flames extended to some of the sails, and also to a part of the ship. There was a general confusion – running with buckets and what not – and, to make matters worse, the fire was rapidly extending to the powder magazine. During the hubbub, Lord Nelson was in the chief cabin writing despatches. His Lordship heard the noise – he couldn't do otherwise – and so, in a loud voice, he called out, 'What's all that d—d noise about?' The boatswain answered, 'My Lord, the loblolly boy's set fire to an empty bottle, and it's set fire to the ship.' 'Oh!' said Nelson, 'that's all, is it? I thought the enemy had boarded us and taken us all prisoners – you and loblolly must put it out, and take care we're not blown up! but pray make as little noise about it as you can, or I can't go on with my despatches,' and with these words Nelson went to his desk, and continued his writing with the greatest coolness.

While waiting, Nelson stressed the importance of morale and ships' companies were encouraged to stage entertainments; on board Lord Northesk's flagship, the *Britannia*, a lieutenant of marines, the son of the admiral's chaplain and secretary, produced amateur theatricals. With the admiral's cabin as the stage, and the bulkhead removed so that the audience could assemble on the upper deck between the guns, plays were acted by the officers, with female parts taken by midshipmen wearing wigs of teased-out rope and red lead for rouge. Watched by the crew and with the admiral in the front row of the audience, they performed not only comedies, with titles ranging from *Miss in her Teens* and *The Mock Doctor*, but also – on the day Nelson's memorandum was delivered on board – a spectacular epic entitled *Columbus, or a World Discovered*. Its playbill boasted:

In the course of the performance will be two splendid processions – a view of the Interior of the Temple of the Sun with a Grand Altar burning incense, etc. – Grand Hymn of the Priestesses, etc. Towards the close of the play the Destruction of the Temple by an Earthquake accompanied by Thunder, Lightning and Hail Storms!! With the rescue of Cora from the ruins by Alonzo!! Doors to be open at 6.30. To begin at 7.

Despite, or perhaps because of, the tension of waiting, Nelson paid particular attention to the worries amongst officers of all ranks, often dealing with them at the dinner-table. Nelson's old friend Captain Tom Fremantle of the *Neptune*, who had fought under him in Corsica, at Tenerife and at the Nile, was anxious about his career. He wrote to his wife, Betsey:

I have seen and dined with Lord Nelson – he shows me the same kindness and attention he has ever done. I had not been with him many minutes before he very handsomely told me I should have my old place in the line of battle, which is his *second*, this is exactly what is the most flattering to me in every point of view. He desired me to come to him whenever I chose and to dine with him as often as I could make it convenient, in short I am quite pleased with his manner towards me.

A few days later, Fremantle wrote again:

I dined again with Lord Nelson a few days ago, and sat with him until 8 o'clock when he detained me to see a play that was performed by the seamen on board the *Victory*, I assure you it was very well conducted, and the voice of the seaman, who was dressed in great form and performed the *female part*, was entertaining to a degree, we poor sloops have not ingenuity to attempt anything of the sort – the weather here is intolerable, I am writing with all the windows open and sleep with my doors so, indeed I have not much benefited by the latter as I have had some very severe attacks of the rheumatism – the whole system here is so completely changed, that it wears quite a different aspect, we are continually with something to change the scene and know precisely how far we may go, which is very pleasant. Lord Nelson often recounts many of our transactions when we were in this country before, and on every occasion is very kind to me.

Among the guests was William Ram, still a midshipman at twenty-one but ambitious and restless, who told his sister in a letter:

I have just dined with Lord Nelson, who had company today, viz. some captains of men of war, amongst whom was Captain Blackwood . . . We had a good deal of conversation and he desires to be remembered to you all . . . Now about my promotion, Lord Nelson's secretary has mentioned that his Lordship *went in person* concerning his appointments and that all his appointments were confirmed, so I am pretty sure of my commission [as lieutenant], and I'll now wait for a captain's commission, you see we are never content, no sooner we get one piece of good fortune than we are distracted to get more, and now adieu.

Soon afterwards he wrote again:

I verily believe from my soul that I am the most discontented fellow alive, nothing will please me, for ever on the fret . . . I am constantly at war with myself . . . knowing that it is *only myself* that I annoy, nobody caring a penny for my peevishness . . . Now, for instance, I begin already to be tired of this station, the sameness that runs through the navy (I mean principally in the line of battleships) is intolerable and tho' in daily hopes of the enemy giving us an opportunity of *signalising ourselves*, yet, alas, day follows day, no enemy comes and the same anxiety is painted on my brow.

Ram's anxiety was about to be relieved as his promotion to lieutenant was confirmed.

Nelson's own calmness and serenity, in contrast to the tension and stress he had sometimes shown at critical moments in the past, was particularly reassuring to those under his command. As he wrote to his friend and agent in London, Alexander Davison:

Day by day, my dear friend, I am expecting the [enemy] fleet to put to sea – every day, hour, and moment; and you may rely that, if it is within the power of man to get at them, that it shall be done; and I am sure that all my brethren look to that day as the finish of our laborious cruise. The event no man can say exactly; but I must think, or render great injustice to those under me, that, let the battle be when it may, it will never have been surpassed. My shattered frame, if I survive that day, will require rest, and that is all I shall ask for. If I fall on such a glorious occasion, it shall be my pride to take care that my friends shall not blush for me. These things are in the hands of a wise and just Providence, and His will be done! I have got some trifle, thank God, to leave to those I hold most dear, and I have taken care not to neglect it. Do not think I am low-spirited on this account, or fancy anything is to happen to me; quite the contrary – my mind is calm, and I have only to think of destroying our inveterate foe.

Outwardly confident, Nelson did, however, worry about the numerical odds against him. Ships of the line had had to be sent away and he now knew that in any battle he would be outnumbered. The Admiralty had promised him further reinforcements but there was no sign of them. On 6 October, he wrote to his influential friend George Rose, vice-president of the Board of Trade:

I think Mr Pitt will do what he can to oblige me. I verily believe the country will soon be put to some expense for my account, either a monument, or a new pension and honours; for I have not the very smallest doubt but that a very few days will put us in battle; the success no man can ensure but the fighting them, if they are to be got at, I pledge myself if the force arrives which is intended. I am *very*, *very* anxious for its arrival, for the thing will be done if a few more days elapse; and I want for the sake of our country that it should be done so effectually as to have nothing to wish for; and what will signify the force the day after the battle? It is, as Mr Pitt knows, annihilation that the country wants and not merely a splendid victory of twenty-three to thirty-six* – honourable to the parties

* Nelson's estimate of the odds at the time.

concerned but absolutely useless in the extended scale to bring Buonaparte to his marrow-bones: numbers can only annihilate.

I think not for myself but the country, therefore I hope the Admiralty will send the fixt force as soon as possible and frigates and sloops of war, for I am very destitute. I do not mean this as any complaint, quite the contrary; I believe they are doing all they can . . . Therefore, if Mr Pitt would hint to Lord Barham that he shall be anxious until I get the force proposed, and plenty of frigates and sloops in order to watch them closely, it may be advantageous to the country: you are at liberty to mention this to Mr Pitt but I would not wish it to go further.

In Cadiz, all was uncertainty. Villeneuve knew that Rosily was on his way and as the senior officer might well take supreme command, although he assumed that he himself would become his deputy. At meetings with his subordinate French admirals – his second-in-command Dumanoir Le Pelley and his third-in-command Charles de Magon* – and the Spanish commander, Admiral Don Frederico Gravina, they discussed their options. Although they had heard rumours that the British were planning an attack on the port, such as that suggested by Sir Sidney Smith, they decided that, since their crews were so much less experienced than the British and they did not have the advantage in numbers of ships that they had expected, they should remain at anchor in Cadiz.

However, Villeneuve privately considered other options. Whatever Rosily's mission, the outcome would almost certainly not be to his own advantage. As his orders from the emperor to sail for the Mediterranean still stood, he decided to carry them out. His own honour would be saved and it was just possible that he might achieve success and professional glory. So he made plans for departure and a possible battle, in which he guessed at Nelson's tactics:

---

* Both Rear-Admiral Pierre Dumanoir Le Pelley and Rear-Admiral Charles de Magon came from aristocratic families in northern France: Dumanoir was from Normandy, and Magon, whose full name was de Magon Clos-Doré, was a Breton. Both had served in the royalist navy before the Revolution and their careers had been revived.

I by no means propose to seek out the enemy; I even wish to avoid him in order to proceed to my destination. But should we encounter him, let there be no ignominious manoeuvring; it would dishearten our crews and bring about our defeat. The enemy will not confine himself to forming a line of battle with our own and engaging us in an artillery duel, in which success is frequently with the more skilful but always with the more fortunate; he will endeavour to envelop our rear, to break through our line and to direct his ships in groups upon such of ours as he shall have cut off so as to surround them and defeat them.

In fact, a 'pell-mell battle'.

It might, however, be difficult to avoid an encounter. On the west coast of Spain the easterly wind required to carry Villeneuve's fleet to sea would also hamper his planned passage of the Straits of Gibraltar. So he must prepare for a fight. To bring his ships' companies up to strength every available seaman was sent on board the ships and they were reinforced by soldiers, who would be able to snipe from the tops (the platforms where the main yards crossed the masts) and also man the ships' guns.

One French captain in particular was not only well prepared for close-quarter fighting but relished the prospect. This was Captain Jean-Jacques Lucas of the *Redoutable*, who described how he trained his men in boarding:

I had had canvas pouches to hold two grenades made for all captains of guns, the cross-belts of these pouches carrying a tin tube containing a small match. In all our drills, I made them throw a great number of pasteboard grenades and I often landed the grenadiers in order to have them explode iron grenades; they had so acquired the habit of hurling them that on the day of the battle our topmen were throwing two at a time. I had a hundred carbines fitted with long bayonets on board; the men to whom these were served out were so well accustomed to their use that they climbed halfway up the shrouds to open a musketry fire. All the men armed with swords were instructed in broadsword practice every day and pistols had become familiar arms to them. The grapnels were thrown aboard so skilfully that they succeeded in hooking a ship even though she was not exactly touching us.

News of Admiral Louis's departure for Gibraltar on 3 October soon reached Villeneuve. Believing that Nelson's fleet – invisible, except for a few frigates, below the horizon – was weaker than it actually was, he decided that if he was going to run for the Straits before the arrival of Rosily, now was the time. But before he sailed, he wanted to be more certain of the strength of the British waiting out of sight. On 18 October, he ordered Admiral Magon to put to sea with seven of the line and a frigate, capture one of the British frigates cruising off Cadiz and discover what he could about the enemy battle-fleet.

At dawn on the 19th, look-outs in the closest British frigate to Cadiz, the *Sirius*, sighted enemy battleships emerging from port. The *Sirius* signalled to Blackwood's *Euryalus*, further out to sea, 'Enemy have their topsails hoisted.' At seven o'clock she hoisted the numeral flags '370', the code for 'Enemy ships are coming out of port'. The *Euryalus* repeated this to the *Phoebe*, lying beyond her, adding, 'Repeat signals to look-out ships west.' The news was passed from her to the frigate *Naiad*, then on through the signal officers of the battleships *Defence*, *Colossus* and *Mars* and thence to the flagship well below the horizon. On board the *Bellerophon*, the signal was seen by the first lieutenant, William Cumby:

I immediately reported this to Captain Cooke, and asked his permission to repeat it. The *Mars* at that time was so far from us that her topgallant-masts alone were visible above the horizon; consequently the distance was so great for the discovery of the *colours* of the flags that Captain Cooke said he was unwilling to repeat a signal of so much importance unless he could clearly distinguish the flags himself, which on looking through his glass he declared himself unable to do.

The very circumstances of the importance of the signal, added to my own perfect conviction of the correctness of my statement founded on long and frequent experience of the strength of my own sight, induced me again to urge Captain Cooke to repeat it, when he said if any other person of the many whose glasses were now fixed on the *Mars* would confirm my opinion he would repeat it. None of the officers or signalmen, however, were bold enough to assent positively, as I did, that the flags were number 370, and I had the mortification to be disappointed in my anxious wish that the *Bellerophon* should be the first to repeat such delightful intelligence to the admiral.

Soon afterwards, the *Mars* hauled the flags down, and I said, 'Now she will make the distant signal 370.' She did make the distant signal 370 as I had predicted; this could not be mistaken and we were preparing to repeat it, the *Mars*'s signal was answered from the *Victory*, and immediately afterwards the dinner signal was annulled and the signal given for a general chase.

In the *Euryalus*, Captain Blackwood, satisfied that he had performed his task and believing a battle to be imminent, wrote to his wife:

What think you, my own dearest love? At this moment the enemy are coming out, and as if determined to have a fair fight; all night they had been making signals, and the morning showed them to us getting under sail. They have thirty-four sail of the line, and five frigates. Lord Nelson, I am sorry to say, has but twenty-seven sail of the line with him; the rest are at Gibraltar, getting water. Not that he has not enough to bring them to close action; but I want him to have so many as to make the most decisive battle of it that ever was, which will bring us a lasting peace, I hope, and some prize-money. Within two hours, though our fleet was at sixteen leagues off, I have let Lord N. know of their coming out, and I have been enabled to send a vessel off to Gibraltar, which will bring Admiral Louis, and the ships in there, out.

Nelson himself, so often prone to prophesying his own death in a coming action, calmly began a letter to Emma:

My dearest beloved Emma, the dear friend of my bosom. The signal has been made that the enemy's combined fleet are coming out of port. We have very little wind, so that I have no hopes of seeing them before tomorrow. May the God of Battles crown my endeavours with success; at all events, I will take care that my name shall ever be most dear to you and Horatia, both of whom I love as much as my own life. And as my last writing before the battle will be to you, so I hope in God that I shall live to finish my letter after the battle. May Heaven bless you prays your

NELSON AND BRONTE

Nelson adapted his tactics as news of the enemy's strength and movements reached him. Because of the absence of Calder's and Louis's ships, his strength was less than he had expected, and there was always the risk that a French squadron might have escaped from Rochefort, or a Spanish squadron from Cartagena, and were on their way to reinforce Villeneuve. Nelson therefore tightened his own plan of attack and dispensed with the mobile reserve. He would fight in two divisions: his own weather column of twelve ships and Collingwood's lee column of fifteen, while the six frigates would hover within sight to relay signals. Meanwhile, as Anderson recorded, he ordered a general chase and to prepare for battle.

On the *Orion*, which was to fight in Nelson's column, Captain Codrington found time to write to his wife that evening:

How would your heart beat for me, dearest Jane, did you but know that we are now under every stitch of sail we can set, steering for the enemy, whom we suppose to be come out of Cadiz! Lord Nelson had just hoisted his *dinner flag* to several captains at 9 o'clock this morning, when to my great astonishment he wore ship [turned with the wind] and made the signal for a general chase to windward. It was nearly calm, and has continued so ever since, till towards evening: but we have now a nice air, which fills our flying kites and drives us along four knots an hour. *Orion*, true to the affection we bear her, has now got ahead of *all* but *Belleisle*, although she started in the very middle of the fleet, half of which were to windward and half to leeward. *Defence* and *Agamemnon* are upon the look-out nearest to Cadiz, and I conclude have seen all the enemy's movements; *Colossus* and *Mars* were stationed next, so as to keep up the communication with the fleet. The above four, and as many more of us, are now to form an advanced squadron; and I trust by the morning we shall all be united and in sight of the enemy.

We are fully prepared in every respect, and I have every confidence in the result being such as will at least keep up and justify the esteem you have for your husband. As to my coming out of the battle alive or dead, that is the affair of chance and the little cherub: but that I shall come out without dishonour is my affair; and yet I have but little apprehension about the matter, so great is my confidence in my ship, and in our excellent admiral. It is not, dear Jane, that I am insensible to the value of life with such a domestic circle as I belong to: no, my heart was never more alive to the sacrifice than at this very moment. But life in such a situation as this, even with the delightful prospect of returning to pass years in the society of a wife and children, whom I love with a religious reverence, is really but a secondary consideration.

However, it will be all over before you get this, and it is, therefore, needless to dwell longer on the subject. I feel a little tired; and, as I have now nothing to do but keep the ship's head the right way, and take care that the sails are well trimmed, in readiness for the morning, I shall even make that over to the officer of the watch and go to my cot; nor do I think I shall sleep the worse for my cabin being only divided from the quarterdeck by a boat's sail. And so, dear, I shall wish thee once more a good night, and that thy husband's conduct in the hour of battle may prove worthy of thee and thy children.

Expecting Villeneuve to make for the Straits of Gibraltar, Nelson did likewise, confident of encountering Louis's squadron hurrying north to meet him. But, on the morning of the 20th, the horizons were clear of any ships but his own. Villeneuve, he guessed, must have returned to Cadiz, and Louis might still be taking on stores and water at Tetuan. Richard Anderson, navigating master of the *Prince* at the rear of Nelson's line, became bored with the waiting, noting in his diary:

'Sunday. Oh, dear, I have to keep watch. Everybody is so busy . . . I don't dislike it. We have no church, or anything. I must read my Bible.'

With the weather turning foul, Nelson feared that a strong westerly wind might force him through the Straits and into the Mediterranean. His fleet, ready for battle, faced anticlimax and frustration. Depression set in and rumours spread, Richard Anderson jotting in his journal: 'Well, the bustle over. Enemy in port again. We chased all night and old ship sailed well. I am tired and we have bad weather today. I am not sorry that the enemy are in port for they are ten sail of the line superior.'

In the captain's cabin of the *Orion*, Codrington again wrote to his wife:

All our gay hopes are fled; and, instead of being under all possible sail in a very light breeze and fine weather, expecting to bring the enemy to battle, we are now under close-reefed topsails, in a very strong wind with thick rainy weather, and the dastardly French we find returned to Cadiz. Had they persevered we should certainly have come up with them, from the decisive dash we made for the Gut of Gibraltar. Of further particulars I know nothing; but Hope [Captain George Hope of the *Defence*], I observe, has been on board the admiral, and he, I conclude, has been just without shot of them all the time. I have no hesitation in saying that *Orion* beat all the fleet, except *Belleisle*; because we were much more advanced than any but her; and, as we gained on her greatly to windward, and also when we each steered the same course, I am not dissatisfied with respect to *her* even. In short, we are all charmed with our little ship, and have every confidence in her power of sailing in whatever point circumstances may direct. I went to bed last night full of hope that Lord Nelson's declaration would be verified; viz. that we should have a good battle, and go home to eat our Christmas dinner.

Nelson himself added a postscript to his letter to Emma:

October 20th. In the morning we were close to the mouth

of the Straits, but the wind had not come far enough to the westward to allow the combined fleets to weather the shoals off Trafalgar; but they were counted as far as forty sail of ships of war, which I suppose to be thirty-four of the line, and six frigates. A group of them was seen off the lighthouse of Cadiz this morning, but it blows so very fresh and thick weather, that I rather believe they will go into the harbour before night. May God Almighty give us success over these fellows, and enable us to get a peace.

Nelson ordered the fleet to wear and steer north-west back towards its original station fifty miles west of Cadiz. As they did so, a frigate signalled that the enemy were indeed at sea but still close to Cadiz. Then, Codrington recorded,

On the Sunday morning, Lord Nelson, as a compliment to Collingwood, called him on board by signal to consult with him, saying to Hardy, jocosely, that he should not be guided by his opinion unless it agreed with his own; and, upon asking him, Collingwood gave his opinion in favour of attacking the fleet immediately. Lord Nelson, however, kept to his own plan of waiting till he could get them further off; and as they did not seem determined to return immediately to Cadiz, but to persevere in attempting to pursue their original intention of pushing for Toulon, he continued waiting upon them, in two columns according to the order of sailing, and the memorable written instruction which was given out to all the captains.

By staying far from land, Nelson hoped to entice the enemy to run for the Straits so that he could be intercepted well away from any refuge. In fact, because of unfavourable winds, Villeneuve had had difficulty in getting his fleet out of Cadiz and they had not all reached the open sea until the morning of the 20th. He began by steering west, because of the south-westerly wind and so that he could take up the order of sailing he had planned: his flagship, the *Bucentaure*, in the centre of the twenty battleships in line ahead, with the remainder of the fleet as a mobile reserve under Admiral Gravina. Then that afternoon the wind shifted to the west – a wind that could carry him into the

Mediterranean. To take advantage of it, Villeneuve ordered his fleet to wear, form three columns and steer south. The squalls of the morning, and now the change of wind and course, caused confusion among captains far less experienced than the British at handling ships in formation at sea. In the event, the eighteen French and fifteen Spanish battleships were only able to steer south in one straggling, intermingled line ahead.

All this was watched and reported by Nelson's frigates. So darkness fell on 20 October. This, it became clear, was the eve of battle. Although Nelson remarked – in an unintended reference to expected casualties – to young midshipmen on the quarter-deck, 'This day or tomorrow will be a fortunate one for one of you young men,' he told his flag-captain, Hardy: 'The 21st of October will be our day.'

Many on board the British ships wrote eve-of-battle letters to their families, some assuming that they would only be sent in the event of their death in action. One such was Midshipman Robert Smith of the *Victory*:

Victory, October 20th, off Cadiz, Sunday evening

My most dear and honor'd parents,

As I expect to be in action tomorrow morning with the enemy of our country, the idea of which I assure you gives me great pleasure, in case I shall fall in the *noble cause* have wrote these few last lines to assure you that I shall die with a clear conscience, pure heart and in peace with all men. Have only a few requests to make, first that you will have the goodness to thank and make my kind respects to all friends for their kind attention to me. Secondly that you will not give way to any uneasiness on my account and further that you my dearest of mothers will not give way to those low spirits which you are subject to, consider that your affectionate son could not die in a more glorious cause and that it is all the fortune of war. Have no doubt had I survived the glorious day should have met with the reward due to my merit from worthy friends and a *good country*. Have requested every profit arising from my stock to be given you with my desk as a small tribute of affection. Shall conclude this last with my kindest duty to you my honor'd parents, love to sister, brothers, and praying the Almighty to receive my soul. Remain your ever dutiful and affectionate son,

R. SMITH

Even after nightfall the British frigates continued to observe the movements of the combined Franco-Spanish fleet by carefully watching their lights. Nelson had ordered, 'Captain Blackwood to keep two frigates in sight of the enemy in the night . . . If the enemy are standing to the southward, or towards the Straits, burn two blue lights together every hour in order to make the greater blaze. If the enemy are standing to the westward, three guns quick every hour.' The French and Spanish were anxiously watching, too. One French officer reported:

Lights were continuously seen at various points of the horizon. They were the signals of the English fleet and the look-out ships that felt the way for them. The reports of cannon, repeated from time to time, and blue lights casting a bright and sudden glare in the midst of profound darkness were soon added to the earlier signals and convinced Admiral Villeneuve that he would vainly attempt to conceal his course from his active foes.

In the *Redoutable*, Captain Lucas saw confusion in the ships around him but made sure that his own would be ready to fight next day:

About nine o'clock at night the flagship made the general signal to the fleet to form in the order of battle at once. To carry out this evolution, those ships most to leeward ought to have shown a light at each masthead, so as to mark their positions. Whether this was done I do not know: at any rate I was unable to see such lights. At that moment, indeed, we were all widely scattered. Another cause of confusion was this. Nearly all the ships had answered the admiral's signals with flares, which made it impossible to tell which was the flagship. All I could do was to follow the motions of other ships near me, which were closing on some to leeward.

The whole fleet was by this time cleared for action, in accordance with orders signalled from the *Bucentaure* earlier in the night. In the *Redoutable*, however, we had cleared for action immediately after leaving Cadiz. A battle being certain, I kept few men on duty during the night, sending most of the officers and men to rest, so that they might be as fresh as possible for the coming fight.

Admiral Gravina's chief of staff, Rear-Admiral Don Antonio de Escano, stared into the night from the quarterdeck of the *Principe de Asturias* and saw 'coloured lights quite close, which could only be from enemy frigates located between the two fleets. At 9 p.m. the enemy fired signal guns and by the length of time between the flash and the sound – eight seconds – they must have been two miles distant.' Meanwhile in the frigate *Euryalus*, Midshipman Hercules Robinson recalled: 'When we had brought the two fleets fairly together, we took our place between the two lines of lights, as a cab might in Regent Street, the watch was called and [Captain] Blackwood turned in quietly to wait for the morning.'

CHAPTER 5

England Expects

For the ships' companies of the opposing fleets – twenty-seven British sail of the line and thirty-three French and Spanish – it was a restless night as they waited for the first light of day and what that might reveal. At about five o'clock in the dim dawn, look-outs on several ships sighted the enemy. The chaplain of the *Revenge*, the Reverend John Greenly, claimed that he had been the first, although it is more likely that it was a seaman high on the mast of the same ship, for another was to write:

As the day began to dawn, a man at the topmast-head called out, 'A sail on the starboard bow!' and in two or three minutes more he gave another call that there was more than one sail, for indeed they looked like a forest of masts rising from the ocean and, as the morning got light, we could plainly discern them from the deck.

On board the *Prince*, despite the early hour, Richard Anderson was hard at work when the enemy was sighted: 'We got 30 butts of water from *Britannia* and in the midst of it a signal is made to chase and signal to prepare for battle.' Ahead, on the *Victory*, Able Seaman John Brown's impression echoed feelings on the *Revenge*: 'On Monday the 21st at day light the French and Spanish fleets was like a great wood on our lee bow, which cheered the hearts of every British tar in the *Victory* like lions anxious to be at it.' In the *Belleisle* an officer recalled:

As the day dawned the horizon appeared covered with ships. The whole force of the enemy was discovered standing to the southward, distant about nine miles between us and the coast near Trafalgar. I was awaked by the cheers of the crew and by their rushing up the hatchways to get a glimpse of the hostile fleet. The delight manifested exceeded anything I ever witnessed, surpassing even those gratulations when our native cliffs are descried after a long period of distant service.

Another seaman, George Hewson, saw them and maintained that 'The human mind cannot form a grander or more noble sight.' Looking east from the deck of the *Euryalus*, Midshipman Hercules Robinson remembered 'a beautiful, misty, sun-shiny morning'. Midshipman William Badcock, in the *Neptune*, observed that

the sun rose, which, as it ascended from its bed of ocean, looked hazy and watery, as if it smiled in tears on many brave hearts which fate had decreed should never see it set. It was my morning watch; I was midshipman of the forecastle, and at the first dawn of day a forest of strange masts was seen to leeward. I ran aft and informed the officer of the watch. The captain was on deck in a moment, and ere it was well light, the signals were flying through the fleet to bear up and form the order of sailing in two columns.

The wind had moderated considerably in the night, but still our fleet, which consisted of twenty-seven sail of the line, four frigates, a schooner, and cutter, was much scattered. Our ship had been previously prepared for battle, so that with the exception of stowing hammocks, slinging the lower yards, stoppering the topsail-sheets, and other minor matters, little remained to be done.

In the *Bellerophon*, the first lieutenant, William Cumby, noted:

About a quarter before six I was roused from my slumbers by my shipmate Overton, the master, who call'd out 'Cumby my boy turn out, here they are all ready for you, thrice and thirty sail of the line close under our lee and evidently disposed to wait our attack.' You may readily conclude I did not long remain in a recumbent position but springing out of bed hurried on my clothes and kneeling down by the side of my cot put up a short but fervent prayer to the great God of battles for a glorious victory to the arms of my country, committing myself individually to

His allwise disposal and begging His gracious protection and favour for my dear wife and children whatever His unerring wisdom might see fit to order for myself . . . I was soon on deck when the enemy's fleet was distinctly seen to leeward [windward] standing to the southward under easy sail, and forming in line on the starboard tack.

In the *Victory*, the commander-in-chief had been awake since before dawn. The ship's surgeon, Dr William Beatty, recorded:

Soon after daylight, Lord Nelson came upon deck. He was dressed as usual in his admiral's frock coat, bearing on the left breast four stars of different Orders, which he always wore with his common apparel. He did not wear his sword . . . it had been taken from the place where it hung up in his cabin and was laid ready on his table; but it is supposed he forgot to call for it . . . He displayed excellent spirits and expressed his pleasure at the prospect of giving a fatal blow to the naval power of France and Spain . . . declaring to Captain Hardy that 'he would not be contented with capturing less than 20 sail of the line'. He afterwards pleasantly observed that 'the 21st of October was the happiest day in the year among his family' but did not assign the reason for this.*

Lord Nelson then ascended the poop to have a better view of . . . the British fleet; and, while there, gave particular directions for taking down from his cabin the different fixtures and for being very careful in removing the portrait of Lady Hamilton. 'Take care of my Guardian Angel,' said he, addressing himself to the persons to be employed in the business . . .

The wind was now from the west but the breezes were very light with a long, heavy swell running.

Across in the *Royal Sovereign*, Admiral Collingwood's valet

---

* Nelson did explain this on other occasions. It was both the anniversary of a successful action fought by his uncle, the late Captain Maurice Suckling, against the French in the Caribbean, and also the day of the fair at Burnham Thorpe, the village where he had been born, in Norfolk.

was to recall how he

entered the admiral's cabin about daylight and found him already up and dressing. He asked me if I had seen the French fleet; and on my replying that I had not he told me to look out at them, adding that, in a very short time, we should see a great deal more of them. I then observed a crowd of ships to leeward; but I could not help looking with still greater interest at the admiral, who, during all this time, was shaving himself with a composure that quite astonished me.

Admiral Collingwood dressed himself that morning with peculiar care; and soon after meeting Lieutenant Clavell [the first lieutenant], advised him to pull off his boots. 'You had better put on silk stockings as I have done: for if one should get a shot in the leg they would be so much more manageable for the surgeon.'

Collingwood came out on the quarterdeck and said to a group of his officers: 'Now, gentlemen, let us do something today which the world will talk of hereafter.' Then, walking round the gun-decks, the Northumbrian told the crews, 'Today, my lads, we must show those fellows what the "Tars of the Tyne" can do!'

The opposing fleets now lay about nine miles apart, steering towards the Straits of Gibraltar, some thirty miles south-west of Cape Trafalgar. At six o'clock, Blackwood of the *Euryalus* was ordered by signal to cross to the *Victory* and was rowed over since the fleet was moving at walking-pace. He recalled:

In a few minutes I went on board and had the satisfaction to find the admiral in good but very calm spirits. On receiving my congratulations at the approach of the moment he so often and for so long had wished for, he replied, 'I mean today to bleed the captains of the frigates as I shall keep you on board until the very last minute.'* His mind seemed entirely directed to the strength and formation of

* Nelson planned to keep his frigate captains with him until the *Victory* was in range of the enemy to ensure they received his final orders, which they might have to repeat by signal to the fleet.

the enemy's line as well as the effects his novel mode of attack was likely to produce.

At half past six, Nelson ordered his fleet to form two columns in which he and Collingwood would attack. It was a slow man-oeuvre to perform in the light wind; it would be about two hours before the formation could come together and six before action could begin. Half an hour later, Nelson noted in his diary, 'At seven, the enemy wearing in succession.' Villeneuve, seeing the British begin to divide into two divisions, had realised that Nelson's fleet was stronger than he had anticipated and that an attack was imminent. He decided to abandon his run for the Straits and head back to Cadiz and, he hoped, safety. As his report put it:

The wind was very light from the west, with a heavy swell on. The enemy's fleet, which was counted as twenty-seven ships of the line, seemed to be heading *en masse* for my rear squadron; with the double object, apparently, of engaging in greatly superior force and on cutting the combined fleet off from Cadiz. I therefore signalled for the fleet to wear all together, and form line of battle in the reverse order. My main idea was to secure the rear squadron from being overpowered by the enemy's attack in force. Through this new disposition the third squadron, under Rear-Admiral Dumanoir, became the advance guard, with the *Neptuno*, commanded by Don Gaetano Valdez, as squadron leader. I myself was in the centre of the fleet, in the *Bucentaure*, and Vice-Admiral Alava followed me with the second squadron. The Squadron of Observation, under the orders of Admiral Gravina, formed the rear guard, with, as second-in-command, Rear-Admiral Magon in the *Algésiras*.

The enemy continued to steer for us under all sail, and at nine o'clock I was able to make out that their fleet was formed in two columns, of which one was heading directly for my flagship and the other towards the rear of the com-bined fleet. The wind was very light, the sea with a swell on, owing to which our formation in line was rendered very difficult to effect; but in the circumstances, considering the nature of the attack that I foresaw the enemy were about to make, the irregularity of our order did not seem a disadvantage, if each ship could have continued to keep to the wind, and close upon the ship next ahead.

I made a signal to the leading ships to keep as close as possible to the wind and to make all sail possible. At eleven o'clock I signalled to the rear squadron to keep closer to the wind and support the centre, which appeared to be the point on which the enemy now appeared to be directing his main attack. The enemy meanwhile came steadily on, though the wind was very light. They had their most powerful ships at the head of the columns. That to the north had four three-deckers.

In the *Intrépide*, Lieutenant des Touches noted the drastic change in Villeneuve's strategy:

At dawn on the 21st the two squadrons became aware of each other and battle seemed inevitable. The admiral [Villeneuve] signalled to us to get into order of battle in a single line on the larboard tack in order to give the most damaged ships the chance to return to Cadiz. We therefore turned about and set course towards the north. The *Intrépide* was part of the vanguard commanded by Rear-Admiral Dumanoir; the *Bucentaure* and the *Santissima Trinidad*,* flying the flags of Vice-Admirals Villeneuve and Gravina, were in the middle of the line of battle. The rearguard extended in the distance under the command of Rear-Admiral Magon in the *Algésiras*. Instead of ordering the vanguard to get into the wind so that the line-ahead formation could be properly formed, the admiral constantly signalled to sail closer to the wind so that the line lost its shape more and more with vessels moving off in all directions, leaving wide gaps which the English were bound to exploit. The English moreover appeared to have no other object than to prevent our escape.

The French and Spanish ships were so intermingled that all cohesion was lost and communication between captains by sig-

* The huge Spanish ship of up to 140 guns.

nal, or voice, was difficult.

At 6.40 a.m., Nelson had the signal 'Prepare for battle' hoisted – the order for the fleet to clear for action. All the bulkheads, screens and furniture had been removed from the gundecks, which were now open and clear from stem to stern, the gun-crews, stripped to the waist, checking their flintlock firing mechanisms and eating cold food brought from the galley, where the cooking fires had been doused; chicken coops and livestock were pushed overboard.

Meanwhile, the *Victory* slowly hauled ahead of the weather line. At about seven, Nelson had returned to his cabin when Lieutenant John Pasco knocked and entered to report the latest signals received. He intended to ask the admiral to reconsider his decision to transfer him to the post of signals officer during the coming engagement; Pasco's grievance was that it was the custom, after a successful battle, for the first lieutenant to be promoted captain. He remembered: 'On entering the cabin, I discovered his Lordship on his knees writing . . . I waited till he rose and communicated what I had to report but could not at such a moment disturb his mind with any grievances of mine.'

Nelson had first made a straightforward entry in his diary, but then he wrote:

At daylight saw the enemy's combined fleet from East to ESE; bore away; made the signal for order of sailing, and to prepare for battle; the enemy with their heads to the southward: at seven the enemy wearing in succession. May the great God, whom I worship, grant to my country, and for the benefit of Europe in general, a great and glorious victory; and may no misconduct in any one tarnish it; and may humanity after victory be the predominant feature in the British fleet. For myself, individually, I commit my life to Him who made me, and may His blessing light upon my endeavours for serving my country faithfully. To Him I resign myself and the just cause which is entrusted to me to defend. Amen. Amen. Amen.

Nelson then invited Hardy and Blackwood into his cabin to witness a codicil to his will:

October the twenty-first, one thousand eight hundred and five, then in sight of the combined fleets of France and Spain, distant about ten miles.

Whereas the eminent services of Emma Hamilton, widow of the Right Honourable Sir William Hamilton, have been of the very greatest service to our king and country, to my knowledge, without her receiving any reward from either our king or country . . .

Could I have rewarded these services, I would not now call upon my country; but as that has not been in my power, I leave Emma Lady Hamilton, therefore, a legacy to my king and country, that they will give her an ample provision to maintain her rank in life. I also leave to the beneficence of my country my adopted daughter, Horatia Nelson Thompson; and I desire she will use in future the name of Nelson only.

In the *Revenge*, sailing in Collingwood's lee column, the seaman William Robinson described preparations:

There was nearly six hours to prepare for battle, while we glided down to them under the influence of a gentle breeze . . . During this time each ship was making the usual preparations such as breaking away the captain's and officers' cabins and sending all the lumber below – the doctors, parson, purser and loblolly men were also busy getting the medicine chests and bandages out; and sails prepared for the wounded to be placed on, that they might be dressed in rotation as they were taken down to the after cockpit.

On board the *Ajax* in the weather column Second Lieutenant Samuel Ellis of the Royal Marines noted:

I was sent below with orders and was much struck with the preparations made by the bluejackets, the majority of whom were stripped to the waist; a handkerchief was tightly bound round their heads and over the ears, to deaden the noise of the cannon, many men being deaf for days after an action. The men were variously occupied – some were sharpening their cutlasses, others polishing the guns, as though an inspection were about to take place instead of a mortal combat, whilst three or four, as if in mere bravado, were dancing a hornpipe. Occasionally they would look out of the ports and speculate as to the various ships of the enemy, many of which had been on former occasions engaged by our vessels.

There was still time to write a final letter home. In the *Royal Sovereign*, at the head of the lee line, Midshipman Thomas Aikenhead wrote to his sister at Portsmouth:

We have just piped to breakfast; thirty-five sail, besides smaller vessels, are now on our beam, about three miles off. Should I, my dear parents, fall in defence of my king, let that thought console you. I feel not the least dread on my spirits. Oh my parents, sisters, brothers, dear grandfather, grandmother, and aunt, believe me ever yours!

Accept, perhaps for the last time, your brother's love; be assured I feel for my friends, should I die in this glorious action – glorious, no doubt, it will be. Every British heart pants for glory. Our old admiral [Collingwood] is quite young with the thoughts of it. If I survive, nothing will give me greater pleasure than embracing my dearest relations. Do not, in case I fall, grieve – it will be to no purpose. Many brave fellows will no doubt fall with me on both sides. Oh! Betsey, with what ardour I shall, if permitted by God's providence, come to England to embrace you all!

On the upper decks of some ships bands played popular, patriotic music such as 'Rule, Britannia', 'Britons Strike Home' and 'The Downfall of Paris', while first lieutenants made sure their ships' companies had something to eat and drink. 'So we piped to dinner and ate a bit of raw pork and half a pint of wine,' remembered Able Seaman John Brown of the *Victory*. Able Seaman John Cash of the *Tonnant*, a 74 that had been captured by Nelson at the Battle of the Nile, noted:

Our good captain called all hands and said, 'My lads, this will be a glorious day for us and the groundwork of a speedy return to our homes.' He then ordered bread and cheese and butter and beer for every man at the guns. I was one of them and, believe me, we ate and drank and were as cheerful as ever we had been over a pot of beer.

There was fatalism, too. In the *Revenge*, William Robinson remembered: 'Some would be offering a guinea for a glass of grog, whilst others were making a sort of mutual verbal will such as, "If one of Johnny Crapeau's shots knocks my head off, you will take all my effects; and if you are killed and I am not, why, I will have all yours." '

There were many practicalities to be attended to as Lieutenant Cumby of the *Bellerophon*, now sailing in the lee column, later attested:

I was soon on deck when the enemy's fleet was distinctly seen to leeward standing to the southward under easy sail, and forming in line on the starboard tack. At six o'clock the signal was made to form the order of sailing and soon after to bear up and steer ENE. We made sail in our station and at twenty minutes past six we answered the signal to prepare for battle and soon afterwards to steer east: we then beat to quarters and cleared ship for action. After I had breakfasted as usual at 8 o'clock with the captn in his cabin, he begged of me to wait a little as he had something to show me, when he produced and requested me to peruse Lord Nelson's private memorandum, addressed to the captains relative to the conduct of the ships in action; which having read he enquired whether I perfectly understood the admiral's instructions. I replied they were so distinct and explicit, that it was quite impossible they could be misunderstood. He then expressed his satisfaction, and said he wished me to be made acquainted with it that in the event of his being 'bowl'd out' I might know how to conduct the ship agreeably to the admiral's wishes. On this I observed that it was very possible that the same shot which disposed of him might have an equally tranquillising effect upon me and under that idea I submitted to him the expediency of the master 'as being the only officer who in such case would remain on the quarterdeck' being also apprised of the admiral's instructions that he might be enabled to communicate them to the next officer whoever he might be that should succeed to the command of the ship. To this Captain Cooke immediately assented and poor Overton the master was desired to read the memorandum, which he did, and here I may be permitted to remark *en passant*, that of the three officers who carried the knowledge of this private memorandum into the action, I was the only one who brought it out.

On going round the decks to see everything in its place, and all in perfect order before I reported to the captain the ship in readiness for action, the fifth or junior lieutenant, George Lawrence Saunders, who commanded the seven foremost guns on each side of the lower deck, pointed out to me some of the guns at his quarters where the zeal of the seamen had led them to chalk in large characters on their guns the words 'Victory or Death', a very gratifying mark of the spirit with which they were going to their work. At eleven o'clock finding we should not be in action for an hour or more we piped to dinner which we had ordered to be in readiness for the ship's company at that hour thinking that Englishmen would fight all the better for having a comfortable meal and at the same time Captain Cooke joined us in partaking of some cold meat etc. on the rudder head, all our bulkheads, tables etc. being necessarily taken down and carried below.

On board the *Neptune*, near the head of the weather column, Midshipman Badcock was impressed by the visual splendour presented by the enemy:

It was a beautiful sight when their line was completed, their broadsides turned towards us, showing their iron teeth. Some of the enemy's ships were painted like ourselves with double yellow streaks, some with a broad single red or yellow streak, others all black and the noble *Santissima Trinidad* with four distinct lines of red with a white ribbon between them, made her seem to be a super man-of-war, which, indeed, she was. Her appearance was imposing, her head splendidly ornamented with a colossal group of figures, painted white, representing the Holy Trinity, from which she took her name.

Yet on the *Santissima Trinidad*, there was some apprehension. According to one young Spanish seaman:

Early in the morning the decks were cleared for action and, when all was ready for serving the guns and working the ship, I heard someone say: 'The sand – bring the sand.' A number of sailors were posted on the ladders from the hatchway to the hold and between decks, and in this way were hauling up sacks of sand . . . they were emptied out on the upper decks, the poop and the fo'c'sle, the sand being spread about so as to cover all the planking. The same thing was done between decks. My curiosity prompted me to ask a lad who stood next to me what this was for. 'For the blood,' he said very coolly. 'For the blood!' I exclaimed, unable to repress a shudder. I looked at the sand – I looked at the men who were busily employed on this task – and for a moment I felt I was a coward.

But there were no qualms on board the French *Redoutable*, where Captain Lucas was trying to keep station as the fleet tacked, so that he could give the flagship *Bucentaure* the protection of his superbly trained sharpshooters when it came to close-quarter fighting. He continued:

By nine o'clock the enemy had formed up in two columns. They were under all sail – they even had studding sails out – and heading directly for our fleet, before a light breeze from the west-south-west . . . The *Redoutable*'s place was third ship astern of the flagship *Bucentaure*. I at once made every effort to take station in the wake of the flagship, leaving between her and myself the space necessary for my two immediate leaders. One of them was not very far out of its station, but the other showed no signs of trying to take post. That ship was at some distance to leeward of the line, which was now beginning to form ahead of the admiral.

Lucas himself decided to concentrate on encouraging his ship's company: 'Preceded by the drums and fifes that I had on board, I paraded at the head of my officers round all the decks; everywhere I found gallant lads burning with impatience to be in the fray; many of them saying to me, "Captain, don't forget to board!" '

In the *Victory*, Nelson was similarly engaged. There was no need for further orders to the fleet: his captains knew enough to carry them into action and, in the 'pell-mell' battle he planned, the scene would be so confused and hidden in gunsmoke that the outcome would only become clear once the superior British gunnery had achieved its purpose. Instead, as a contemporary described, he attended to the morale of his flagship, visiting every part of it with Captain Hardy:

Lord Nelson went over the different decks of the *Victory*, saw and spoke to the different classes of seamen, encouraged them with his usual affability and was much pleased with the manner in which the seamen had barricaded the hawse-holes of the ship.* All was perfect death-like silence, till just before the action began. Three cheers were given his Lordship as he ascended the quarterdeck ladder. He had been particular in recommending cool, steady firing, in preference to a hurrying fire without aim, or precision.

In a letter home, one seaman recorded: 'We cleared away our guns whilst Lord Nelson went round the decks and said, "My noble lads, this will be a glorious day for England, whoever lives to see it. I shan't be satisfied with 12 ships this day, as I took at the Nile." '

During Nelson's tour, an Irish seaman was observed cutting a notch into a wooden gun-carriage, adding it to those that, he explained, already marked victories; he was carving the new one before action in case he did not survive. Nelson laughed and said, 'You'll make notches enough in the enemy's ships.'

Some were more reflective. Lieutenant Louis Roteley of the Royal Marines remembered the advice his father had given him when he had first been appointed to the *Victory*: 'Louis, you will soon be in battle. I foresee a tremendous contest but, whatever you do, be sure to keep your head erect in battle. Never bow to a

* Ports for mooring cables through which the enemy might be able to board.

Frenchman's shot; it is folly, for when you hear the balls whistle you are safe, the ball has passed harmless before you can hear it.'

Close behind the *Royal Sovereign*, in the *Belleisle* (like the *Tonnant*, a prize captured from the French), Second Lieutenant Paul Harris Nicolas of the Royal Marines noticed a sombre mood:

The officers now met at breakfast; and though each seemed to exult in the hope of a glorious termination to the contest so near at hand, a fearful presage was experienced that all would not again unite at that festive board. One was particularly impressed with a persuasion that he should not survive the day, nor could he divest himself of this presentiment, but made the necessary disposal of his property in the event of his death. The sound of the drums, however, soon put an end to our meditations, and after a hasty and, alas, a final farewell to some, we repaired to our respective posts.

At eleven o'clock that morning, Nelson and his officers stood on the poop of the *Victory* – the highest deck at the stern of the ship – from which they could see the two British divisions under full sail dipping towards the enemy, now only three miles away. There was still an hour before action would be joined and time for any final instructions to be issued, but the two columns seemed to be in order, except for the 64-gun *Africa*, which had missed a signal to deploy during the night and was away to the north.

To starboard, Collingwood's line was led by his flagship, the *Royal Sovereign*, like the *Victory* mounting one hundred guns. The fourteen ships astern of her were mostly 74s but the fourth in line, the *Tonnant*, mounted eighty guns; the eighth, the *Dreadnought*, ninety-eight. Nelson, on the other hand, was leading his column with his flagship followed by two more heavy ships, the *Téméraire* and the *Neptune*, both of ninety-eight guns; the fifth in the line was Lord Northesk's flagship, the 100-gun *Britannia*. Out on the flanks of the columns cruised four frigates to repeat signals and assist any crippled battleships, and also a despatch-vessel, the schooner *Pickle*, which could be employed to carry news of whatever happened that day.

Both Dr Beatty and Captain Blackwood, who was still on board the *Victory*, worried about Nelson. Beatty wished the admiral would change into a less conspicuous uniform coat so as to present a less obvious target when the action became close; but the doctor was advised not to say this by the admiral's secretary. Blackwood's warnings were also ignored, as he explained:

About ten o'clock, Lord Nelson's anxiety to close with the enemy became very apparent: he frequently remarked that they put a good face upon it; but always quickly added, 'I'll give them such a dressing as they never had before,' regretting at the same time the vicinity of the land. At that critical moment I ventured to represent to his Lordship, the value of such a life as his, and particularly in the present battle; and I proposed hoisting his flag in the *Euryalus*, whence he could better see what was going on, as well as what to order in case of necessity. But he would not hear of it, and gave as his reason the force of example; and probably he was right. My next object, therefore, was to endeavour to induce his Lordship to allow the *Téméraire*, *Neptune* and *Leviathan* to lead into action before the *Victory*, which was then the headmost.

After much conversation, in which I ventured to give it as the joint opinion of Captain Hardy and myself, how advantageous it would be to the fleet for his Lordship to keep as long as possible out of the battle, he at length consented to allow the *Téméraire*, which was then sailing abreast of the *Victory*, to go a-head, and hailed Captain Harvey to say such were his intentions, if the *Téméraire* could pass the *Victory*. Captain Harvey being rather out of hail, his Lordship sent me to communicate his wishes, which I did; when, on returning to the *Victory*, I found him doing all he could to increase rather than diminish sail, so that the *Téméraire* could not pass the *Victory*: consequently when they came within gunshot of the enemy, Captain Harvey, finding his efforts ineffectual, was obliged to take his station astern of the admiral . . .

During the five hours and a half that I remained on board the *Victory*, in which I was not ten times from his side, he frequently asked me, what I should consider as a victory? the certainty of which he never for an instant seemed to doubt, although from the situation of the land he questioned the possibility of the subsequent preservation of the prizes. My answer was, 'That considering the handsome way in which the battle was offered by the enemy, their apparent determination for a fair trial of strength, and the proximity of the land, I thought if fourteen ships were captured, it would be a glorious result'; to which he always replied, 'I shall not, Blackwood, be satisfied with anything short of twenty.'

Nelson's plan of attack was about to be realised. Always flexible, at its most basic it remained that of making a dangerous approach in two columns at right angles to the enemy before breaking through and enveloping their centre and rear for a gunnery engagement, which would prove decisive before the van could turn and come to their aid. But this meant that the leading British ships would have to face the concentrated broadsides of the enemy line for perhaps twenty minutes before their own could be brought to bear. Nelson knew that this would not be quite so dangerous as it seemed. Whereas his own ships were pitching to the swell, the enemy were broadside to the sea and rolling, which would make accurate gunnery far more difficult. Their problems would be exacerbated because their guns were fired by slow-matches with a delay between the order to fire and the actual firing; whereas the British had the new flintlock mechanism, which was almost instantaneous.

The two British columns did not approach in exact line astern. Collingwood's lee column was, it seemed to some who watched, advancing in loose echelon to starboard so as to come into action in quick succession, thereby sharing their vulnerability to enemy gunfire. Nelson always intended to confuse the enemy with his tactics. At this time, his own weather column seemed to be aiming for the enemy's van when, as all knew, he intended to break through the centre close to Villeneuve's flagship.

At 11.35, Nelson turned to Captain Blackwood, as the latter recalled:

I was walking with him, on the poop, when he said, 'I'll

now amuse the fleet with a signal'; and he asked me if I did not think there was one yet wanting? I answered that I thought the whole of the fleet seemed very clearly to understand what they were about, and to vie with each other who should first get nearest to the *Victory*, or *Royal Sovereign*. These words were scarcely uttered, when his last well-known signal was made, 'England expects every man will do his duty.' The shout with which it was received throughout the fleet was truly sublime. 'Now', said Lord Nelson, 'I can do no more. We must trust to the great Disposer of all events, and the justice of our cause. I thank God for this great opportunity of doing my duty.'

The acting signals officer Lieutenant Pasco, whose recollections of the incident might be more reliable, remembered it differently:

His Lordship came to me on the poop, and after ordering certain signals to be made, about a quarter to noon he said: 'Mr Pasco, I wish to say to the fleet, "England confides that every man will do his duty." ' And he added, 'You must be quick, for I have one more to make, which is for close action.' I replied, 'If your Lordship will permit me to substitute the word "expects" for "confides" the signal will sooner be completed, because the word "expects" is in the vocabulary, but the word "confides" must be spelt.' His Lordship replied in haste, and with seeming satisfaction, 'That will do, Pasco; make it directly.' When it had been answered by a few ships in the van, he ordered me to make the signal for close action, and to keep it up.

Blackwood and Captain Prowse of the *Sirius* were told to return to their frigates. It was an emotional moment, particularly for Blackwood who, like so many young officers, saw Nelson as a father-figure. As they turned to board their boats, Blackwood took the admiral's left hand and said, 'I trust, my Lord, that on my return to the *Victory*, which will be as soon as possible, I shall find your Lordship well and in possession of twenty prizes.' Nelson replied, 'God bless you, Blackwood. I shall never speak to you again.'

The British fleet was swooping over the swell under every sail that could be set, even studding sails extending from the yards like wings. It was clear that Collingwood's division, nearly a mile to the south of Nelson's, would be in action first and would soon come within extreme range of the enemy. As Collingwood steered for the sixteenth ship from the enemy's rear, at 11.50, flashes and billows of smoke were seen from the French line; at a range of half a mile, the *Fougueux* had fired a broadside at the *Royal Sovereign* and, a moment later, the whole of the enemy's rear division followed with the sound of rolling thunder. Collingwood could not bring his own broadside to bear on the ships ahead but, exactly at noon, he too opened fire, not with any chance of hitting a target but to conceal his ship for a moment in a cloud of her own gunsmoke. Seeing that the weather line was yet to come into action, Collingwood remarked, 'What would Nelson give to be here!' Watching from his own quarterdeck, Nelson exclaimed, 'See how that noble fellow Collingwood takes his ship into action! How I envy him!'

Nelson had no need to be envious for long. He planned to break the enemy line close to Villeneuve's flagship, the *Bucentaure*, but she was yet to be identified and in any case he wanted to keep the enemy guessing. No captain seemed to have taken notes during Nelson's briefing in the *Victory* when he had joined the fleet, or certainly not kept any, and details of the exact course he steered are not clear. But in the efficient Captain Codrington's ship, the *Orion*, lying towards the rear of Nelson's line, an entry was made in the log: 'The *Victory*, after making a feint of attacking their van, hauled to starboard so as to reach their centre and then wore round to pass under the lee of the *Bucentaure*.' This was confirmed by the French Admiral Dumanoir, commanding the enemy van, who later said: 'The left column of the English, having Admiral Nelson at its head, bore at first on the French vanguard, which I commanded, but, finding it too compact, they exchanged some shots with us, then struck at the centre of our line.'

This showed the cunning of Nelson's tactics. By steering for the head of the enemy line he ensured that they would hold their course and formation and this would delay any move they might make in turning to support the centre and rear, which were his true objectives. He turned away from the van to the centre, where he presumed Villeneuve's flagship lay, while keeping at the limit of the enemy broadsides. Once Nelson identified the *Bucentaure*, he put his helm over to break through the line. With action imminent, he gave orders to cut away the studding sails, so that they fell overboard, and to clew up the mainsails to lessen the risk of fire.

Nelson had no more signals to make. Some hundreds of yards from the *Victory*, Villeneuve was about to give his own final orders on the quarterdeck of the *Bucentaure*. He had heard the first gunfire at the rear of his fleet and could see the *Victory* leading her line of battleships towards him, Union flags flying from their topmast stays and white ensigns from their sterns. All the French and Spanish ships hoisted their national colours, while the Spaniards had hung large wooden crosses from the boom above each ship's stern and the French displayed their eagles – the carved and gilded Napoleonic emblem carried into action by every ship and regiment – at the foot of their mainmasts. Just as the British were coming into the extreme range of his guns, Villeneuve seized the *Bucentaure*'s eagle, waved it above his head and shouted to those around him, 'My friends, I am going to throw this on board the English ship. We will go and fetch it back, or die!' Having already made the signal for his captains to open fire at their own discretion as the British came within range, Villeneuve ordered his last signal to be hoisted: 'Every ship which is not in action is not at her post and must take station to bring herself as speedily as possible under fire.' Then, as one of his brother-officers put it, 'It only remained for him to show himself personally the bravest of his captains.'

CHAPTER 6

Collingwood

The first ships to open fire at Trafalgar were in the rear of the French line. Amongst the British, the lee line was the first to join close action. Their commanders were in sharp contrast. Flying his flag in the 74-gun *Algésiras* was the fierce little Breton, Rear-Admiral Charles de Magon. Napoleon's staff considered him 'a daring and impetuous fellow'; the year before, he had been chosen to lead the invasion fleet across the Channel to the beaches of Kent. When Villeneuve had turned back from the Channel after the action with Calder, Magon had 'stamped and foamed at the mouth', then, as the admiral passed in his flagship, 'gave vent to furious exclamations and flung at him in his rage whatever happened to be at hand, including his field-glass and even his wig, both of which fell into the sea'. Approaching him in the *Royal Sovereign* was Vice-Admiral Sir Cuthbert Collingwood: tall, quiet, reflective, munching an apple as he went into action. His flag-captain, Edward Rotherham, showed equal sang-froid; when advised to remove his cocked hat, trimmed with gold lace, to avoid becoming a target for sharpshooters, he replied, 'I have always fought in a cocked hat and I always will.'

The *Royal Sovereign* was the only British ship yet in action but she still could not reply effectively to enemy broadsides. Midshipman Hercules Robinson, watching from the *Euryalus*, grasped Collingwood's optimistic calculation that 'fire would scarcely be opened until the approaching ship was within four hundred yards and, as this ground would be over in five or six minutes, she would not have to encounter more than a couple of broadsides into her bows and then would have ample revenge in a double-shotted broadside into her opponent's stern'.

But to protect them from those broadsides that would sweep his decks from bow to stern, Collingwood ordered his men to lie down between the guns, ready to spring into action once his target was reached. This was not the *Fougueux*, which had first fired upon him, but the huge, black-painted *Santa Ana* of 112 guns, the flagship of the Spanish Rear-Admiral Ignacio Alava, which lay immediately ahead of the *Fougueux*. Here, the *Royal Sovereign* broke through the enemy line. As she passed the stern of the *Santa Ana*, cliff-like and richly carved with its rows of windows lighting the admiral's and captain's quarters, Collingwood gave the order to fire and his port broadside, triple-shotted, raked her from stern to bow. It was devastating, killing or wounding scores of men and knocking fourteen guns from their carriages. Then Collingwood directly fired his starboard broadside into the bow of the *Fougueux*, albeit at longer range.

He now ordered the helm hard over and the *Royal Sovereign* swung against the far side of the *Santa Ana*. The Spanish were ready and loosed their starboard broadside, which made the British ship heel under the impact. The British had reloaded their port-side guns and fired them at point-blank range. Midshipman George Castle, who was with the 32-pounder guns on the lower gun-deck of the *Royal Sovereign*, wrote later: 'I can assure you it was glorious work. I think you would have liked to have seen me thump into her quarter.'

Still the *Royal Sovereign* fought alone and enemy ships closed in on her, the *Fougueux* raking her from stern to bow. Collingwood was on the poop as two more French ships and a Spaniard sailed through the smoke, and ordered the marines around him to take cover from the small-arms fire that could be expected to follow the broadsides. He himself was hit in the leg, as he recollected: 'It was by a splinter – a pretty severe blow. I had a good many thumps; one in the back, which I think was the wind of a great shot, for I never saw anything that did it.'

Soon afterwards, on the quarterdeck, the ship's navigating master, William Chalmers, was standing beside Collingwood when, as the admiral recalled:

A great shot almost divided his body: he laid his head upon my shoulder and told me he was slain. I supported him till two men carried him off. He could say nothing to me but to bless me; but as they carried him down, he wished he could but live to read the account of the action in a newspaper.

After the shock of the first impact, the *Royal Sovereign*'s ship's company, despite the killed and wounded, fired their guns with the rhythm of long training. One seaman remembered:

They fought us pretty tightly for French and Spanish. Three of our mess are killed and four of us winged. But to tell you the truth of it, when the game began I wished myself at Warnborough with my plough again; but when they had given us one duster and I found myself snug and tight I bid fear kiss my bottom and set to in good earnest and thought no more about being killed than if I were at Murrell Green Fair; and I was presently as busy and as black as a collier. How my fingers got knocked overboard I don't know; but off they are and I never missed them till I wanted them. You see by my writing that it was my left hand so I can write to you and fight for my king yet.

Midshipman George Castle saw that the flagship was surrounded.

I looked once out of our stern ports – but I saw nothing but French and Spaniards round firing at us in all directions – it was shocking to see many brave seamen mangled so, some with their heads half shot away, others with their entrails mashed lying panting on the deck, the greatest slaughter was on the quarterdeck and poop – we had seven ships on us at once – the *Belleisle* was next to us in the action, and she kept off a great deal of fire from us, likewise the *Tonnant*.

The *Royal Sovereign* fought alone against five enemies for a quarter of an hour before help could reach her. This came first from the *Belleisle*, commanded by Captain William Hargood. Pointing at the great *Santa Ana*, looming through the smoke, Hargood told his officers, 'Gentlemen, I have only this to say: that I shall pass under the stern of that ship. Put in two round shot and then grape and give her that. Now go to your quarters and mind not to fire until each gun will bear with effect.'

Then, according to one of the *Belleisle*'s marine lieutenants, John Owen:

All sail was accordingly made and, on passing the *Tonnant*, the two captains greeted each other, Captain Tyler hoping that we should each of us have an enemy ship in tow before night, and the band playing 'Rule, Britannia' . . .

As we were steering directly for them [the enemy] we could only remain passive, and perseveringly approach the position we were to occupy in this great battle. This was a trying moment. Captain Hargood had taken his station at the forepart of the quarterdeck on the starboard side, occasionally standing on a carronade slide, whence he issued his orders for the men to lie down at their quarters, and with the utmost coolness directed the steering of the ship. The silence on board was almost awful, broken only by the firm voice of the captain, 'Steady!' or 'Starboard a little!' which was repeated by the master to the quartermaster at the helm; and occasionally by an officer calling to the now impatient men, 'Lie down there, you sir!' As we got nearer and nearer to the enemy the silence was, however, broken frequently by the sadly stirring shrieks of the wounded, for of them, and killed, we had more than fifty before we fired a shot; and our colours were three times shot away and rehoisted during the time.

Lieutenant Nicolas, in the same ship, remembered:

The shot began to pass over us, and gave us intimation of what we should in a few minutes undergo . . . A shriek soon followed – a cry of agony was produced by the next shot – and the loss of the head of a poor recruit was the effect of the succeeding, and, as we advanced, destruction rapidly increased. A severe contusion of the breast now prostrated our captain, but he soon resumed his station. Those only who had been in a similar situation to the one I am attempting to describe can have a correct idea of such a scene.

I was half disposed to follow the example [in lying down] but, turning round, my much esteemed and gallant senior fixed my attention; the serenity of his countenance and the composure with which he paced the deck, drove more than half my terrors away, and, joining him, I became somewhat infused with his spirit, which cheered me on to act the part that became me. My experience is an instance of how much depends on the example of those in command when exposed to the fire of the enemy, more particularly in the trying situation in which we were placed for nearly thirty minutes, from not having the power to retaliate.

Lieutenant Owen continued:

Seeing that our men were fast falling, the first lieutenant ventured to ask Captain Hargood if he had not better show his broadside to the enemy and fire, if only to cover the ship with smoke? The gallant man's reply was somewhat stern but emphatic: 'No, we are ordered to go through the line, and go through she shall, by ——!'

This state of things had lasted about twenty minutes, and it required the tact of the more experienced officers to keep up the spirits of those around them, by observing that 'We should soon begin our work'; when our energies were joyfully called into play by 'Stand to your guns!'

We were just then passing slowly through the line, and our fire was opened on a ship on each side within less than pistol shot. The enemy's ship on our starboard side now bore up and gallantly closed with us, running us on board on the beam, where her position soon became so hot and uncomfortable, that she was glad to drop astern much disabled, not, however, till she had knocked away our main-topmast and mizen-mast. This ship was the *Fougueux*.

An officer on the gun-decks of the *Belleisle* described the scene there:

At every moment the smoke accumulated more and more thickly, stagnating on board between-decks, at times so densely as to blur over the nearest objects and blot out the men at the guns from those close at hand on each side. The guns had to be trained as it were mechanically by means of orders passed down from above and on objects that the men fighting the guns hardly ever got a glimpse of. In these circumstances you frequently heard the order on the main and lower decks to level the guns 'two points abaft the beam', 'point-blank' and so on. In fact, the men were as much in the dark as to external objects as if they had been blindfolded and the only comfort to be derived from this serious inconvenience was that every man was so isolated from his neighbour that he was not put in mind of his danger by seeing his messmates go down all round. All that he knew was that he heard the crash of the shot smashing through the rending timbers and then followed at once the hoarse bellowings of the captains of the guns, as men were missed at their posts, calling out to survivors, 'Close up there! Close up!'

Lieutenant Owen went on:

In the meantime another French ship – the *Achille* – had placed herself on our larboard quarter, where she remained with comparative impunity on account of our mizen-mast having fallen in that direction and impeded our fire. Another ship of the line had placed herself on our larboard bow and another on our starboard.

About two o'clock the mainmast fell over the larboard side, and half an hour afterwards the foremast, also, fell over the starboard bow. Thus was the *Belleisle* a total wreck, without the means of returning the fire of the enemy except from the very few guns still unencumbered by the wreck of the masts and rigging. Every exertion, however, continued to be made for presenting the best resistance, and offering the greatest annoyance to the enemy; guns were run out from the sternports on each deck, and all that intelligence could suggest, and discipline effect, was done. Our loss was, however, becoming severe: the first and junior lieutenants had both been killed on the quarterdeck early in the action; and about the same time the captain was knocked down and severely bruised by a splinter, but refused to leave the deck.

As we were lying in this dismasted state surrounded by the enemy's ships, and not having seen the colours of a friendly ship for the previous two hours, the captain, seeing me actively employed in my duty, was kind enough to bring me a bunch of grapes,* and seemed pleased when I told him that our men were doing nobly, and that the ship had been greatly distinguished.

The ships near the head of the lee line which now came to the relief of the *Royal Sovereign* and the *Belleisle* had, unlike Collingwood, a clear view of Nelson's weather line turning towards the centre of the enemy and striking it in an eruption of flame and smoke. But otherwise they had no idea of what was happening a mile to the north; all eyes were upon the enemy ahead. The second ship to come surging into battle to support the admiral was the *Mars*, a 74, commanded by a big, genial Scot, Captain George Duff, whose young son was on board as a volunteer, training to become an officer. As the ship sailed towards the stabbing flame and billowing smoke around the *Royal Sovereign* and the *Belleisle*, Duff saw that he was on a collision course with the *Santa Ana* and put the helm over, so exposing his ship's stern to raking fire from the French *Pluton*. The wind had dropped and the ship drifted towards her enemies, unable to manoeuvre. Captain Thomas Norman of the Royal Marines then saw the *Fougueux* making towards them through the smoke and shouted a warning to Captain Duff. 'Do you think our guns will bear?' asked the captain. 'I think not,' replied Norman, 'but I cannot see for smoke.' 'Then we must point our guns on the ships on which they will bear,' ordered Duff. 'I shall go and look but the men below may see better as there is less smoke there.' The captain crossed the quarterdeck and looked over the side, just able to see the *Fougueux* through the smoke on the starboard quarter. He told a midshipman to pass the order to the lieutenants on the gun-decks to train their guns further aft when the French ship fired a broadside at point-blank range.

Midshipman James Robinson reported what he heard and saw:

Captain Duff walked about with steady fortitude and said, 'My God, what shall we do? Here is a Spanish three-decker raking us ahead and a French one under our stern!'

* These must have come from the potted vine that adorned Captain Hargood's stern cabin. It was not unusual for captains at the time to furnish their quarters in individual style.

In a few minutes our poop was totally cleared, the quarter-deck and the foc's'le nearly the same and only the boat-swain and myself and three men left alive . . . I am struck to remark the beautiful and steady manner Captain Duff brought the ship into battle. He stood with his arms across, looked with *undaunted fortitude* until his head and neck were entirely severed from his body.

Amongst the thirty dead was the marine, Captain Norman; a further sixty-five men lay wounded. The ship was almost crippled, her masts damaged or shot away. Seamen spared by the lethal broadside ran up to their headless captain and, said Robinson, 'They held his body up and gave three cheers to show they were not discouraged by it and then returned to their guns.'

Collingwood's flagship had taken a battering but had broken through the enemy line, as had the *Belleisle*, although she had been dismasted and virtually wrecked. Sixteen French and Spanish battleships were trying to seal the breach in their line, among them the *Algésiras*, the flagship of Admiral Magon, who commanded the rear division. Lieutenant Owen of the *Belleisle* watched as the *Algésiras* joined the mêlée:

A French ship of eighty guns with an admiral's flag came up, and poured a raking broadside into our stern which killed and wounded forty petty officers and men, nearly cut the rudder in two, and shattered the whole of the stern with the quarter galleries. She then in the most gallant manner locked her bowsprit in our starboard main shrouds, and attempted to board us with the greater part of her officers and ship's company. She had riflemen in her tops who did great execution. Our poop was soon cleared, and our gallant captain shot through the left thigh and obliged to be carried below. During this time we were not idle. We gave it to her most gloriously with the starboard lower and main-deckers, and turned the forecastle guns loaded with grape on the gentleman who wished to give us a fraternal hug. The marines kept up a warm and destructive fire on the boarders. Only one man made good his footing on our quarterdeck, when he was pinned through the calf of his right leg by one of the crew with his half-pike, whilst another was going to cut him down, which I prevented, and desired him to be taken to the cockpit. At this period the *Bellerophon*, seeing our critical position, gallantly steered between us and our first French antagonist and sheeted her home until she struck her colours. Our severe contest with the French admiral lasted more than half an hour, our sides grinding so much against each other that we were obliged to fire the lower deck guns without running them out.

Simultaneously, Admiral Magon engaged both the *Bellerophon* and the *Tonnant*, as the French admiral's assistant flag-lieutenant, Lieutenant Pierre Philibert, described:

We collided with [the *Tonnant*] by driving our bowsprit into its mainmast shrouds. They then fired several volleys of canister shot at us, which totally carried away our rigging. Our well-sustained fire soon reduced it to the same state as ourselves. From that moment it was no longer possible to see anything of our fleet . . . Fighting alongside the *Tonnant*, our foremast snapped close to the deck; it had already received several shot and was carried away by the fall of the mizen-mast from the English ship . . . Several times the English vainly tried to gain control; all those who came on board were killed.

Magon decided to counter-attack, as Philibert reported:

[He] gave orders to board and all who were told off for this service advanced enthusiastically; although supported by a vigorous musketry fire, almost all fell victim to their valour and daring because at this moment the enemy ship poured into us a whole volley from the carronades on his upper works and loaded with bullets.

The admiral was hit twice but, refusing to go below, he tried to rally the survivors, shouting, 'Save the honour of the flag!', when he was shot in the chest and died instantly. Philibert continued:

Our 18-pounder battery was almost deserted, several guns were wrecked. We then brought together all our forces in the 36-pounder battery [the lower gun-deck], which continued to be employed on both sides with the same vigour. The *Tonnant*, with whom we were entangled, set fire to our boatswain's storeroom with burning wads impregnated with sulphur* and killed three of our men there.

As the duel reached its climax, Lieutenant Hoffman watched the battle from the wreckage of the *Tonnant*'s upper deck:

The wind was very light, and it was nearly noon before we closed with the enemy. We remarked they had formed their ships alternately French and Spanish. All our ships that had bands were playing 'Rule, Britannia', 'Downfall of Paris', etc. Our own struck up 'Britons, Strike Home'. We were so slow in moving through the water in consequence of the lightness of the wind that some of the enemy's ships gave us a royal salute before we could break their line, and we lost two of the band and had nine wounded before we opened our fire . . . We were saved the trouble of taking in our studding-sails, as our opponents had the civility to effect it by shot before we got into their line. At length we had the honour of nestling his Majesty's ship between a French and a Spanish 74, and so close that a biscuit might have been thrown on the decks of either of them. Our guns were all double-shotted. The order was given to fire: being so close every shot was poured into their hulls, down came the Frenchman's mizen-mast, and after our second broadside the Spaniard's fore and cross-jack yards. A Spanish three-decker now crossed our bows and gave us a raking broadside which knocked away the fore and main top-masts, the main and foreyards with the jib-boom and sprit-sail yard, part of the head, and killed and wounded twenty-two of the men. One midshipman was cut literally in half. This was the more provoking as we could not return her the compliment, having full employment with those we first engaged . . .

* At such close range, probably burning wads from the British guns.

I must retrograde a little here and relate a few occurrences which took place during the action, and of which I was an eyewitness. We had hoisted our colours before the action in four different places – at the ensign-staff, peak, and in the fore and main top-mast shrouds, so that if one was shot away the others might be flying. A number of our fleet had done the same, and several of the enemy followed our example. The French admiral's ship who so gallantly attempted to board us had his flag hoisted in three places. One of our men, Fitzgerald, ran up his rigging and cut away one of them and placed it round his waist, and had nearly, after this daring exploit, reached his ship, when a rifleman shot him and he fell between the two ships and was no more seen. The principal signalman, whose name was White, and a captain of one of the guns on the poop, had his right great toe nearly severed from his foot. He deliberately took his knife and cut it away. He was desired to go below to the doctor. 'No, sir,' was his reply; 'I am not the fellow to go below for such a scratch as that. I wish to give the beggars', meaning the enemy, 'a few more hard pills before I have done with them.' Saying this, he bound his foot up in his neck-handkerchief and served out double allowance until his carronade was dismounted by the carriage of it being shattered to pieces. He then hopped to another gun, where he amused himself at the Frenchman's expense.

Later Hoffman himself went below:

On entering the cockpit I found fourteen men waiting amputation of either an arm or a leg. A marine who had sailed with me in a former ship was standing up as I passed, with his left arm hanging down. 'What's the matter, Conolly?' said I to him. 'Not much, sir,' replied he: 'I am only winged above my elbow, and I am waiting my turn to be lopped.' His arm was dreadfully broken by a grape-shot. I regret to mention that out of sixteen amputations only two survived. This was in consequence of the motion of the ship during the [later] gale. Their wounds broke out afresh, and it was impossible to stop the haemorrhage.

One of them, whose name was Smith, after his leg was taken off, hearing the cheering on deck in consequence of another of the enemy striking her colours, cheered also. The exertion he made burst open the vessels, and before they could be again dressed he fell back and died.

Another eyewitness described the scene on the *Tonnant*'s orlop deck, where he watched the surgeon, Forbes Chevers, at work:

It may well be imagined that, with 26 killed and 50 wounded, C. had hot work in the cockpit of the *Tonnant* during the action. The place was utterly dark, half of its depth being below the water-line. C. did all his amputations by the light of tallow candles, held torch-like by two assistants, to whom he said, 'If you look straight into the wound, and see all that I do, I shall see perfectly.' I have myself tried this plan, which is of infallible accuracy when any work of this kind has to be done at night. A consequence was that, when he washed his face at the first opportunity, he found that his eyebrows had been burnt off. He received most admirable assistance from Mr George Booth, the purser, who, having no duty elsewhere, shared the labours of the surgeon. Excellent aid was also given by a very powerful and resolute woman, the wife of a petty officer, whose name I deeply regret I cannot recall. She and Mr Booth (whom I saw many years afterwards), a small but singularly agile man, carried the sailors who had been operated upon to their temporary berths, taking them up in their arms as if they had been children, in a manner in which C. himself, a tall and very strong young man, always spoke of with expressions of wonder.

Meanwhile, on deck, Hoffman continued to observe the battle:

At length both ships caught fire, and our firemen, with all the coolness and courage so inherent in British seamen, got the engine and played on both ships, and finally extinguished the flames, although two of them were severely wounded in doing so. At length we had the satisfaction of seeing her three lower masts go by the board, ripping the partners up in their fall, as they had been shot through below the deck, and carrying with them all their sharp-shooters to look sharper in the next world; for as all our boats were shot through we could not save one of them in this. The crew were then ordered with the second lieutenant to board her. They cheered, and in a short time carried her. They found the gallant French Admiral Magon killed at the foot of the poop ladder, and the captain dangerously wounded. Out of eight lieutenants, five were killed with three hundred petty officers and seamen and about one hundred wounded. We left the second lieutenant and sixty men in charge of her and took some of the prisoners on board when she swung clear of us. We had pummelled her so handsomely that fourteen of her lower-deck guns were dismounted and her larboard bow exhibited a mass of splinters.

Fifth in Collingwood's line and astern of the *Tonnant* was the *Bellerophon*, commanded by Captain John Cooke. Her first lieutenant, William Cumby, described her entry into action:

It had been Captn Cooke's original intention not to have fired a shot till we were in the act of passing through the enemy's line but finding that we were losing men as we approached their ships from the effect of their fire and also suffering in our masts and rigging he determined on opening our fire a few minutes sooner from the double motive of giving our men employment and at the same time of rendering the ship a less ostensible mark to be shot at by covering her with smoke. At twenty minutes past twelve we opened our fire and at half-past twelve we were engaged on both sides passing thro their line close under the stern of a Spanish 74 [the *Monarca*] into whom from the lightness of the wind being still further lulled by the effect of the carronade, we fired our carronades three times, and every long gun on the larboard side at least twice. Luckily for us by this operation she had her hanging magazine blown up and was completely beaten for in hauling up to settle her business to leeward we saw over the smoke the topgallant sails of another ship close under our starboard bow which proved to be the French 74 *L'Aigle* as the name on her stern showed us, and although we hove all aback to avoid it we could not sufficiently check our ship's way to prevent our running her on board with our starboard bow on her larboard quarter our foreyard locking with her mainyard which was squared.

By the captain's directions I went down to explain to the officers on the main and lower decks the situation of the ship with respect to this new opponent and to order them to direct their principal efforts against her, having so done as I was returning along the main deck I met my poor messmate Overton the master carried by two men with his leg dreadfully shatter'd and before I reached the quarter-deck ladder, having stopped to give some directions by the way, I was met by a quartermaster who came to inform me that the captain was very badly wounded and as he believed dead.

I went immediately on the quarterdeck and assumed the command of the ship, this would be about a quarter past one o'clock when I found we were still entangled with *L'Aigle* on whom we kept up a brisk fire and also on our old opponent on the larboard bow the *Monarca*, who by this time was nearly silenced tho' her colours were still flying. At the same time we were receiving the fire of two other of the enemy's ships, one nearly astern of the other on the lar-board quarter. Our quarterdeck, poop and forecastle were at this time almost cleared by musquetry from troops on board *L'Aigle*, her poop and gangway completely com-manding those decks and the troops on board her ap-pearing very numerous. At this moment I ordered all the remaining men down from the poop and calling the board-ers had them mustered in readiness to repel any attempt that might be made by the enemy to board us, their posi-tion rendering it quite impracticable for us to board them in the face of such a fire of musquetry so advantageously situated. But whatever advantage they had over us on these upper decks was greatly overbalanced by the superiority of our fire on the lower and main decks. *L'Aigle* soon ceasing entirely to fire on us from her lower deck the ports of which were lowered down whilst the fire from ours was vigorously maintained the ports having been by my orders haul'd up close against the side when we first fell on board her to prevent their being torn from their hinges, when the ships came in contact. Whilst thus closely engaged and rubbing sides with *L'Aigle* she threw many hand grenades on board us, both on our forecastle and gangway and in at the ports, some of these exploded and dreadfully scorched several of our men, one of them I took up myself from our gangway where the fuse was burning and threw it overboard. One of these grenades had been thrown in at a lower deck port and in its explosion had blown off the scuttle of the gunner's storeroom, setting fire to the storeroom and forcing open the door into the magazine passage. *Most* providentially, this door was so placed with respect to that opening from the passage into the magazine, that the same blast which blew open the storeroom door, shut to the door of the magazine, otherwise we must all in both ships inevitably have been blown up together. The gunner who was in the storeroom at the time went quietly up to Lieutenant Saunders on the lower deck and acquainting him the storeroom was on fire, requesting a few hands with water to extinguish it: these being instantly granted he returned with them and put the fire out without its having been known to any person on board except to these employed in its extinction.

At forty minutes past one o'clock *L'Aigle* hoisted her jib, and dropp'd clear of us under a tremendous raking fire from us as she paid off: our ship at this time was totally unmanageable, the main and mizen topmasts hanging over the side, the jibboom, spankerboom and gaff shot away and not a brace or bowline serviceable. We observed that *L'Aigle* was engaged by the *Defiance* and soon after two o'clock she struck. On the smoke clearing away we observed that several of the enemy's ships had struck their colours, and amongst them our first opponents the *Monarca* of whom we took possession. We were now without any opponent within reach of our guns, and our fire consequently ceasing I had a message from the surgeon stating that the cockpit was so crowded with wounded men

that it was quite impossible for him to attempt some operations which were highly requisite and begging I would
allow him to bring some subjects up into the captain's
cabin for amputation if the fire was not likely to be renewed for a quarter of an hour. I gave him the requested
permission with an understanding that he must be prepared to go down again if any of the enemy's van who had
not been engaged should approach us. It had been my
unvarying rule from the commencement of the action to
avoid speaking to any of my messmates and friends who
might be wounded, not wishing to trust my private feelings at a time when all my energies were called for in the
discharge of my public duty, and on this ground I had
passed poor Overton as I have already related without
exchanging a word. But now my much esteemed messmate
Captain Wemyss of the marines . . . came up the quarterdeck ladder wounded just at the moment I approached it
and not being able to avoid speaking to him without apparent unkindness I said, 'Wemyss my good fellow I'm sorry
you've been wounded, but I trust you will do well' to which
he replied with the utmost cheerfulness ''tis only a mere
scratch and I shall have to apologise to you by and by for
having left the deck on so trifling an occasion': he was then
entering the cabin to have his right arm amputated! . . .

I cannot and must not omit to record the spirited and
gallant conduct of a young midshipman named Pearson
of about fourteen years of age, 'tis so creditable to our profession and to our country. This youngster the son of a
clergyman in the West of England who held I believe the
living of Queen's Camel, had joined *Bellerophon* as his first
ship just before we left England in the preceding May. He
was stationed on the quarterdeck and when he saw Captn
Cooke fall he ran to his assistance, but ere he reached his
captain he was himself brought down by a splinter in the
thigh. As I was coming up to take command of the ship I
met on the quarterdeck ladder little Pearson in the arms of
a quartermaster who was carrying him to the surgeons in
the cockpit. I here made an exception to my general rule of
silence on such occasions and said 'Pearson my boy I'm
sorry you've been hit but never mind, you and I'll talk over

this day's work fifty years hence depend upon it' – he smiled and I passed on.

An eyewitness to the mortal wounding of Captain Cooke described what happened:

He had discharged his pistols very frequently at the enemy, who as often attempted to board, and he had killed a French officer on his own quarterdeck. He was in the act of reloading his pistols . . . when he received two musket-balls in the breast. He immediately fell, and upon the quartermaster going up and asking him if he should take him down below, his answer was, 'No, let me lie quietly one minute. Tell Lieutenant Cumby never to strike.'

The signal midshipman of the *Bellerophon*, John Franklin, told an admiring story about one of his men:

Christopher Beaty, yeoman of signals, seeing the ensign shot away a third time, mounted the mizen-rigging with the largest Union Jack he could lay his hands upon, deliberately stopped the four corners of it with as much spread as possible to the shrouds, and regained the deck unhurt. The French riflemen in the tops and on the poop of *L'Aigle*, seemingly in admiration of such daring conduct, suspended their fire for the few seconds that he remained aloft.

Seen from a distance, the close-quarter fighting around the *Royal Sovereign* was a tumult in the smoke. But gradually observers realised that not only had Collingwood broken through the enemy line, he had defeated the rear squadron. The first phase of 'the Nelson touch' concept had been achieved.

CHAPTER 7

Nelson

Twenty minutes after the first shot was fired at Collingwood's flagship, Nelson was in action. Like the *Royal Sovereign*, the *Victory* led her division bows-on towards the enemy line of battle, unable to bring her broadside to bear – although a few forward-firing guns in the bows were able to reply – while having to suffer the enemy's concentrated fire. At the speed she could make, which was barely walking-pace, the ordeal could be expected to last for as long as fifteen to twenty minutes.

The flagship's log recorded that the French first fired on the *Victory* at 11.50 a.m., and that fourteen minutes later she herself had fired long-range shots at the enemy's van as the helm was put over and – having made her feint – she steered down the line towards the combined fleet's centre. However, the chronometers and watches in the British ships were not synchronised and Blackwood, nearby in his frigate, noted that the enemy had opened fire at 12.21 p.m. and that the *Victory* had replied as best she could two minutes later. Such was the fog of war.

Nelson himself stood on the quarterdeck below the poop with Hardy, John Scott, his secretary, and others including Captain Charles Adair of the Royal Marines. Along the enemy line they could see the huge shape of the *Santissima Trinidad* and just astern of her Villeneuve's flagship, the *Bucentaure*, which loosed a shot at the *Victory* at the range of a mile. This initial firing was only spasmodic and no hits were registered.

Suddenly shot howled overhead and one punched through the *Victory*'s main-topgallant sail. They were in range. Then flame flashed down the enemy line, which disappeared behind its own gunsmoke as five battleships opened fire.

Shot crashed into the *Victory*, showering the decks with flying splinters of timber. John Scott was talking to Hardy when he was whirled away, cut in two by a roundshot. 'Is that poor Scott that is gone?' asked Nelson. Told that it was, he simply said 'Poor fellow' and continued strolling to and fro with Hardy, while Midshipman Thomas Goble, a master's mate aged nineteen, was told to take Scott's place beside the admiral. A bar-shot – two roundshot linked by a bar and designed to cut rigging – scythed through a file of marines on the poop, killing eight. Nelson again turned to Adair and ordered, 'Disperse your men round the ship.' By this command he deprived himself of their protection against snipers up the enemy's masts when close action began.

One of Adair's officers, Lieutenant Louis Roteley, described what happened:

Previous to breaking the enemy's line their fire was terrific. The *Victory* was steering for the four-decker [the *Santissima Trinidad*], when four ships ahead and four astern together with that huge leviathan brought their broadsides to bear upon the bows of the *Victory*. It was like a hail-storm of bullets passing over our heads on the poop, where we had forty marines stationed with small arms. It has been stated that Lord Nelson ordered them to lie down at their quarters until wanted, but no such order was given, and no man went down until knocked down: had such orders been given many a life would have been saved, as not a man was hit below the waist. Their steadiness indeed was observed by Nelson, whose eye was everywhere, and who declared he had seen nothing which surpassed it in any of his previous battles. He also made this remark during the battle, 'The young marine is doing well,' which I have taken for my motto.

This I learnt from Sir Thomas Hardy, when returning me his thanks on the quarterdeck for my conduct in the battle. The poop became a slaughterhouse, and soon after the commencement the two senior lieutenants of marines, and half the original forty, were placed *hors de combat*. Captain Adair then ordered me to bring him up a re-inforcement of marines from the great guns. I need not inform a seaman the difficulty of separating a man from his gun. In the excitement of action the marines had thrown off their red jackets and appeared in check shirts and blue trousers. There was no distinguishing marine from sea-man – they were all working like horses. I was now upon the middle deck: we were engaging on both sides, every gun was going off. A man should witness a battle in a three-decker from the middle deck, for it beggars all description. It bewilders the senses of sight and hearing. There was the fire from above, the fire from below, besides the fire from the deck I was upon, the guns recoiling with violence, reports louder than thunder, the deck heaving and the side straining. I fancied myself in the infernal regions, where every man appeared a devil. Lips might move, but orders and hearing were out of the question: everything was done by signs.

One roundshot shattered the *Victory*'s wheel, so she had to be steered by forty men heaving the massive wooden tiller three decks below to shouted orders relayed from the quarterdeck. Another shot smashed through the upper-deck woodwork and a splinter struck the silver buckle of Hardy's left shoe. Nelson stopped, smiled and said, 'This is too warm work, Hardy, to last long.'

Nelson hoped to break the enemy line by passing under the stern of the *Santissima Trinidad*, just ahead of the *Bucentaure*, raking both ships as he did so. But the enemy line was closing up and there was no space to sail through so he decided to steer for the stern of Villeneuve's flagship, although the gap between her and the next ship astern was also closing. There seemed to be an almost solid barrier of enemy ships and ramming was probably inevitable. Hardy asked Nelson which of the enemy they should engage. 'I cannot help it,' replied the admiral. 'Go on board where you please: take your choice.'

From the quarterdeck of the *Bucentaure*, Villeneuve had seen the ships of his rear open fire on Collingwood's line and had given the order to his whole fleet 'to get into action as soon as possible'. This applied equally to his van of nine ships commanded by Admiral Dumanoir, which, after Nelson's feint, had not itself been directly threatened by the British. Then the *Victory* swung towards the stern of the *Bucentaure* and fired a raking, double-shotted broadside through the windows of the great cabin.

As the *Victory* had passed close under the stern of the enemy flagship – the ships touching one another as they rolled – she had fired her forecastle carronade and loaded with a 68-pound round-shot and a keg of five hundred musket balls through the stern windows. Then, as she had slid past, so close that the French ensign at the stern almost brushed her opponent, the *Victory*'s port broadside – double- and triple-shotted – was loosed in succession. At what was described as 'the deafening crash made by their shot in the French ship's hull, the British crew were nearly suffocated with the clouds of black smoke that entered the *Victory*'s port holes; and Lord Nelson, Captain Hardy and others that were walking the quarterdeck had their clothes covered with the dust which issued from the crumbled woodwork of the *Bucentaure*'s stern'.

Villeneuve recollected a shattering quarter-hour:

The port column, led by the *Victory*, with the flag of Admiral Nelson, came on in much the same way. She appeared as if she was aiming to break the line between the *Santissima Trinidad* and the bows of the *Bucentaure*. Whether, however, they found our line too well closed up at that point, or from some other reason, when they were almost within half pistol-shot – while we, for our part, prepared to board and had our grappling-irons ready for throwing – they swung off to starboard and passed astern of the *Bucentaure*. The *Redoutable* had the station of the [French] *Neptune*, which had fallen to leeward, and she heroically fulfilled the duties of the second astern to the flagship. She ran on board the *Victory*, but the lightness of the wind had not prevented the *Victory* passing close under the stern of the *Bucentaure* and firing into us as she passed several treble-shotted broadsides, with effects that were murderous and destructive. At that moment I made the signal, 'All ships not engaged owing to their stations, are to get into action as soon as possible!' It was impossible for me to see how things were going in the centre and rear of the fleet because of the dense smoke which enveloped us.

To the *Victory* succeeded two others of the enemy, three-deckers, and several 74s. These one after the other came up and filed by, slowly past the stern of the *Bucentaure*. I had just made the signal to the van to put about when the main- and mizen-masts both came down. The

English ships which had passed through astern of us were attacking us from leeward, but, unfortunately, without suffering any serious loss in return from our batteries. The greater part of our guns were already dismounted and others were disabled or masked by the fall of the masts and rigging. Now, for one moment, the smoke-fog cleared and I saw that all the centre and rear had given way. I found, also, that my flagship was the most to windward of all. Our foremast was still standing, however. It offered a means for our making sail to get to leeward to join a group of ships at a little distance which did not seem much damaged: but immediately afterwards the foremast came down like the others. I had had my barge kept ready, so that in the event of the *Bucentaure* being dismasted, I might be able to go on board some other ship, and rehoist my flag there. When the mainmast came down I gave orders for it to be cleared for launching, but it was found to be unserviceable, damaged irreparably, either from shot or crushed in the fall of the masts. Then I had the *Santissima Trinidad* hailed – she was just ahead of us – and asked them either to send a boat or take us in tow. But there was no answer to the hail. The *Trinidad* at that moment was hotly engaged. A three-decker was attacking her on the quarter astern, and another enemy was on the beam to leeward.

As the *Victory* had swung towards the stern of Villeneuve's flagship, officers on her upper deck had also identified the ship immediately ahead of her as the *Santissima Trinidad* by her bulk. But the ship astern and rapidly coming up with the *Bucentaure* was seen only as another French 74. She was, in fact, Captain Lucas's *Redoutable*, the most dangerous ship in the enemy fleet.

Captain Lucas had tried to prevent the raking of the flagship by closing the gap between the *Redoutable* and the *Bucentaure* and had almost succeeded:

I pressed on and closed on the flagship so as, in effect, to keep the *Redoutable*'s bowsprit touching the taffrail of the *Bucentaure*. I made up my mind to sacrifice my ship, if necessary, in defence of the flagship. This I told my officers and men, who answered me with shouts and cheers, repeated over and over again, of '*Vive l'empereur!*', '*Vive l'amiral!*', '*Vive le commandant!*'

As the *Redoutable* ran alongside the *Victory*, Lucas continued:

In less than a minute our decks swarmed with armed men, who rapidly spread to the poop, the nettings and the shrouds; it is not possible to say who was first. Then a heavy fire of musketry was opened . . . But our fire was so fast, and so superior that in less than a quarter of an hour we had silenced the *Victory* altogether. More than two hundred grenades were thrown on board her, with the utmost success; her decks were strewn with dead and wounded.

The *Victory* had not been silenced but, as the *Redoutable*'s gun-crews rushed on deck to board, her guns were indeed still. As Dr Beatty explained, 'It was supposed at different times that she [the *Redoutable*] had surrendered; and, in consequence of this opinion, the *Victory* twice ceased firing upon her by orders transmitted from the quarterdeck.' On the British gun-decks, men were only aware of noise, smoke, flame and exertion. One of the *Victory*'s seamen, David Johns, remembered: 'We was so involved in smoke and fire not to be seen by any of our frigates looking on for about half an hour and they thought we was blown up, or sunk, having no less than 5 ships on us at the time.'

Lieutenant Roteley, who had been sent to call up reinforcements from below, returned to the upper deck:

With the assistance of two sergeants and two corporals – and in some cases by main force – I succeeded in separating about twenty-five men from the great guns, and with this force I ascended to a purer air. The battle now raged at its greatest height. The *Redoutable* had fallen on board us on our starboard side, and the soldiers from their tops were picking off our officers and men with deadly aim. We were also engaged with the *Santissima Trinidad* and the *Bucentaure*, though at a greater distance, on our larboard.

The reinforcement arrived at a most critical moment: Captain Adair's party was reduced to less than ten men, himself wounded in the forehead by splinters, yet still using his musket with effect. One of his last orders to me was, 'Roteley, fire away as fast as you can!' when a ball struck him on the back of the neck and he was a corpse in a moment.

While the men fighting could only see the violence around them, a pattern to the battle was emerging. There were two intense focal points, where first Collingwood and then Nelson had broken through the Franco-Spanish line. The flagships of the British lee and weather columns had taken the initial impact but they were now supported by the heavy ships that had been placed in, or near, the van and had moved forward. Astern of them, the rest of the two columns, mostly lighter 74s, were slowly making their way towards the storms of smoke and flame ahead.

In the *Victory*, Nelson and Hardy still paced the quarter-deck. Then, after the flagship had been in action for an hour and her upper decks were a shambles of blood and wreckage, Dr Beatty wrote of the admiral:

About fifteen minutes past one o'clock, which was in the heat of the engagement, he was walking the middle of the quarterdeck with Captain Hardy, and in the act of turning near the hatchway with his face towards the stern of the *Victory*, when the fatal ball was fired from the enemy's mizen-top; which, from the situation of the two ships (lying on board of each other), was brought just abaft, and rather below, the *Victory*'s main-yard, and of course not more than fifteen yards distant from that part of the deck where his Lordship stood. The ball struck the epaulette on his left shoulder, and penetrated his chest. He fell with his face on the deck. Captain Hardy, who was on his right (the side furthest from the enemy) and advanced some steps before his Lordship, on turning round, saw the serjeant-major (Secker) of marines with two seamen raising him from the deck; where he had fallen on the same spot on which, a little before, his secretary had breathed his last, with whose blood his Lordship's clothes were much soiled. Captain Hardy expressed a hope that he was not severely wounded; to which the gallant chief replied: 'They have done for me at last, Hardy.' 'I hope not,' answered Captain Hardy. 'Yes,' replied his Lordship, 'my backbone is shot through . . .'

Captain Hardy ordered the seamen to carry the admiral to the cockpit; and now two incidents occurred strikingly characteristic of this great man, and strongly marking that energy and reflection which in his heroic mind rose superior even to the immediate consideration of his present awful condition. While the men were carrying him down the ladder from the middle deck, his Lordship observed that the tiller ropes were not yet replaced; and desired one of the midshipmen stationed there to go upon the quarter-deck and remind Captain Hardy of that circumstance, and request that new ones should be immediately rove. Having delivered this order, he took his handkerchief from his pocket and covered his face with it, that he might be conveyed to the cockpit at this crisis unnoticed by the crew.

Several wounded officers, and about forty men, were likewise carried to the surgeon for assistance just at this time; and some others had breathed their last during their conveyance below. Among the latter were Lieutenant William Andrew Ram, and Mr Whipple, captain's clerk. The surgeon had just examined these two officers, and found that they were dead, when his attention was arrested by several of the wounded calling to him, 'Mr Beatty, Lord Nelson is here: Mr Beatty, the admiral is wounded.' The surgeon now, on looking round, saw the handkerchief fall from his Lordship's face; when the stars on his coat, which also had been covered by it, appeared. Mr Burke, the purser, and the surgeon, ran immediately to the assistance of his Lordship, and took him from the arms of the seamen who had carried him below. In conveying him to one of the midshipmen's berths, they stumbled, but recovered themselves without falling. Lord Nelson then enquired who were supporting him; and when the surgeon informed him, his Lordship replied, 'Ah, Mr Beatty! you can do nothing for me. I have but a short time to live: my back is shot through.' The surgeon said, 'he hoped the wound was not so dangerous as his Lordship imagined, and that he might still survive long to enjoy his glorious victory.' The Reverend Dr Scott, who had been absent in another part of the cockpit administering lemonade to the wounded, now came instantly to his Lordship; and in his anguish of grief wrung his hands, and said: 'Alas, Beatty, how prophetic you were!' alluding to the apprehensions expressed by the surgeon for his Lordship's safety previous to the battle.

Few in the *Victory* knew that Nelson had been hit, such was the noise and smoke. Nor could there be any chance of telling Collingwood by signal, or by boat, not that there was any immediate need to do so, for now the battle was ship-to-ship with little or no communication possible. In any case, Nelson was still alive and in command, just able to give orders to Hardy, who, when he could, left the quarterdeck for the dim-lit horrors of the orlop deck, where Nelson lay. Some on the upper deck did know. Amongst them was Midshipman John Pollard, aged nineteen, who was stationed on the poop of the flagship. He later claimed to have avenged Nelson, having seen the snipers in the maintop of the *Redoutable*:

They were in a crouching position and rose breast-high to fire. I pointed them out . . . and I remained firing at the top until not a man was to be seen; the last one I discovered coming down the mizen rigging and from my fire he fell also. King, a quartermaster, was killed in the act of handing me a parcel of ball-cartridge.

In the *Redoutable*, Captain Lucas still intended to board the *Victory*, but:

It proved difficult to board her on account of the motion of the two ships and the height of the *Victory*'s upper deck and battery. Therefore I gave the order to cut away the main yard so that [falling across the gap between the ships] it might act as a bridge. And now Midshipman Yon and four men leaped on board the *Victory* by means of her anchor.

The French were killed, or driven back to fight their guns, firing upwards through the *Victory*'s decks, showering them with wood-splinters which shattered the legs of the newly promoted Lieutenant William Ram, but not killing him.

Now the second ship in Nelson's division, the *Téméraire*, came bursting through the enemy line astern of the *Redoutable*, but the French *Neptune* lay ahead of her, firing at the *Victory*. She now loosed a raking broadside into the bows of the *Téméraire*, bringing down an avalanche of upper masts, yards, sails and rigging. The big ship was scarcely under control but Captain Eliab Harvey was able to steer her alongside the *Redoutable*, on the far side from the *Victory*, and fire his heavy guns into her with such effect that he feared the shot might pass straight through the French ship and hit the flagship. Captain Lucas of the *Redoutable* said of the onslaught:

It is impossible to describe the carnage produced by the murderous broadside of this ship. More than two hundred of our brave men were killed or wounded by it. I was also wounded at this time, but not enough to make me leave my post. Not being able to do anything on the *Victory*'s side, I ordered the remainder of my crew to man the batteries on the other side and fire at the *Téméraire* those guns not dismounted when she came alongside . . .

The *Téméraire* hailed us to surrender and not to prolong a hopeless resistance; my reply was to order some soldiers near me to fire back, which they very promptly did. Almost at the same moment the *Redoutable*'s mainmast fell on board the English ship, and the two topmasts of the *Téméraire* then came down, falling on board us. Our whole poop was stove in – the helm, rudder and stern-post all shattered to splinters; all the stern-frame and the decks shot through. The broadsides of the *Victory* and *Téméraire* had either smashed or dismounted all our guns. In addition, an 18-pounder on the lower deck and a 32-pounder carronade on the forecastle had burst, killing or wounding a great many men. The hull was riddled – shot through from side to side; deck beams were shattered and port lids torn away or knocked to pieces. Four of our six pumps were so damaged as to be useless. The quarterdeck ladders were broken, which made it difficult to communicate with other parts of the ship. The decks were everywhere strewn with dead men, lying under the debris. Out of a crew of 643 men we had 522 *hors de combat*. Of these, three hundred were killed and 222 wounded, nearly all the officers among them. The batteries and upper decks were practically abandoned – bare of men – and we were no longer able to offer any resistance.

No one who had not seen the *Redoutable* could form any idea of her awful condition. I know of nothing on board that had not been hit by shot. In the midst of this horrible carnage and devastation my splendid fellows who had not been killed – even the wounded, below on the orlop – kept cheering: '*Vive l'empereur!*', 'We're not taken yet!', 'Is the captain still alive?' Some tarred canvas at the stern caught fire about this time, but fortunately the flames were checked, and we soon managed to put them out.

Lieutenant Andrew Green, the signals officer of the British *Neptune*, logged the course of the engagement:

The *Victory* open'd her fire and endeavouring to pass under the stern of the French admiral in the *Bucentaure*, the *Redoutable*, closed so near the *Bucentaure*, to support his commander-in-chief, that the *Victory* was obliged to lay that ship on board, when both ships paid off before the wind. The *Téméraire* in following gallantly Lord Nelson's ship, fell on the opposite side the *Redoutable*, from the same cause and the *Intrépide* alongside the *Téméraire*, the four ships lock'd in and on board each other, and their sterns to us. We put the ship's helm a-starboard and the *Neptune* passed between the *Victory* and *Bucentaure* with which ship we were warmly engaged (the *Conqueror's* jib boom nearly touching our taffrail) we passed on to the *Santissima Trinidad* whose stern was entirely exposed to our fire without her being able to return a single shot with effect. At fifty minutes past one observed her main and mizen-masts fall overboard, *gave three cheers*, she then paid off and brought us nearly on her lee beam, in about a quarter of an hour more, her foremast fell over her stern.

Meanwhile, down in the darkness of the orlop deck of the *Victory*, in the cockpit where the wounded were taken, Nelson was being examined by Dr Beatty:

His Lordship was laid upon a bed, stripped of his clothes and covered with a sheet. While this was effecting, he said to Dr Scott, 'Doctor, I told you so. Doctor, I am gone'; and, after a short pause, he added in a low voice, 'I have to leave Lady Hamilton and my adopted daughter Horatia as a legacy to my country.' The surgeon then examined the wound, assuring his Lordship that he would not put him to much pain in endeavouring to discover the course of the ball; which he soon found had penetrated deep into the chest and had probably lodged in the spine. This being explained to his Lordship, he replied, 'he was confident his back was shot through'. The back was then examined externally but without any injury being perceived; on which his Lordship was requested by the surgeon to make him acquainted with all his sensations. He replied that 'he felt a gush of blood every minute within his breast; that he had no feeling in the lower part of his body; that his breathing was difficult and attended with very severe pain about that part of the spine where he was confident the ball had struck; for', said he, 'I felt it break my back.'

These symptoms, but more particularly the gush of blood, which his Lordship complained of, together with the state of his pulse indicated to the surgeon the hopeless situation of the case.

The *Victory* and the *Téméraire* had been followed into action by the British *Neptune* of ninety-eight guns and two 74s, the *Leviathan* and the *Conqueror*, which burst through the enemy line, loosing broadsides into the *Bucentaure* as they passed. Even so, less than a third of Nelson's division was in action and those that had broken through were soon surrounded by enemy ships. The *Téméraire*, locked alongside the *Redoutable*, was now attacked by the *Fougueux*, which had moved up the line from the fight with the head of Collingwood's line and now crashed into Harvey's ship. But Harvey continued to concentrate on the *Redoutable*, which, with five-sixths of her men dead or wounded, still refused to surrender. Then a mast, shot through, crashed to her deck, forming a bridge across which stormed Harvey's men to take possession of her. Captain Lucas finally surrendered at 2.20 that afternoon.

But it was the *Bucentaure* that was the target for every British ship within gunshot. Crippled, and with half her ship's company of some eight hundred killed or wounded, she could not fight on. Captain Jean-Jacques Magendie, Villeneuve's flag-captain, who directly commanded the ship, had been visiting the gun-decks. When he returned to the admiral's side he found that it was all over:

Our rigging completely dismantled, having lost all the men on the upper decks, the 24-pounder battery entirely out of commission and abandoned through dead and wounded men, the starboard side fouled by the masts; incapable of defending ourselves, with nearly 450 men killed or wounded; not having been helped by any other vessel, everyone appearing engaged, and there being none within reach, nor any frigate to which the admiral could move his flag; not even having a small boat in which he could embark, all of them having been crippled, as well as the one we had kept in the sea since before the battle, we were isolated in the middle of five enemy vessels that were firing very vigorously at us. At that moment I went back on to the deck because Admiral Villeneuve had been forced to order our ship to surrender so as to avoid more brave men being killed who were unable to fight back, which was done after three and a quarter hours of the most furious fighting almost always within pistol range. The remains of the eagle were thrown into the sea as well as all the signals.

Captain Magendie himself lowered the flag as Villeneuve looked away. A boarding party was sent by boat from the *Conqueror*. According to the *Conqueror*'s log:

The officer in charge of the boat was Captain James Atcherley, of the marines, who had with him but five hands, a corporal and two privates of his corps, and two seamen. On the captain's stepping upon the *Bucentaure*'s quarterdeck, M. Villeneuve and his two captains presented their swords.

'To whom', asked Admiral Villeneuve, in good English, 'have I the honour of surrendering?'

'To Captain Pellew of the *Conqueror*.'

'I am glad to have struck to the fortunate Sir Edward Pellew.'

'It is his brother, sir,' said Captain Atcherley.

'His brother! What! are there two of them? *Hélas!*'*

– but, conceiving that it more properly belonged to Captain Pellew to disarm officers of their rank, Captain Atcherley declined the honour of receiving them. Having secured the magazine and put the key in his pocket, and placed two of his men as sentries, one at each cabin-door, Captain Atcherley, accompanied by the French admiral and his two captains, pulled off with his three remaining hands, and at length boarded, not the *Conqueror*, who had proceeded in chase, but the *Mars*, her sister-ship.

On board the *Bucentaure*, Atcherley had observed:

The dead, thrown back as they fell, lay along the middle of the decks in heaps, and the shot, passing through these, had frightfully mangled the bodies . . . More than four hundred had been killed and wounded, of whom an extraordinary proportion had lost their heads. A raking shot, which entered in the lower deck, had glanced along the beams and through the thickest of the people, and a French officer declared that this shot alone had killed or disabled nearly forty men.

---

* Captain Israel Pellew of the *Conqueror* was the younger brother of Rear-Admiral Sir Edward Pellew – later Admiral Viscount Exmouth – who had become famous in 1797 as a frigate captain by destroying, with another frigate, a French 74.

After Captain Duff's death, the first lieutenant had assumed command of the *Mars*, leading the 74 into battle in close support of the lee column's flagship. From his post on the *Mars*'s quarterdeck, Midshipman James Robinson saw the prisoners arrive.

Villeneuve was a thinnish, tall man, a very tranquil, placid, English-looking Frenchman; he wore a long-tailed uniform coat, high and flat collar, corduroy pantaloons of a greenish colour, with stripes two inches wide, half-boots with sharp toes, and a watch-chain with long gold links.

– a well-bred man and, I believe, a very good officer; he has nothing in his manner of the offensive vapouring and boasting which we, perhaps too often, attribute to Frenchmen.

But then Robinson's opinion changed. Villeneuve,

seeing Captain Duff lying dead upon deck, began to smile to some of his attendants, which one of our sailors observing, came running up to him and laid hold of him and said when my captain lived he was able to revenge himself an insult. Now he is dead it is my duty to revenge it for him, at the same time throwing Villeneuve from him, covered the dead body with a flag that was lying near him.

Now both commanders-in-chief were out of action, but that was of little consequence for the battle was already beyond their control. Nelson, lying in the gloom of the orlop deck of his flagship, had the satisfaction of knowing not only that he had pierced the enemy line but that he had broken it up and so brought about the pell-mell battle that had been his intention.

CHAPTER 8

Pell-mell

When Admiral Villeneuve surrendered his sword on board the *Mars*, the vortex of battle around the *Victory* and the *Royal Sovereign* widened as more ships followed them through the enemy line. Duels began, then broke off, as one or other opponent veered to support a friend or to avoid an enemy. The ships at the rear of the British columns had yet to join the fight but were on their way whereas, surprisingly, the van of the Franco-Spanish fleet was still sailing north, apparently heading for Cadiz, and remained a mile and a half away from the fighting. One of Villeneuve's last acts had been to signal Admiral Dumanoir ordering him for the second time to turn and join the centre. Despite being mostly obscured by smoke, the flags were seen by ships in the van but virtually no action was taken. Dumanoir himself did try to turn his flagship, the *Formidable*, but the wind had dropped and in the heavy swell he was finding it difficult if not impossible. But those embroiled in the action were mostly unaware of this, so intense was the fighting.

Although the *Bucentaure* and the *Redoutable* had surrendered, the *Victory* was still heavily engaged. Most of those fighting lost count of time and the sequence of events. But even while battling with both the *Bucentaure* and the *Redoutable*, the British flagship's crew was always aware of the great *Santissima Trinidad* beyond. She was a dangerous adversary. Lieutenant Lawrence Halloran of the Royal Marines, on board the *Britannia*, recollected the terrible effect of a single shot from the Spanish four-decker:

A shot struck the muzzle of the gun at which I was stationed (the aftermost gun on the larboard side of the lower deck), and killed or wounded everyone there stationed, myself and Midshipman Tompkins only excepted. The shot was a very large one, and split into a number of pieces, each of which took its victim. We threw the mangled body of John Jolley, a marine, out of the stern port, his stomach being shot away; the other sufferers we left to be examined. The gun itself was split, and our second lieutenant, Roskruge, who came down at that moment with some orders, advised me to leave the gun as useless. He had scarcely left us, when he was brought down senseless with a severe wound in his head . . . Amongst the wounded who suffered at my gun was an Italian, who was stooping to take up a shot for the gun, when it was split, and both his arms were blown off.

Once both the *Victory*'s immediate opponents had surrendered, she swiftly turned her attention to the *Santissima Trinidad*. A member of *Victory*'s company wrote:

We ceased firing the starboard guns, kept a fire from the larboard guns [as] on the quarter we had several of the enemy's ships firing on us. We were then engaged with the *Santissima Trinidad* . . . We raked [her] for a considerable time and the *Neptune*, breaking the line, fired a broadside into her which carried away her mainmasts and she struck.

Soon the *Santissima Trinidad* was being battered by broadsides from the *Neptune* on one side and the *Conqueror* on the other. An officer in the *Conqueror* watched the suffering of the great ship:

In a short time this tremendous fabric gave a deep roll with the swell to leeward, then back to windward; and on her return every mast went by the board, leaving her an unmanageable hulk on the water. Her immense topsails had every reef out, her royals were sheeted home but lowered, and the falling of this mass of spars, sails, and rigging, plunging into the water at the muzzles of our guns, was one of the most magnificent sights I ever beheld.

The *Africa* bore down ahead of the *Santissima Trinidad*. Meeting no return to her fire, and seeing no colours hoisted on board the latter, Captain Digby concluded that the four-decker had surrendered, and sent Lieutenant John Smith in a boat to take possession. Upon the lieutenant's reaching the quarterdeck, and asking an officer who advanced to meet him, whether or not the *Santissima Trinidad* had surrendered, the Spaniard replied, '*Non, non,*' pointing to one Spanish and four French sail of the line then passing to windward. As, for want of masts, the *Santissima Trinidad* was settling fast to windward of the two fleets, and he had only a boat's crew with him, Lieutenant Smith quitted the Spanish ship (the crew of which, singularly enough, permitted him to do so), and returned on board the *Africa*.

A Spanish officer described his ship's condition.

The scene on board the *Santissima Trinidad* was simply infernal. She could not move. The English shot had torn our sails to tatters. It was as if huge invisible talons had been dragging at them. Fragments of spars, splinters of wood, thick hempen cables cut up as corn is cut by the sickle, fallen blocks, shreds of canvas, bits of iron, and hundreds of other things that had been wrenched away by the enemy's fire, were piled along the deck. Blood ran in streams about the deck, and in spite of the sand, the rolling of the ship carried it hither and thither until it made strange patterns on the planks. The ship creaked and groaned as she rolled, and through a thousand holes and crevices in her hull the sea spurted in and began to flood the hold.

Soon afterwards another Spanish officer hung a large British Union flag over the *Santissima Trinidad*'s side in token of surrender. Other French and Spanish ships, dismasted and heaped with dead and wounded after hard fighting, were forced to strike their colours, too. A typical case was that of the *Fougueux*. After two hours' cannonade, when Captain Louis Baudoin was mortally wounded, his second-in-command, Commander François Bazin, recollected:

I took over the command. I continued firing from the gundecks and only kept a few men with me to repel boarding or to prevent a footing from being made on board. But the enemy by her superior fire riddled us with grape and in less than half an hour our decks were beaten in in several places; after having seen all those about me fall dead or wounded, I summoned the fourth lieutenant, the only one left on his feet, and questioned him as to the condition of the lower deck battery: he assured me that it was practically out of action and that he had no people left. The only officer in the 18-pounder battery sent me word that he had only 15 men and that all the guns were dismounted.

Seeing the impossibility of repelling boarding or of defending the ship against the number of enemies who were getting aboard, I gave orders to cease firing and dragged myself, in spite of my wounds, as far as the captain's cabin to get and to throw into the sea the box containing the signals and instructions for the ship, and, reappearing on the quarterdeck, I was taken and was conveyed on board the English ship: the enemy hauled down the colours and gradually the slaughter ceased entirely. That was the issue of this fight, in which the *Fougueux* lost three-quarters of her crew.

Down on the orlop deck of the *Victory*, Nelson was subjected to the noise of the guns – particularly the thirty three-ton 32-pounders, manned by more than two hundred men on the lower gun-deck immediately above his head: the blast of the broadsides, the crash of the recoil and the rumble of the gun-carriages being hauled back to the gun-ports, thick smoke eddying down the hatchway. Dr Beatty described Nelson's situation:

The true nature of his wound was concealed by the surgeon from all on board except only Captain Hardy, Dr Scott, Mr Burke [the purser], and Messrs Smith and Westerburgh, the assistant surgeons.

The *Victory*'s crew cheered whenever they observed an enemy's ship surrender. On one of these occasions, Lord Nelson anxiously enquired what was the cause of it; when Lieutenant Pasco, who lay wounded at some distance, raised himself up and told him that another ship had struck, which appeared to give him much satisfaction. He now felt an ardent thirst, and frequently called for drink, and to be fanned with paper, making use of these words:

'fan, fan', and 'drink, drink'. This he continued to repeat, when he wished for drink, and the refreshment of cool air, till a very few minutes before he expired. Lemonade, and wine and water were given to him occasionally. He evinced great solicitude for the event of the battle, and fears for the safety of his friend Captain Hardy. Dr Scott and Mr Burke used every argument they could suggest to relieve his anxiety. Mr Burke told him 'the enemy were decisively defeated, and that he hoped his Lordship would still live to be himself the bearer of the joyful tidings to his country.' He replied, 'It is nonsense, Mr Burke, to suppose I can live: my sufferings are great, but they will all be soon over.' Dr Scott entreated his Lordship 'not to despair of living', and said, 'he trusted that Divine Providence would restore him once more to his dear country and friends.' 'Ah, Doctor!' replied his Lordship, 'it is all over; it is all over.'

Many messages were sent to Captain Hardy by the surgeon, requesting his attendance on his Lordship; who became impatient to see him, and often exclaimed: 'Will no one bring Hardy to me? He must be killed: he is surely destroyed.' The captain's aide-de-camp, Mr Bulkeley, now came below, and stated that 'circumstances respecting the fleet required Captain Hardy's presence on deck, but that he would avail himself of the first favourable moment to visit his Lordship.' On hearing him deliver this message to the surgeon, his Lordship enquired who had brought it. Mr Burke answered, 'It is Mr Bulkeley, my Lord.' 'It is his voice,' replied his Lordship: he then said to the young gentleman, 'Remember me to your father.'

An hour and ten minutes however elapsed, from the time of his Lordship being wounded, before Captain Hardy's first subsequent interview with him; the particulars of which are nearly as follows: they shook hands affectionately, and Lord Nelson said: 'Well, Hardy, how goes the battle? How goes the day with us?' 'Very well, my Lord,' replied Captain Hardy: 'we have got twelve or fourteen of the enemy's ships in our possession; but five of their van have tacked and show an intention of bearing down upon the *Victory*. I have therefore called two or three of our fresh ships round us, and have no doubt of giving them a drubbing.' 'I hope', said his Lordship, 'none of *our* ships have struck, Hardy.' 'No, my Lord,' replied Captain Hardy, 'there is no fear of that.' Lord Nelson then said: 'I am a dead man, Hardy. I am going fast: it will be all over with me soon. Come nearer to me. Pray let my dear Lady Hamilton have my hair, and all other things belonging to me.' Mr Burke was about to withdraw at the commencement of this conversation; but his Lordship perceiving his intention, desired he would remain. Captain Hardy observed, that 'he hoped Mr Beatty could yet hold out some prospect of life.' 'Oh! no,' answered his Lordship; 'it is impossible. My back is shot through. Beatty will tell you so.' Captain Hardy then returned on deck, and at parting shook hands again with his revered friend and commander.

His Lordship now requested the surgeon, who had been previously absent a short time attending Mr Rivers, to return to the wounded, and give his assistance to such of them as he could be useful to; for, said he, 'you can do nothing for me.' The surgeon assured him, that the assistant surgeons were doing everything that could be effected for those unfortunate men; but on his Lordship several times repeating his injunctions to that purpose, he left him, surrounded by Dr Scott, Mr Burke, and two of his Lordship's domestics. After the surgeon had been absent a few minutes, attending Lieutenant Peake, and Reeves, of the marines, who were wounded, he was called by Dr Scott to his Lordship, who said: 'Ah, Mr Beatty! I have sent for you to say, what I forgot to tell you before, that all power of motion and feeling below my breast are gone; and *you*', continued he, 'very well *know*, I can live but a short time.' The emphatic manner in which he pronounced these last words, left no doubt in the surgeon's mind, that he adverted to the case of a man who had some months before received a mortal injury of the spine, on board the *Victory*, and had laboured under similar privation of sense and muscular motion. The case had made a great impression on Lord Nelson: he was anxious to know the cause of such symptoms, which was accordingly explained to him; and he now appeared to apply the situation and fate of this man to himself. The surgeon answered, 'My Lord, you told me so before': but he now examined the extremities, to ascertain the fact; when his Lordship said, 'Ah, Beatty! I am too certain of it: Scott and Burke have tried it already. *You know* I am gone.' The surgeon replied: 'My Lord, unhappily for our country, nothing can be done for you'; and having made this declaration, he was so much affected, that he turned round and withdrew a few steps, to conceal his emotions. His Lordship said: 'I know it. I feel something rising in my breast', putting his hand on his left side, 'which tells me I am gone.' Drink was recommended liberally, and Dr Scott and Mr Burke fanned him with paper. He often exclaimed, 'God be praised, I have done my duty'; and upon the surgeon's enquiring whether his pain was still very great, he declared, 'it continued so very severe, that he wished he was dead. Yet', said he, in a low voice, 'one would like to live a little longer, too': and after a pause of a few minutes, he added, in the same tone, 'What would become of poor Lady Hamilton if she knew my situation!'

Captain Hardy now came to the cockpit to see his Lordship a second time, which was after an interval of about fifty minutes from the conclusion of his first visit. Before he quitted the deck, he sent Lieutenant Hill to acquaint Admiral Collingwood with the lamentable circumstance of Lord Nelson's being wounded. Lord Nelson and Captain Hardy shook hands again, and while the captain retained his Lordship's hand, he congratulated him, even in the arms of death, on his brilliant victory; 'which', he said, 'was complete; though he did not know how many of the enemy were captured, as it was impossible to perceive every ship distinctly. He was certain, however, of fourteen or fifteen having surrendered.' His Lordship answered, 'That is well, but I bargained for twenty.'

While on deck, Nelson had seen the high, wispy clouds forecasting wind, had noted the heavy swell and knew that a storm was gathering in the Atlantic. However decisive his victory might prove, he realised that most of his ships were so damaged aloft that they would be unable to make sail and ride it out. He therefore gave another order, as Beatty remembered:

Then [he] emphatically exclaimed, '*Anchor*, Hardy, *anchor*!' To this the captain replied, 'I suppose, my Lord, Admiral Collingwood will now take upon himself the direction of affairs.' 'Not while I live, I hope, Hardy!' cried the dying chief; and, at that endeavoured ineffectually to raise himself from the bed. 'No,' added he, 'do *you* anchor, Hardy.' Captain Hardy then said, 'Shall *we* make the signal, Sir?' 'Yes,' answered his Lordship, 'for, if I live, I'll anchor.' The energetic manner in which he uttered these his last orders to Captain Hardy, accompanied with his efforts to raise himself, evinced his determination never to resign the command while he retained the exercise of his transcendent faculties and that he expected Captain Hardy still to carry into effect the suggestions of his exalted mind; a sense of his duty overcoming the pains of death.

In fact, after his first visit to the dying Nelson, Hardy had sent a boat on a dangerous mission through the flying shot, across to the *Royal Sovereign* – still fighting Admiral Alava's *Santa Ana*, she was now only half a mile away – with a message telling Admiral Collingwood that Nelson had been wounded. The boat ran alongside the *Royal Sovereign* just as the duel with the Spanish ship reached its climax. After a two-hour fight, the *Santa Ana*'s foremast and mainmast had crashed over the side and she was drifting helplessly. Admiral Alava had no option but to strike his colours. When Hardy's boat arrived, Blackwood of the *Euryalus* was on board and about to cross to the *Santa Ana* to accept her surrender. Hardy's message was handed to Collingwood, who later remembered: 'Though the officer was directed to say that the wound was not dangerous, I read in his countenance what I had to fear.'

As he put it afterwards in a letter to a woman friend:

It was about the middle of the action when an officer came from the *Victory* to tell me he was wounded. He sent his love to me and desired me to conduct the fleet. I asked the officer if the wound was dangerous and he, by his look, told what he could not speak, nor I reflect upon now without suffering again the anguish of that moment.

Blackwood was hoping to be sent over to the *Victory* to see Nelson but had to board the *Santa Ana*, where he learned that Admiral Alava was mortally wounded. Leaving him to die, as he thought, in relative peace, Blackwood took the captain prisoner; in fact, Admiral Alava survived his wound.

On Blackwood's return to the *Royal Sovereign*, his prisoner asked the name of the ship; when told, he patted a gun and remarked, 'I think she should be called the "Royal Devil".' Blackwood was then told by Collingwood that the ship was so crippled that he would probably shift his flag to the *Euryalus* – now at the heart of the battle while most of Collingwood's lee division was fighting with the enemy's rear well astern of her – in order to give him mobility in exercising what he knew would soon become the supreme command.

No British ship fought harder, or suffered more, than the *Belleisle* at the forefront of the lee column. Dismasted, immobile and alone, she had defied a succession of enemy ships before relief arrived at last, as Lieutenant Owen recorded:

To our great joy, at half-past three the *Swiftsure*, English 74, came looming through the smoke, passed our stern, and giving us three cheers, placed herself between us and the French ship which had been so long more attentive to us than was agreeable; shortly afterwards the *Polyphemus* took the enemy's ship off our bow, and thus we were at length happily disengaged after nearly four hours of struggle, perhaps as severe as ever fell to the lot of a British man of war.

A beaten Spanish 80-gun ship, the *Argonauta*, having about this time hoisted English colours, the captain was good enough to give me the pinnace to take possession of her; the master accompanied me with eight or ten seamen or marines who happened to be near us. On getting up the *Argonauta*'s side, I found no living person on her deck, but on my making my way, over numerous dead and a confusion of wreck, across the quarterdeck, was met by the second captain at the cabin door, who gave me his sword which I returned, desiring him to keep it for Captain Hargood to whom I should soon introduce him. With him I accordingly returned to the *Belleisle*, leaving the master in charge of the prize, on board which I had seen only about six officers, the remainder (amongst whom was the captain, wounded) and all the men being below out of the way of the shot.

Captain Hargood took the Spaniard to his cabin, where he shortly afterwards assembled as many of the officers as could be spared from duty, to the most acceptable refreshment of tea . . .

During the time we were enjoying our welcome meal, Captain Hargood observed that my trousers were torn and bloody, and sent for the surgeon, who came reeking from the cockpit, which was crowded with wounded, to examine my hurt, which while the battle lasted I was scarcely conscious of, but after it was over recollected that I had been knocked down early in the action by a splinter, which tore away a small portion of muscle from the left thigh. The surgeon also looked at Captain Hargood's hurt, which was an extensive bruise reaching from the throat nearly to the waist, but he desired not to be returned wounded.

Away in the smoke-clouded mêlée on the port side of the *Belleisle*, the *Bellerophon*, the *Colossus* and the *Revenge*, commanded by Captain Richard Moorsom, began to burst through the enemy line to cut off the five rear ships. Midshipman William Robinson described the approach:

While we were running down to them, of course we were favoured with several shots, and some of our men were wounded. Upon being thus pressed, many of our men thought it hard that the firing should be all on one side and became impatient to return the compliment: but our captain had given orders not to fire until we got close in with them, so that all our shots might tell; indeed, these were his words. 'We shall want all our shot when we get close in: never mind their firing: when I fire a carronade from the quarterdeck, that will be a signal for you to begin, and I know you will do your duty as Englishmen.' In a few minutes the gun was fired, and our ship bore in and broke the line, but we paid dear for our temerity, as those ships we had thrown into disorder turned round, and made an attempt to board. A Spanish three-decker ran her bow-sprit over our poop, with a number of her crew on it, and, in her fore rigging, two or three hundred men were ready to follow; but they caught a Tartar, for their design was discovered, and our marines with their small arms, and the carronades on the poop, loaded with canister shot, swept them off so fast, some into the water and some on the decks, that they were glad to sheer off. While this was going on aft, we were engaged with a French two-deck ship on our starboard side, and on our larboard bow another, so that many of their shots must have struck their own ships and done severe execution. After being engaged about an hour, two other ships fortunately came up, received some of the fire intended for us, and we were now enabled to get at some of the shot-holes between wind and water and plug them up: this is a duty performed by the carpenter and his crew. We were now unable to work the ship, our yards, sails, and masts being disabled, and the braces completely shot away. In this condition we lay by the side of the enemy, firing away, and now and then we received a good raking from them, passing under our stern. This was a busy time with us, for we had not only to endeavour to repair our damage, but to keep to our duty. Often during the battle we could not see for the smoke whether we were firing at a foe or friend, and as to hearing, the noise of the guns had so completely made us deaf, that we were obliged to look only to the motions that were made . . .

As we were closely engaged throughout the battle, and the shots were playing their pranks pretty freely, grape as well as canister, with single and double headed thunderers all joining in the frolic; what was termed a *slaughtering one*, came in at one of the lower deck ports, which killed and wounded nearly all at the gun, and amongst them, a very merry little fellow, who was the very life of the ship's company, for he was ever the mirth of his mess, and on what-ever duty he might be ordered, his spirits made light the labour. He was the ship's cobbler, and withal a very good dancer; so that when any of his messmates would *sarve* us out a tune, he was sure to trip it on light fantastic toe, and find a step to it. He happened to be stationed at the gun where this messenger of death and destruction entered, and the poor fellow was so completely stunned by the head of another man being knocked against his, that no one doubted but that he was dead. As it is customary to throw overboard those, who, in an engagement are killed outright, the poor cobbler, amongst the rest, was taken to the port-hole to be committed to the deep, without any other ceremony than shoving him through the port: but, just as they were about to let him slip from their hands into the water, the blood began to circulate, and he commenced kicking. Upon this sign of returning life, his shipmates soon hauled the poor snob [cobbler] in again, and, though wonderful to relate, he recovered so speedily, that he actually fought the battle out; and, when he was afterwards joked about it, he would say, 'it was well that I learned to dance; for if I had not shown you some of my steps, when you were about to throw me overboard, I should not be here now, but safe enough in *Davy Jones's Locker*.'

The *Revenge*'s chaplain, the Reverend John Greenly, recorded his own impressions:

I had a very narrow escape, a 42-pounder came within 6 inches of me and entirely shattered a beam: the captain ordered me off twice but I went up when I could from the wounded. We had a dreadful carnage: Capt. Moorsom (very slightly wounded in the cheek but would not quit the deck) fought his ship as coolly as if at dinner . . . We have 27 killed and 45 wounded very badly, some of them the *Centurion*'s late crew, one master is wounded, two midshipmen killed, 2 wounded, all our yards were shot away and topmasts and lower masts terribly mauled. The killed on board the enemy must have been dreadful, as one of the ships which struck to us was employed all the morning in throwing their dead bodies overboard. We were so disabled that we could not take possession of our prizes, the *Polyphemus* and another have got them astern of them. I would not have been out of this action for any consideration, though the sight of the dead and dying are dreadful.

Such narrow escapes were commonplace. One befell Midshipman William Hicks of the *Conqueror*, at the heart of the weather column:

I was aide-de-camp to Sir I. Pellew, and had just reported to the first lieutenant that I had obeyed an order which he had commanded me to convey to the officers on the lower deck, and had walked a few yards from him, when I saw a grape-shot which had struck a canister case close by. I took it up and put it in my pocket. Turning round I saw the first lieutenant and sixth lying close by me. I ran to them, saying 'I hope you are not seriously hurt', and lifting Mr Lloyd's head the blood gushed into my shoes. Both were dead.

Casual courage was displayed everywhere. Close by the *Conqueror*, Captain Henry Bayntun noted one particular example in his ship, the *Leviathan*:

The *St Augustin*, of 74 guns, bearing the pendant of Commodore Cagigal, gave us an opportunity of closing with him, which was immediately embraced. A shot took off the arm of Thomas Main, when at his gun on the forecastle; his messmates kindly offered to assist him in going to the surgeon; but he bluntly said, 'I thank you, stay where you are; you will do more good there': he then went down by himself to the cockpit. The surgeon would willingly have attended him, in preference to others, whose wounds were less alarming; but Main would not admit of it, saying, 'Avast, not until it comes to my turn, if you please.' The surgeon soon after amputated the shattered part of the arm; during which, with great composure, smiling, and with a steady clear voice, he sang the whole of 'Rule, Britannia'.

In the lee column, astern of the *Revenge* came the *Defiance*, a 74 commanded by Captain Philip Durham, who steered his ship in the wakes of the *Bellerophon*, the *Colossus* and the British *Achilles* into the cauldron around *L'Aigle*, which had suffered so when Collingwood first broke the line. Amongst the

officers on her upper deck was a handsome young Irish midshipman, now a master's mate, named James (known as Jack)
Spratt, who had particular reason to hope for close-quarter
fighting as he was eager to make a mark and be promoted lieutenant. He recalled:

I took great pleasure in instructing the ship's boarders
in the French and English sword exercises, which I [was]
fully expert at, intermingling with it a little of my country's shillelagh [Irish blackthorn cudgel], which I saw the
sailors were very deficient in. This pleased my commander
so much that he promised if he came into general action he
intended giving me an opportunity of signalising myself
. . . I attended those fellows who could, at length, pick a
tooth out of an enemy's jaw without disturbing its neighbour.

When going into action . . . my captain, Sir Philip H.
Durham, ordered up the boarders on the quarterdeck and
told them should we be boarded, or have occasion to board
the enemy, that he was sure Mr Spratt would lead them on
to glory. The men gave three cheers and I made a low bow
and returned to my fighting quarters.

We were soon after in close engagement with the combined fleets of France and Spain and lately with *L'Aigle*,
80 guns [in fact a 74], which after a well-contested action
her firing slackened gradually from our superior broadsides. She seemed very much torn up yet her colours were
flying but our gallant captain ordered our firing to cease to
save human life, both ships being within pistol-shot.

About this time the wind had died away and a dead calm
ensued, during this interval both ships preparing for an
awful contest. We were to board the enemy . . . each view-
ing the other with glistening arms in hand, impatient for
the encounter. Both ships' boats being shot through and
rendered useless, and so no prospect of closing with the
enemy, I asked my captain leave to board by swimming as I
well knew that 50 or 60 of the boarders, who I had taught
for some years, could swim like sharks. This request he
received with astonishment, saying I was too prompt but
finally consented.

So I gave the word, 'You, you, my brave fellows, who can swim, follow me.' I plunged overboard from the starboard gangway with my cutlass between my teeth and my tomahawk under my belt and swam to the stern of *L'Aigle*, where by the assistance of her rudder chains I got into her gunroom stern-port *alone*. My men in the loud clamour of a general engagement not hearing what I said, or misunderstanding me, did not follow.

So I fought my way under God's guidance through a host of gallant French, all prepared with arms in hand and through all decks until I got on her poop. The position was no sinecure for 15 minutes: I now showed myself to our crew from the enemy's taffrail and gave them a cheer with my hat on the point of my cutlass.

Our ship at this moment contrived to steer alongside and now came the tug of war, both ships lashed side by side by our gallant boatswain, Mr Foster, who was shot through the heart by a rifleman from the cat lashings* and received a second shot as he was carrying below. A division of my boarders flew to my support and a timely one indeed for I was that moment attacked by 3 grenadiers with fixed bayonets and from the taffrail by the assistance of a rope, the signal halyards which I held in my hands, I sprung over their heads upon an arms chest and disabled two of them before they could act against me with their muskets. The 3rd man I grappled by the collar and forced over the break of the poop but on falling he fell [head] first and broke his neck; I got off better by falling on his body.

I found myself now in a desperate conflict on the French quarterdeck. The first division of boarders being nearly cut up was reinforced by a fresh division which soon cleared the quarterdeck of every soul but one officer, who had done his duty well as long as in his power, and trying to escape below was seized by two of our men with uplifted tomahawks. He cried for quarter and threw himself at my feet and I was obliged to throw myself on him and cover his body to save him from our men, who said they would open his soul case in a minute.

I had scarcely performed this piece of service and was

* Tackle for hauling anchors in the bows.

in the act of rising up when a grenadier from the starboard gangway with fixed bayonet thought to run me through but I parried his thrust with my blade, he then retired a little, levelling his piece at my breast, which I struck downwards with my trusty old friend the cutlass so that the ball, which would otherwise have passed through my body, shivered and shattered the bone of my right leg which was in advance. I felt something like an electric shock and darted at him but my right leg turned up between my thighs with my shinbone resting on the deck. I backed in between two of the quarterdeck great guns with my back to the bulwark to prevent being cut down from behind, where I was immediately attacked by my old tormentor in front and one at each side, slashing at me furiously. I was obliged to hollow out for my boarders who, when the smoke cleared off, saw my perilous situation and ran my old tormentor through the body and nearly put me on the same spit. I now found myself very weak from hard work and loss of blood and on one knee with my shinbone on my right leg sticking in the deck. I tied it round with my neck handkerchief above the wound, which acted as a turnicat [tourniquet].

The ship about this time was completely carried and I feel satisfaction to this day for saving the life of the French officer, a Monsieur Salmon, which afterwards caused a great laugh in the fleet to think that the little fish saved the larger one.

I saw several gallant encounters that day. One in particular between one of my boarders, a tobacco-twister* from Dublin and a powerful Frenchman. Both fixed their eyes on each other at a distance and cautiously approached, firing their pistols in each other's faces without effect, they then closed and fought furiously with their swords without advantage to either. Pat, getting impatient at the length of the contest, closed, both grappling, but the Irish tobacco-twister gave his adversary such a twist that brought his heels upwards and was soon on the flat of his back. The cunning Frenchman however picked up a cocked pistol close by him, which he fired upwards and

* A maker of tobacco twist, or plug, for chewing.

drove a ball through Pat's body that came out near the spine but he despatched the Frenchman. This brave Irishman lay in Gibraltar Hospital for many months in a bad state and not expected to survive but he was at length made a good cure of, his surname was Flyn, a carrotty-headed fellow . . .

I forgot to remark that a rifleman's 2nd shot from the maintop killed my brave and particular friend Lieut. Symonds, who assisted in hauling down the French colours, so gallantly defended, and which I sent over to my gallant captain by a black man, one of my boarders, who received them with expression of high admiration on our conduct on the occasion.

At this time I presented myself on the captured ship's quarterdeck [and], her boats being shot away, I swung myself to our ship by one of her boat-tackle falls and landed on a lower deck port, saturated with blood and salt water and was drawn into the port pretty well done up after so much hard work.

At last [I] got to the cockpit where the doctors thought amputation necessary for the safety of my life, which I would not submit to, hoping one day to be able again to follow the profession which I was so proud of.

The horrors of surgery in the cockpit on the orlop deck were, of course, shared by both sides. In the French *Pluton*, an army officer described how

A cannonball piercing the second battery killed three men and wounded several others, of whom I was one. I fell, bathed in my own blood and that of the dead men. I remained there for some time unconscious. When I came to, I recognised one of my soldiers by the sound of his voice and begged him to lead me to the surgeon's post. He told me that he would already have done it, if he hadn't believed me dead. On my arrival they dressed my wounds. Happily I had no fractures. I had received three wounds, one to the left eye which I believed I would lose, but which opened after four days; one to the left hand which would be the longest to heal; and that which caused me the greatest pain . . . the blow I received on my chest, near the collar bone, and from one shoulder to the other . . . After that, when I was laid out on a mattress, I was again wounded in the head in two places by the splinters thrown up by a cannonball as it passed through the orlop deck . . . What made me worse was that yet again I could not see, and that afterwards a dozen wounded men fell on my body and made me suffer considerably. They were obliged to dress my wounds again, and they put me in a room belonging to a naval officer. If I was no longer witness to the combat, and its terrible consequences, I could not help trembling at hearing it. I learned that my sub-lieutenant had been killed, as well as my first sergeant, my drummer and two other soldiers, and 23 were very badly wounded. The number of killed and wounded on our ship was put down as 400.

Ships fought each other then drifted away, their place taken by another, perhaps to receive the surrender of an enemy they had only just engaged. Usually the identity of an opponent was unknown until they surrendered. When the *Defiance* fought a Spanish 74 for twenty-five minutes her ship's company did not discover her name until, as Midshipman Thomas Huskisson noted:

We sent a boat on board and found her to be *St Ildefonzo* bearing the pendant of a brigadier or commodore, who was severely wounded, but his captain re-turned in the boat and delivered up his sword to Captain Hope, immediately afterwards very coolly he took a match out of one of the match-tubs on the quarter deck, lighted his *segar* and smoked it as unconcernedly as if nothing particular had occurred.

Among the most effective Spanish ships in the rear of the combined fleet was the 74-gun *San Juan Nepomuceno*, commanded by the able young Commodore Don Cosme Churruca. Hoping to rake the crippled *Bellerophon*, he was about to administer what he intended to be the *coup de grâce* when through the smoke appeared the slow-sailing 98-gun *Dreadnought*, arriving late into action. She was not alone, for the *Tonnant* and the *Defiance* also began to fire on Churruca's ship, as a Spanish account recalled:

The *San Juan Nepomuceno* was at the end of the line. The *Royal Sovereign* and the *Santa Ana* opened fire and then all the ships in turn came into action. Five English vessels under Collingwood attacked our ship; two, however, passed on, and Churruca had only three to deal with.

We held out bravely against these odds till two in the afternoon, suffering terribly, though we dealt double havoc on the foe. Our leader seemed to have infused his heroic spirit into the crew and soldiers, and the ship was handled and her broadsides delivered with wonderful promptitude and accuracy. The new recruits learnt their lesson in courage in no more than a couple of hours' apprenticeship, and our defence struck the English with astonishment.

They were in fact forced to get assistance, and bring up no less than six against one. The two ships that had at first sailed past us now returned, and the *Dreadnought* came alongside of us, with not more than half a pistol-shot between her and our stern. You may imagine the fire of these six giants pouring balls and small shot into a vessel of 74 guns!

Churruca, meanwhile, who was the brain of all, directed the battle with gloomy calmness. Knowing that only care and skill could supply the place of strength, he economised our fire, trusting entirely to careful aim, and the consequence was that each ball did terrible havoc on the foe. He saw to everything, settled everything, and the shot flew round him and over his head without his ever once changing colour even.

It was not the will of God, however, that he should escape alive from that storm of fire. Seeing that no one could hit one of the enemy's ships which was battering us with impunity, he went down himself to judge of the line of fire and succeeded in dismasting her. He was returning to the quarterdeck when a cannonball hit his right leg with such violence as almost to take it off, tearing it across the thigh in the most frightful manner. He fell to the ground, but the next moment he made an effort to raise himself, supporting himself on one arm. His face was as white as death, but he said, in a voice that was scarcely weaker than his ordinary tone: 'It is nothing – go on firing!'

He did all he could to conceal the terrible sufferings of his cruelly mangled frame. Nothing would induce him, it would seem, to quit the quarterdeck. At last he yielded to our entreaties and then he seemed to understand that he must give up the command. He called for Moyna, his second in command, but was told that he was dead. Then he called for the officer in command on the main deck. That officer, though himself seriously wounded, at once came to the quarterdeck and took command.

It was just before he went below that Churruca, in the midst of his agonies, gave the order that the flag should be nailed to the mast. The ship, he said, must never surrender so long as he breathed.

The delay, alas! could be but short. He was going fast. He never lost consciousness till the very end, nor did he complain of his sufferings. His sole anxiety was that the crew should not know how dangerous his wound was; that no one should be daunted or fail in his duty. He specially desired that the men should be thanked for their heroic courage. Then he spoke a few words to Ruiz de Apodoca, and after sending a farewell message to his poor young wife, whom he had married only a few days before he sailed, he fixed his thoughts on God, whose name was ever on his lips. So with the calm resignation of a good man and the fortitude of a hero, Churruca passed away.

After he was gone, it was too quickly known, and the men lost heart . . . Their courage was really worn out. It was but too plain that they must surrender . . . A sudden paralysis seemed to seize on the crew; their grief at losing their beloved leader apparently overpowered the disgrace of surrender.

Quite half the *San Juan*'s crew were *hors de combat*, dead or wounded. Most of the guns were disabled. All the masts, except the mainmast, had gone by the board. The rudder was useless. And yet, in this deplorable plight even, they made an attempt to follow the *Principe de Asturias*, which had given the signal to withdraw; but the *San Juan*

Nepomuceno had received her death blow. She could neither sail nor steer.

The *Defiance* then ran in close. Captain Durham, as one
account had it, was 'just going to pour in a broadside' when
he saw Spanish officers on the enemy's deck 'making signals
with their hats and ordered the crew of the *Defiance* not to fire,
upon which the Spaniard hauled down his colours without firing
a shot'. The apparent surrender was also seen from the deck of
the *Tonnant*, according to Lieutenant Benjamin Clement:

We were hard at it on the Spanish ship, when at last down
came her colours. I hailed him and asked him if he had
struck, when he said 'yes' I came aft and informed the
first lieut. when he ordered me to board her. We had no
boat but what was shot, but he told me I must try: so I
went away in the jolly boat with 2 men, and had not got
above a quarter of the way when the boat swampt . . . I
cannot swim, but the two men that were with me could,
one a black man, the other a quartermaster, he was the
last man in her, when a shot struck her and knocked her
quarter off, and she turned bottom up . . . Macnamara,
the black man, staid by me on one side, and MacKay, the
quartermaster, on the other, until I got hold of the jolly
boat's fall that was hanging overboard. I got my leg
between the fall, and as the boat was lifted by the sea, so
was I, and as she descended I was ducked; I found myself
weak, and thought I was not long for this world, but Macnamara swam to the ship and got a rope, and came to me
again, making it fast under my arms, when I swang off and
was hauled into the stern port.

In the end it was a boarding-party from the *Dreadnought*
which accepted the *San Juan*'s formal surrender. They left a
prize-crew on board.

The French and Spanish had tried to double their own line at
the rear to halt the procession of British ships breaking through,
and there the pell-mell battle was most intense. Villeneuve's
second-in-command, Admiral Gravina, was fighting in his flagship, the *Principe de Asturias*, when the last three-deck battle-

ship in Collingwood's line, the *Prince* of ninety-eight guns, came up. As the admiral's chief of staff, Escano, related:

She discharged all her guns at grape-shot range into our stern. [Admiral Gravina] was wounded in the left leg; he was obliged to go below but while it was being temporarily dressed he gave orders that he should be conveyed back and placed sitting at his post on deck.

Weakened by loss of blood he fell fainting; but quickly coming to himself and not perceiving the national colours, he ordered them to be hoisted without delay and he resumed command.

In this critical position we sighted the [French] *Neptune* and the *San Justo* that were coming up to our aid, which was observed by the enemy, who obliged them to sheer off.

By mid-afternoon, the British seemed to have won the battles with the centre and rear of the combined fleet. Admiral Gravina's *Principe de Asturias* was still fighting, although breaking away from the mêlée to the east and signalling that other ships should follow, which suggested he might no longer have the will to continue the contest. The *Principe de Asturias* was sighted from the wreck of the *Algésiras*, herself a prize of the *Tonnant*, by Lieutenant Philibert, who could at last see further than the smoke and enemies alongside:

The smoke which had enveloped us up to then having cleared, our first glances searched for our fleet; there no longer existed any line on either side; we could see nothing more than groups of vessels in the most dreadful state, towards the place more or less where we judged that our battle fleet ought to be. We counted 17 ships from the two navies totally dismasted – their masts gone right down to the deck – and many others partially dismasted . . . Several vessels that we judged to be from our fleet were not attacking, although they appeared to be in good condition, to judge by their masts and sails. Two French ships were hugging the wind in order to reach the vanguard, but afterwards they rejoined the *Principe*, Admiral Gravina's ship, which, as far as we could see, was flying the flag for the general and unconditional recall.

But there still remained another element. Villeneuve had, before his surrender, repeatedly signalled to the commander of his van, Rear-Admiral Dumanoir le Pelley, to turn and come to his aid, but seemingly to little avail. However, the officers in the ten ships of the van were becoming increasingly worried by their commander's apparent inactivity. Lieutenant des Touches of the *Intrépide* put it bluntly:

The leading division, although not a single British ship threatened it, remained inactive. Our captain, Infernet, with his eyes fixed on the *Formidable*, expected Admiral Dumanoir every moment to make the signal to go about and take part in the battle. But no signal went up. Time passed, and the van division slowly drew off from where the fighting was going on: it soon became but too plain that its chief was keeping out of the battle. Admiral Villeneuve, meanwhile, while he still had a mast standing on which to hoist a signal, was ordering our ships to put about and come into action.

In fact Dumanoir had tried to comply earlier, but the wind was so light and the swell so heavy that his ships had been unable to turn and head south until they launched their boats to tow them round. When they eventually succeeded, Dumanoir himself led four battleships in company with his flagship *Formidable* and steered south, to windward of the battle itself, but making for the *Bucentaure*, which he knew to be in the centre of the line. However, the little 64-gun *Africa*, which had become separated from Nelson's column and was still trying to rejoin it, gallantly fired on the French van as it sought to pass, distracting Dumanoir from his aim. As he finally came within sight of Villeneuve's flagship, he found his way barred by the 74s *Minotaur* and *Spartiate*, which, at the rear of Nelson's weather division, had only just reached the battle, and soon dissuaded him from pressing his attack further.

The rest of the combined fleet's van appeared to scatter: two of them – one the *Intrépide* – headed for the flashing, smoking heart of the battle as if set on joining Villeneuve; but the others held back to leeward as if ready to run for Cadiz and safety. On board the *Intrépide*, Lieutenant des Touches was still critical:

Happily, Captain Infernet took another view of his duty, and his honour. Although we were immediately under the orders of M. Dumanoir, we had already made several unsuccessful attempts to put about; but the wind had been entirely stilled by the cannonading. In the end, after incessant efforts and by the aid of the only boat we had available, we were able to wear round, whereupon the captain called out 'Lay her head for the *Bucentaure!*'

It was now the hottest moment of the battle. We could hardly make out, in the midst of the smoke and confusion of the battle, the situation of our flagship, surrounded as she was by the enemy, and having near her only the *Redoutable*, a small 74, crushed by the overpowering mass of the *Victory*. The enemy's superiority in gunnery was so great that, in a very short time, our crews were decimated, whilst on the British side the losses were comparatively trivial.

When at length we drew near where the *Bucentaure* and the *Redoutable* lay, their masts had fallen, their fire was almost silenced; yet the heroism of those on board kept up an unequal and hopeless struggle, fighting against ships that were practically undamaged, from the ports of which broadside after broadside flashed incessantly. It was into the thick of this fray that our Captain Infernet led us. It was a reckless and forlorn hope, a mad enterprise. It was noble madness, but, though we knew it, we all supported him with joyful alacrity – and would that others had imitated his example! . . .

I passed the entire battle on the forecastle, where I was in charge of manoeuvring and musketry. It was from here, too, that I was to lead my boarding company; this was my most ardent wish but I was unfortunately unable to fulfil it . . .

What took much of my attention was to prevent the masts and yards from coming down, and I was able to keep the foremast standing for a considerable time, by means of which we were able to manoeuvre the ship to some extent.

While the fighting was very hot the British *Orion* crossed our bows in order to pour in a raking fire. I got my men ready to board and pointing out to a midshipman her position and what I wanted to do, I sent him to the captain with a request to have the ship laid on board the *Orion*.

I saw to the rest, and seeing the ardour of my men, I already imagined myself master of the British 74 and taking her into Cadiz with her colours under ours. With keen anxiety I waited; but there was no change in the *Intrépide*'s course.

Then I dashed off to the quarterdeck myself. On the way I found my midshipman lying flat on the deck, terrified at the sight of the *Britannia*, which ship had come abreast of us within pistol shot and was thundering into us from her lofty batteries. I treated my emissary as he deserved – I gave him a hearty kick – and then I hurried aft to explain my project personally to the captain. It was then, though, too late. The *Orion* swept forward across our bows, letting fly a murderous broadside – and no second chance presented itself.

At the moment I reached the poop the brave Infernet was brandishing a small curved sabre which struck off one of the pieces of wooden ornamental work by the rail. The sword blade went close to my face, and I said laughingly, 'Do you want to cut my head off, Captain?'

'No, certainly not you, my friend,' was the reply, 'but that's what I mean to do to the first man who speaks to me of surrender.'

Nearby was a gallant colonel of infantry, who had distinguished himself at Marengo. He was terribly perturbed at the broadside from the *Britannia*. In vain he tried to dodge and shelter behind the stalwart form of the captain, who at length saw what he was doing.

'Ah, Colonel,' called out the captain, 'do you think I am sheathed in metal then?'

In spite of the gravity of the moment we could not keep from laughing.

But by now, indeed, the decks had been almost swept clear, our guns were disabled, and the batteries heaped up with dead and dying. It was impossible to keep up a resistance which meant the doom of what remained of our brave ship's company, and ourselves, without the means of striking back and inflicting harm on the enemy.

His captain, Infernet, was to report:

I was dismantled to such a degree that all my rigging was cut to pieces and several guns on deck and in the batteries dismounted. I ordered the few hands remaining on deck to go below to the batteries in order to engage to starboard and larboard; at this minute the mizen-yard where my colours were flying was carried away by a shot; I immediately ordered a flag to be flown from the mizen shrouds to starboard and larboard and continued the fight.

The wheel, the tiller-sweep, the tiller ropes and the tiller were shattered to a thousand pieces; I at once had the spare tiller rigged and steered with it, always fighting desperately. The mizen-mast fell; four or five minutes later the mainmast did the same; I still fought – and I am able to say so to the honour of those whom I commanded – undauntedly; I was then surrounded by seven enemy ships, which were all firing into me and I was making all possible resistance; I was firing with the stern-chasers, musketry from the upper-works and from the foretops.

The foremast fell; I was then left without masts or sails; seeing myself surrounded by enemies and not being able to escape, having, moreover, no French ships in sight to come to my assistance, the enemy keeping up a terrible fire into me, having about half my crew killed . . . I was obliged to yield to the seven enemy ships that were engaging me.

The intense confusion of the fighting around the *Victory* was described by Captain Edward Codrington of the *Orion*, at the rear of Nelson's line:

We all scrambled into battle as soon as we could, and I believe have done our best *in imitation* of the *noble example* before us. I was in the middle of the battle before I fired a gun, not liking to waste our fire, and my men behaved as coolly as possible . . . *Each* ship engaged must have fought with a dozen enemies, and those headmost in the line had much the greater part of the action. It was all confusion . . .

I suppose no man ever before saw such a sight so clearly as I did, or rather as we did; for I called all my lieutenants up to see it. After passing *Santa Ana* dismasted, and her opponent the *Royal Sovereign* little better, on our larboard side, besides three of our ships and some of those of the enemy all lumped together on our starboard bow, we passed close to the *Victory*, *L'Indomptable*, *Téméraire*, and *Bucentaure* (French), all abreast or aboard each other, each firing her broadside and boarding the other at the same time.

In this situation the two French ships were soon settled but as we were the only ship thereabout not firing (for even the *Agamemnon*, far astern of us, was blazing away and wasting her ammunition), we were the only people who could have a distinct uninterrupted view of that grand and awful scene. The shot both from friends and foes were flying about us like hailstones, and yet did us hardly any damage whatever; and, to the honour of *Orion*'s crew, they did not attempt to break my orders to reserve their fire till I could put the ship where I wished . . . I still persevered in my reserve in spite of the firing all around us, until I saw an unfortunate Frenchman, the *Swiftsure*, not closely occupied; and going close under his stern we poured him in such a dose as carried away his three masts and made him strike his colours. Having repeatedly pointed out to my men the waste of shot from other ships, I had now a fine opportunity of convincing them of the benefit of cool reserve. In my next attempt to close with a French two-decker which annoyed the *Victory*, my second ahead (*Ajax*) cut me out, and I could only fire at a little distance. I then made for Admiral Gravina in the *Prince of Asturias*, but the *Dreadnought* again cut me out here, and yet, like the *Ajax*, did not close and make a finish of it . . .

Seeing *Leviathan* make a fine and well-judged attack on a Spanish 74, *St Augustin* (in the van of the enemy when there were eight or nine others, French and Spanish untouched, which ought to have come to her support), I made sail to assist her. *L'Intrépide*, however, was the only one which wore and came to action gallantly, keeping up a very good fire both on *Leviathan* and the Spaniard, of whom she was taking possession. After several fruitless attempts to pass by one or two of our ships, who kept up a distant cannonade on her, I managed, first to back all sail so as to get under *Ajax*'s stern, and then to make all sail so as to pass close across *Leviathan*'s head, who hailed me and said he hoped laughing that *I* should make a *better fist of it* (if not *elegant*, still very cheering to me to meet so much confidence and good opinion); and then to bear down sufficiently to get our starboard guns to bear on *L'Intrépide*'s starboard quarter, and then to turn gradually round from thence under his stern, pass his broadside, and bring to on his larboard bow. He had said he would not strike till his masts and rudder were shot away; and this we did for him in so handsome a way that he had no time to do us much injury.

The French *Swiftsure* (once captured from the British), had been fighting for more than three hours against a succession of British battleships when the *Orion* came up. As Captain Charles Villemadrin reported:

A three-decker passed me astern and as it was almost a calm at that time, she had leisure to discharge three broadsides into me which brought down my mainmast, carried away part of the taffrail, the wheel, and dismounted most of the guns on the main deck, and killed many of the people. In this painful situation, the senior surgeon twice sent a midshipman from the lower deck to inform me that he was unable to make room for any more wounded, that the space cleared in the hold and the orlop deck were thronged. I then sent all the men that I had available – both from the main deck and from the upper works – to the lower deck to continue the fire. At 3 o'clock, I lost my foremast and I continued in action until 3.40 when having no longer any hope of being supported – seeing the fleet at a great distance and having at hand only the *Achille*, who caught fire an instant later, and [having] 5 feet of water in the hold – I gave orders to cease fire and I hauled down my colours. I cannot say exactly how many people I lost, but it must have amounted to nearly 260 to 300 men killed and wounded, amongst whom were 3 officers and a midshipman killed and two officers wounded. At 4 o'clock a boat came from the *Colossus* to fetch me.

Meanwhile, deep in the battered hull of the *Victory*, Hardy knelt beside Nelson, as Dr Beatty recounted what Nelson told Hardy:

[Nelson] then told Captain Hardy, 'he felt that in a few minutes he should be no more'; adding in a low tone, 'Don't throw me overboard, Hardy.' The captain answered: 'Oh! no, certainly not.' 'Then,' replied his Lordship, 'you know what to do: and', continued he, 'take care of my dear Lady Hamilton, Hardy: take care of poor Lady Hamilton. Kiss me, Hardy.' The captain now knelt down, and kissed his cheek; when his Lordship said, 'Now I am satisfied. Thank God, I have done my duty.' Captain Hardy stood for a minute or two in silent contemplation: he knelt down again, and kissed his Lordship's forehead. His Lordship said: 'Who is that?' The captain answered: 'It is Hardy'; to which his Lordship replied, 'God bless you, Hardy!' After this affecting scene Captain Hardy withdrew, and returned to the quarterdeck, having spent about eight minutes in this his last interview with his dying friend.

Lord Nelson now desired Mr Chevalier, his steward, to turn him upon his right side; which being effected, his Lordship said: 'I wish I had not left the deck, for I shall soon be gone.' He afterwards became very low; his breathing was oppressed, and his voice faint. He said to Dr Scott: 'Doctor, I have *not* been a *great* sinner'; and after a short pause, '*Remember*, that I leave Lady Hamilton and my daughter Horatia as a legacy to my country; and', added he, 'never forget Horatia.' His thirst now increased, and he called for 'drink, drink', 'fan, fan', and 'rub, rub', addressing himself in the last case to Dr Scott, who had been rubbing his Lordship's breast with his hand, from which he found some relief. These words he spoke in a very rapid manner, which rendered his articulation difficult: but he every now and then, with evident increase of pain, made a greater effort with his vocal powers, and pronounced distinctly these last words: 'Thank God, I have done my duty'; and this great sentiment he continued to repeat as long as he was able to give it utterance.

His Lordship became speechless in about fifteen minutes after Captain Hardy left him. Dr Scott and Mr Burke, who had all along sustained the bed under his shoulders (which raised him in nearly a semi-recumbent posture, the only one that was supportable to him), forbore to disturb him by speaking to him; and when he had remained speechless about five minutes, his Lordship's steward went to the surgeon, who had been a short time occupied with the wounded in another part of the cockpit, and stated his apprehension that his Lordship was dying. The surgeon immediately repaired to him, and found him on the verge of dissolution. He knelt down by his side, and took up his hand, which was cold, and the pulse gone from the wrist. On the surgeon feeling his forehead, which was likewise cold, his Lordship opened his eyes, looked up, and shut them again. The surgeon again left him, and returned to the wounded, who required his assistance; but was not absent five minutes before the steward announced to him, that 'he believed his Lordship had expired.' The surgeon returned, and found that the report was but too well founded: his Lordship had breathed his last, at thirty minutes past four o'clock; at which period Dr Scott was in the act of rubbing his Lordship's breast, and Mr Burke supporting the bed under his shoulders.

Around the *Victory*, the battle raged on. At about four o'clock, the *Prince* had found herself near a stationary French 74, the *Achille*, which lay with her mizen-mast and main topmast hanging over her side, and fired a broadside into her, bringing the mainmast down too. A second broadside cut the foremast down and started a fire. Seeing this, Captain Richard

Grindall sheered away, fearing that she might blow up, or that the fire might spread to his own ship. It was about half past four. The *Achille*'s sails caught fire and fell blazing on to her shattered upperworks, which also ignited. The surviving officers ordered the crew over the side and then, as a watcher in the *Prince* described it:

It was a sight the most awful and grand that can be conceived. In a moment the hull burst into a cloud of smoke and fire. A column of vivid flame shot up to an enormous height in the atmosphere and terminated by expanding into an immense globe, representing, for a few seconds, a prodigious tree in flames, speckled with many dark spots, which the pieces of timber and bodies of men occasioned while they were suspended in the clouds.

The end of the *Achille* was heard in Cadiz:

The ships were not visible from the ramparts, but the crowd of citizens assembled there had their ears assailed by the roaring of the distant cannon; the anxiety of the females bordered on insanity; but more of despair than of hope was visible in every countenance. At this dreadful moment, a sound louder than any that had preceded it, and attended with a column of dark smoke, announced that a ship had exploded. The madness of the people was turned to rage against England; and exclamations burst forth, denouncing instant death to every man who spoke the language of their enemies. Two Americans, who had mixed with the people, fled, and hid themselves, to avoid this ebullition of popular fury; which, however, subsided into the calmness of despair, when the thunder of the cannon ceased. They had no hope of conquest, no cheering expectations of greeting their victorious countrymen, nor of sharing triumphal laurels with those who had been engaged in the conflict; each only hoped that the objects of his own affection were safe.

The *Achille* blew up an hour after Nelson died, the explosion marking, in effect, the end of the Battle of Trafalgar. It was signalled in a symbolic way when, a few minutes later, the mizen-mast of the *Victory*, shot through, crashed over the side. It was nearly time for Admiral Collingwood to leave his battered flagship. Not only was the *Royal Sovereign* unmanageable, she was virtually uninhabitable, as Collingwood noted in his quietly humorous way: 'I have a great deal of destruction of my furniture and stock; I have hardly a chair that has not a shot in it and many have lost both legs and arms, without hope of pension. My wine broke in moving and my pigs were slain in battle.' This was, of course, trivial, and he was overwhelmingly conscious of the great events of 21 October, writing soon afterwards: 'Oh! had Nelson lived! how complete had been my happiness – how perfect my joy! Now, whatever I have felt with pleasure has been so mixed with the bitterness of woe that I cannot exult in our success.'

In the *Euryalus*, Captain Blackwood wrote in his log:

At 5.25, made sail for the *Royal Sovereign*. Observed the *Victory*'s mizen-mast go overboard, about which time the firing ceased, leaving the English fleet conquerors . . . At 5.55, Admiral Collingwood came on board and hoisted his flag (blue at the fore). At 6.15, sent a spare shroud hawser on board the *Royal Sovereign* and took her in tow and at the same time sent all our boats with orders from Admiral Collingwood to all the English ships we could discover near us that they were to take the captured ships in tow and follow the admiral. At the time saw Cape Trafalgar being SE by E about 8 miles.

It was time to assess the victory and count the cost. Seventeen French and Spanish ships had been captured and one had blown up. Fifteen enemy ships had escaped: four sailing south-east towards the Straits of Gibraltar with Dumanoir and eleven, led by Gravina, running for Cadiz. No British ship had been lost. It was too early to count the cost in human life.

CHAPTER 9

The Reckoning

The explosion of the *Achille* seemed a fitting climax to the battle. As the sound of the gunfire died away, the task of counting the cost could begin. In the *Revenge*, the seaman William Robinson remembered:

We were now called to clear the decks, and here might be witnessed an awful and interesting scene, for as each officer and seaman would meet . . . they were enquiring for their mess-mates. Orders were now given to fetch the dead bodies from the after cockpit, and throw them overboard; these were the bodies of men who were taken down to the doctor during the battle, badly wounded, and who by the time the engagement was ended were dead. Some of these, perhaps, could not have recovered, while others might, had timely assistance been rendered, which was impossible; for the rule is, as order is requisite, that every person shall be dressed in rotation as they are brought down wounded, and in many instances some have bled to death. The next call was 'all hands to splice the mainbrace', which is the giving out of a gill of rum to each man, and indeed they much needed it, for they had not ate nor drank from breakfast time: we had now a good night's work before us; all our yards, masts, and sails were sadly cut, indeed the whole of the sails were obliged to be unbent, being rendered completely useless.

In the magazines of the British ships, gunners began to check their expenditure of ammunition. In the *Victory*, the 32-, 24- and 12-pounder guns had fired in total:

Powder – 14,390 lbs
Paper cartridges – (32 pdr) 937; (24) 1,234; (12) 1,799
Roundshot – (32) 997; (24) 872; (12) 800

Double-headed shot – (32) 10; (24) 11; (12) 14
Grapeshot – (32) 10; (24) 20; (12) 156
Tin case* – (12) 150

The flagship had fired more than 30 tons of shot that day.

The relief at surviving the battle and grief for lost comrades was expressed by the Royal Marine Second Lieutenant Paul Nicolas of the *Belleisle*:

Eager enquiries were expressed, and earnest congratulations exchanged, at this joyful moment. The officers came to make their report to the captain, and the fatal results cast a gloom over the scene of our triumph. I have alluded to the impression of our first lieutenant that he should not survive the contest.†

This gallant officer was severely wounded in the thigh, and underwent an amputation: but his prediction was realised, for he expired before the action had ceased. The junior lieutenant was likewise mortally wounded on the quarterdeck. These gallant fellows were lying beside each other in the gun-room preparatory to their being committed to the deep; and here many met to take a last look at their departed friends, whose remains soon followed the promiscuous multitude, without distinction of either rank or nation, to their wide ocean grave.

In the act of launching a poor sailor over the poop he was discovered to breathe; he was, of course, saved . . .

The upper-deck presented a confused and dreadful appearance: masts, yards, sails, ropes and fragments of wreck were scattered in every direction; nothing could be more horrible than the scene of blood and mangled remains with which every part was covered, and which, from the quantity of splinters, resembled a shipwright's yard strewed with gore.

From our extensive loss – thirty-four killed and ninety-six wounded – our cockpit exhibited a scene of suffering which rarely occurs. I visited this abode of suffering with the natural impulse which led many others thither –

---

* i.e. case-shot – tins packed with musket balls.
† See p. 72.

namely, to ascertain the fate of a friend or companion. So many bodies in such a confined space and under such distressing circumstances would affect the most obdurate heart. My nerves were but little accustomed to such trials but even the dangers of battle did not seem more terrific than the spectacle before me.

On a long table lay several anxiously looking for their turn to receive the surgeon's care, yet dreading the fate he might pronounce. One subject was undergoing amputation, and every part was heaped with sufferers: their piercing shrieks and expiring groans were echoed through this vault of misery; and even at this distant period the heart-sickening picture is alive in my memory. What a contrast to the hilarity and enthusiastic mirth which reigned in this spot the preceding evening!

At all other times the cockpit is the region of conviviality and good humour, for here it is that the happy midshipmen reside, at whose board neither discord nor care interrupt the social intercourse. But a few short hours since, on these benches, which were now covered with mutilated remains, sat these scions of their country's glory, who hailed the coming hour of conflict with cheerful confidence, and each told his story to beguile the anxious moments; the younger ones eagerly listening to their experienced associates, and all united in the toast of 'May we meet again at this hour tomorrow!'

About five o'clock the officers assembled in the captain's cabin to take some refreshment. The parching effect of the smoke made this a welcome summons, although some of us had been fortunate in relieving our thirst by plundering the captain's grapes which hung round his cabin; still, four hours' exertion of body with the energies incessantly employed, occasioned a lassitude, both corporeally and mentally, from which the victorious termination so near at hand could not arouse us; moreover there sat a melancholy on the brows of some who mourned a messmate who had shared their perils and their vicissitudes for many years. Then the merits of the departed heroes were repeated with a sigh, but their errors sunk with them into the deep . . .

A boat with a lieutenant from the cutter *Entreprenante* shortly after came on board, on his return from the *Victory*, to announce the death of the immortal Nelson. The melancholy tidings spread through the ship in an instant and the paralysing effect was wonderful.

Our captain [Hargood] had served under the illustrious chief for years, and had partaken in the anxious pursuit of the enemy across the Atlantic, with the same officers and crew. 'Lord Nelson is no more!' was repeated with such despondency and heartfelt sorrow that everyone seemed to mourn a parent. All exertion was suspended: the veteran sailor indulged in silent grief; and some eyes evinced that tenderness of heart is often concealed under the roughest exterior.

News of Nelson's death had spread quickly through the *Victory*. A few were so shocked by what they had experienced that they barely registered it, for example Able Seaman Benjamin Stevenson, who wrote to his sister in his untutored style: 'I Dare say you will here Anough of it in the Niewspapers but I am sorry to say that Lord Nelson fel in the Action. it would be A good thing for a great many of us if he had lived but it was god almightys pleasure to call upon him.'

But stunned acceptance soon gave way to an outpouring of emotion that spread throughout the fleet. Many reacted like one seaman in the *Victory*, who exclaimed, 'Great God! I would rather the shot had taken off my head and spared his life.' And a boatswain's mate, who sobbed so heartily that he could not pipe the hands to quarters, blurted out, 'Hang me, I can't do it! I wouldn't have cared if it had been my old father, brother or sisters if there were fifty more of them – but I can't think of parting with Nelson.' An unnamed sailor of the *Royal Sovereign* wrote home:

Our dear Admiral Nelson is killed! So, we have paid pretty sharply for licking 'em. I never set eyes on him, for which I am both sorry and glad; for, to be sure, I should have liked to have seen him. But then all the men in our ship, who have seen him, are such soft toads they have done nothing but blast their eyes and cry ever since he was killed. God bless you! chaps that fought like the devil sit down and cry like a wench.

In the *Prince*, Richard Anderson, the navigating master, jotted in his diary:

Oh, what a day. Such a fight. I believe seventeen are taken. Thank God we escaped unhurt altho' we was close to the enemy [the *Achille*] and dismasted him and set him on fire. Oh, dreadful to relate, we saved 240 men ourselves and 10 minutes later he blew up with a dreadful explosion. We took in tow the *Santissima Trinidad*. We have been so busy and I have had everything knock'd down. No place to write and full of prisoners. Oh, what a time we have had. I never had harder service . . . The greatest loss is the loss of our Noble Nelson. We all cry for him.

An unknown officer of the *Britannia* – ' "Old Ironsides" as our brave sailors call her' – wrote to a friend describing the extent of the victory, adding:

Our greatest loss, the brave, the amiable Lord Nelson, the idol of the profession, the armament and defence of his country, the greatest warrior of his age, has purchased with his invaluable life the advantages I have cited; he died as he had lived an hero and in the arms of Victory. Nelson's merits are indelibly engraved on every British breast, his memory will be immortal and

> If there were in heaven a throne
> For the most brave of men and best of friends,
> It was reserved for him.

I cannot dwell on the affecting subject of the premature fate of the best of friends and worthiest of men without tears and I must therefore close this letter.

In the same ship, a foretopman named James West wrote home:

I am sorry to inform you I am wounded in the left shoulder, and that William Hillman was killed at the same time. The shot that killed him and three others, wounded me and five more! Another of my messmates, Thomas Crosby, was also killed; they both went to their guns like men, and died close to me. Crosby was shot in three places. Pray inform their poor friends of their death, and remind them that they died at the same time as Nelson, and in the moment of glorious victory! Remember me to all my relations and friends, tell them I am wounded at last, but that I do not much mind it, for I had my satisfaction of my enemies, as I never fired my gun in pain; I was sure to hit them; I killed and wounded them in plenty. Should have written you sooner, but the pain in my shoulder would not let me.

Also on board the *Britannia* was Midshipman John Wells, who found time to sit down and, using a shot-box as a desk, wrote to his parents:

I am very happy to say that the *Britannia* was certainly a very fortunate ship during the whole time, as we had not above 10 killed and 41 wounded, although we were the 4th ship in action and the last out of it and I doubt not but it will be found that she does honour to all who belong to her, as our fire was not directed to one particular ship but as soon as one had struck to us we immediately made to others and at one time had 5 ships blazing away upon us, but we soon tired them out. As I told you before, I was stationed at the signals and colours in time of action and, being on the quarterdeck, I had an opportunity of seeing the whole of the sport, which I must own rather daunted me before the first or second broadside but after them I think I never should have been tired of drubbing the jokers, particularly when my shipmates began to fall around me, which in the room of disheartening an Englishman only encourages him as the sight of his countryman's blood makes his heart burn for revenge.

I am very sorry to inform you that my worthy friend, our signal lieutenant, was knocked down by a double-headed shot close by my side and immediately expired, much lamented by his brother officers and everyone in the ship. I had several very narrow escapes from the enemy's shot but, thanks be to the Lord, He has still spared me through His great goodness. Too much credit cannot be given to Lord Northesk and Captain Bullen for their gallant conduct during the engagement, indeed it was the case with every officer and man in the ship.

Immediately the enemy had struck, I went on board one of the French prizes to take possession of her and when I got there I may well say I was shocked to see the sight as I believe there were not less than 3 or 4 hundred bodies lying about the decks cut and mangled all to pieces, some dying and others dead. We took the remainder of the men that were alive on board of our own ships at which they seemed very glad and from the information we can get from them they really came out of Cadiz with an intention of fighting, not thinking us to be above 17 sail of the line and under the command of Sir Robert Calder (but he was not with us at all) and that Lord Nelson was in England sick, so they thought they were an equal match for our 17 with their 43 and, in fact, made so sure of taking us into Cadiz that several private gentlemen came out of Cadiz as passengers on purpose to see the action and have the pleasure of towing us in but they were once more deceived in our wooden walls. Amongst the prisoners in our ship there are 5 or 6 of these gentlemen of pleasure and I think they are in a fair way for seeing an English prison before they return to Cadiz again.

In the surviving French ships, officers began to wonder why, despite the courage with which they had fought, they had been so decisively defeated. Lieutenant des Touches of the *Intrépide*, which had been captured, concluded:

The audacity with which Admiral Nelson had attacked us, and which had so completely succeeded, arose from the complete scorn which, not without reason, he professed for the effects of our gunfire. At that time our principle was to aim at the masts and, in order to produce any real damage, we wasted masses of projectiles which, if they had been aimed at the hulls, would have felled a proportion of the crews. Thus our losses were always incomparably higher than those of the English, who fired horizontally and hit our wooden sides, letting fly splinters which were more murderous than the cannonball itself. We were still using the linstock match to fire our guns, which despatched the ball with an excruciating delay, so that if the ship was rolling, as it was on October 21, complete broadsides flew over the enemy's mastheads without causing the slightest damage. The English had flintlocks, rather crude, but very superior to our linstocks . . . they used . . . a horizontal fire thanks to which, if they did not score a direct hit, they at least scored a useful hit by ricochet.

Admiral Collingwood's first act on boarding the *Euryalus* – pitching and tossing with a rising Atlantic swell – was to sit at the table in the stern cabin and draft a general order to be circulated throughout the fleet, giving credit where he believed it was due, just as Nelson would have done:

The ever-to-be-lamented death of Lord Viscount Nelson, Duke of Bronte, the commander-in-chief, who fell in the action of the 21st, in the arms of victory, covered with glory, whose memory will be ever dear to the British navy, and the British nation; whose zeal for the honour of his king, and for the interests of his country, will be ever held up as a shining example for a British seaman, – leaves to me a duty to return my thanks to the right hon. rear-admiral, the captains, officers, seamen, and detachments of Royal Marines serving on board his Majesty's squadron now under my command, for their conduct on that day; but where can I find language to express my sentiments of the valour and skill which were displayed by the officers, the seamen, and marines in the battle with the enemy, where every individual appeared an hero, on whom the glory of his country depended. The attack was irresistible, and the issue of it adds to the page of naval annals a brilliant instance of what Britons can do when their king and their country need their service . . .

The Almighty God, whose arm is strength, having of

His great mercy been pleased to crown the exertions of his Majesty's fleet with success, in giving them a complete victory over their enemies on the 21st of this month; and that all praise and thanksgiving may be offered up to the Throne of Grace, for the great benefit to our country and to mankind, I have thought proper that a day should be appointed of general humiliation before God, and thanksgiving for His merciful goodness, imploring forgiveness of sins, a continuation of His divine mercy, and His constant aid to us in defence of our country's liberties and laws, without which the utmost efforts of man are nought.

Collingwood then began the lengthy task of composing his official despatch to the Admiralty. These would be the words read by the British public informing them of the great victory and its dreadful price:

Euryalus, off Cape Trafalgar, October 22nd, 1805

Sir,

The ever to be lamented death of Vice-Admiral Lord Viscount Nelson, who, in the late conflict with the enemy, fell in the hour of victory, leaves to me the duty of informing my Lords Commissioners of the Admiralty, that on the 19th instant it was communicated to the commander-in-chief from the ships watching the motions of the enemy in Cadiz, that the combined fleet had put to sea. As they sailed with light winds westerly, his Lordship concluded their destination was the Mediterranean, and immediately made all sail for the Straits entrance with the British squadron, consisting of twenty-seven ships, three of them 64s, where his Lordship was informed by Capt. Blackwood (whose vigilance in watching, and giving notice of the enemy's movements, has been highly meritorious) that they had not yet passed the Straits.

On Monday the 21st instant, at daylight, when Cape Trafalgar bore E by S about seven leagues, the enemy was discovered six or seven miles to the eastward, the wind about west, and very light; the commander-in-chief immediately made the signal for the fleet to bear up in two columns, as they are formed in order of sailing; a mode of attack his Lordship had previously directed, to avoid the inconvenience and delay in forming a line of battle in the usual manner. The enemy's line consisted of thirty-three ships (of which eighteen were French and fifteen Spanish), commanded in chief by Admiral Villeneuve; the Spaniards, under the direction of Gravina, wore, with their heads to the northward, and formed their line of battle with great closeness and correctness; but as the mode of attack was unusual, so the structure of their line was new; it formed a crescent convexing to leeward – so that, in leading down to their centre, I had both their van and rear abaft the beam. Before the fire opened, every alternate ship was about a cable's length to windward of her second a-head and a-stern, forming a kind of double line, and appeared, when on their beam, to leave a very little interval between them; and this without crowding their ships. Admiral Villeneuve was in the *Bucentaure* in the centre, and the *Prince of Asturias* bore Gravina's flag in the rear; but the French and Spanish ships were mixed without any apparent regard to order of national squadron.

As the mode of our attack had been previously determined on, and communicated to the flag-officers and captains, few signals were necessary, and none were made except to direct close order as the lines bore down.

The commander-in-chief in the *Victory* led the weather column; and the *Royal Sovereign*, which bore my flag, the lee.

The action began at twelve o'clock, by the leading ships of the columns breaking through the enemy's line, the commander-in-chief about the tenth ship from the van, the second in command about the twelfth from the rear, leaving the van of the enemy unoccupied; the succeeding ships breaking through in all parts, astern of their leaders, and engaging the enemy at the muzzles of their guns, the conflict was severe. The enemy's ships were fought with a gallantry highly honourable to their officers, but the attack on them was irresistible; and it pleased the Almighty Disposer of all events to grant his Majesty's arms a complete and glorious victory. About three p.m. many of the enemy's ships having struck their colours, their line gave way; Admiral Gravina, with ten ships, joining their frigates to leeward, stood towards Cadiz. The five head-most ships in their van tacked, and standing to the south-ward to windward of the British line, were engaged, and the sternmost of them taken; the others went off, leaving to his Majesty's squadron nineteen ships of the line (of which two are first-rates, the *Santissima Trinidad* and the *Santa Ana*) with three flag officers; viz. Admiral Villeneuve, the commander-in-chief; Don Ignacio Maria d'Alava, vice-admiral; and the Spanish rear-admiral, Don Baltazar Hidalgo Cisneros.

After such a victory it may appear unnecessary to enter into encomiums on the particular parts taken by the sev-eral commanders; the conclusion says more on the subject than I have language to express; the spirit which animated all was the same: when all exert themselves zealously in their country's service, all deserve that their high merits should stand recorded; and never was high merit more conspicuous than in the battle I have described.

The *Achille* (a French 74), after having surrendered, by some mismanagement of the Frenchmen took fire, and blew up; two hundred of her men were saved by the tenders.

A circumstance occurred during the action, which so strongly marks the invincible spirit of British seamen, when engaging the enemies of their country, that I cannot resist the pleasure I have in making it known to their Lord-ships. The *Téméraire* was boarded by accident, or design, by a French ship on one side, and a Spaniard on the other: the contest was vigorous; but in the end the combined ensigns were torn from the poop, and the British hoisted in their places.

Such a battle could not be fought without sustaining a great loss of men. I have not only to lament, in common with the British navy and the British nation, in the fall of the commander-in-chief, the loss of a hero whose name will be immortal, and his memory ever dear to his coun-try; but my heart is rent with the most poignant grief for the death of a friend, to whom, by many years' intimacy, and a perfect knowledge of the virtues of his mind, which inspired ideas superior to the common race of men, I was bound by the strongest ties of affection; a grief to which even the glorious occasion in which he fell, does not bring the consolation which perhaps it ought: his Lordship received a musket ball in his left breast about the middle of the action, and sent an officer to me immediately with his last farewell, and soon after expired.

I have also to lament the loss of those excellent officers, Captains Duff of the *Mars* and Cooke of the *Bellerophon*: I have yet heard of none others.

I fear the numbers that have fallen will be found very great when the returns come to me; but it having blown a gale of wind ever since the action, I have not yet had it in my power to collect any reports from the ships.

The *Royal Sovereign* having lost her masts, except the tottering foremast, I called the *Euryalus* to me, while the action continued, which ship lying within hail, made my signals, a service Captain Blackwood performed with great attention. After the action I shifted my flag to her, that I might more easily communicate my orders to, and collect, the ships, and towed the *Royal Sovereign* out to seaward. The whole fleet were now in a very perilous situation; many dismasted; all shattered; in thirteen fathoms water, off the shoals of Trafalgar; and when I made the signal to prepare to anchor, few of the ships had an anchor to let go, their cables being shot; but the same good Providence which aided us through such a day preserved us in the night, by the wind shifting a few points, and drifting the ships off the land, except four of the captured dismasted ships, which are now at anchor off Trafalgar, and I hope will ride safe until those gales are over.

Having thus detailed the proceedings of the fleet on this occasion, I beg to congratulate their Lordships on a victory which, I hope, will add a ray to the glory of his Majesty's crown, and be attended with public benefit to our country.

I am, etc.,

C. COLLINGWOOD

Those, like Collingwood, who had known Nelson best began a lifelong grieving. The Reverend Alexander Scott, who had been with Nelson at the end, later told a woman friend:

You always mentioned Lord Nelson *con amore* and it is about him – I can neither think nor talk of anything else. Let the country mourn their hero; I grieve for the loss of the most fascinating companion I ever conversed with – the greatest and most simple of men – one of the nicest and most innocent – interesting beyond all, on shore, in public and even in private life. Men are not always themselves and put on their behaviour with their clothes, but if you live with a man on board a ship for years; if you are continually with him in his cabin, your mind will soon find out how to appreciate him. I could for ever tell you the qualities of this beloved man. I have not shed a tear for years before the 21st of October and since, whenever alone, I am quite like a child.

Captain Blackwood wrote to his wife:

The first hour since yesterday morning that I could call my own is now before me, to be devoted to my dearest wife, who, thank God, is not a husband out of pocket! My heart is sad, and penetrated with the deepest anguish. A victory, such a one as has never been achieved, yesterday took place in the course of five hours; but at such an expense, in the loss of the most gallant of men, and best of friends, as renders it to me a victory I never wished to have witnessed – at least, on such terms. After performing wonders by his example and coolness, Lord Nelson was wounded by a French sharpshooter, and died in three hours after, beloved and regretted in a way not to find example. To any other person, my Harriet, but yourself, I could not and would not enter so much into the detail, particularly of what I feel at this moment. But you, who know and enter into all my feelings, I do not even at the risk of distressing you, hesitate to say that in my life I never was so shocked or so completely upset as upon my flying to the *Victory*, even before the action was over, to find Lord Nelson was then at the gasp of death. His unfortunate decorations of innumerable stars, and his uncommon gallantry, was the cause of his death; and such an admiral has the country lost, and every officer and man so kind, so good, so obliging a friend as never was. Thank God, he lived to know that such a victory, and under circumstances so disadvantageous to the attempt, never before was gained. Almost all seemed as if inspired by the one common sentiment of conquer or die. The enemy, to do them justice, were not less so. They waited the attack of the British with a coolness I was sorry to witness, and they fought in a way that must do them honour. As a spectator, who saw the faults, or rather mistakes on both sides, I shall ever do them the justice to say so. They are, however, beat, and I hope and trust it may be the means of hastening a peace. Buonaparte, I firmly believe, forced them to sea to try his luck, and what it might procure him in a pitched battle. They had the flower of the combined fleet, and I hope it will convince Europe at large that he has not yet learnt enough to cope with the English at sea. No history can record such a brilliant victory . . . They were attacked in a way no other admiral ever before thought of, and equally surprised them. Lord Nelson (though it was not his station) would lead, supported by Captain Hardy, and Fremantle in *Téméraire* and *Neptune*. He went into the thickest of it, was successful in his first object, and has left cause for every man who had a heart never to forget him . . .

I fear I shall tire you with all this long account; but so entirely am I depressed with the private loss I have had, that really the victory, and all the prize-money I hope to get (if our prizes arrive safe) appear quite lost by the chasm made by Lord Nelson's death. I am, therefore, persuaded you will not think a tribute like this too much. I can scarcely credit he is no more, and that we have in the sight of the Spanish shore obtained so complete, so unheard-of, a victory.

CHAPTER 10

Storm

On the night of the battle, Captain Blackwood noted in his log 'a great swell from the westward' but it was not until next morning, the 22nd, that he recorded 'strong gales with heavy rain'. Early that afternoon he added, 'Cape Trafalgar SE by S, 7 or 8 miles. Set storm staysail. Down topgallant yards and struck the masts. At 4, strong gales and rain. At 8, ditto gales with heavy squalls and rain. Burnt blue lights every hour.' Next morning, it was, 'The fore topmast staysail split and blown away by a heavy squall from the westward.' This was the beginning of the storm that Nelson had forecast. It was to be not just another Atlantic gale but a hurricane.

Shortly before Nelson died he had ordered Hardy to pass on his instructions for the fleet to anchor after the action as he feared the ships – both victors and their prizes – would be so crippled aloft that they would be unable to claw their way off the lee shore in a westerly gale and would be driven on to the rocks of Cape Trafalgar. But many of the ships, particularly those that had been raked bow to stern, had had their anchors, cables, cat-heads – the heavy beam from which the anchor was suspended – and capstans shot away.

The coming of the storm interrupted the securing of the prizes. Once an enemy had surrendered, a prize-crew was put on board, usually consisting of one or two officers and a few seamen, and they supervised the removal of prisoners to British ships, or put them under guard in their own ships, while most of the wounded were left below under the care of their own surgeons. Midshipman Badcock of the *Neptune* was sent to the *Santissima Trinidad*, where a shock awaited him:

I was on board our prize the *Trinidad* getting prisoners out of her, she had between 3 and 400 killed and wounded, her beams were covered with blood, brains and pieces of flesh and the after part of her decks with wounded, some without legs and some without an arm; what calamities war brings on and what a number of lives were put an end to on the 21st . . .

She was a magnificent ship and ought now to be in Portsmouth harbour. Her topsides it is true were perfectly riddled by our firing . . . but from the lower part of the sills of the low-deck ports to the water's edge few shot of consequence had hurt her between wind and water and those were all plugged up. She was built of cedar and would have lasted for ages, a glorious trophy of the battle but 'sink, burn and destroy' was the order of the day and, after a great deal of trouble, scuttling her in many places, hauling up her lower-deck ports – that, when she rolled, a heavy sea might fill her decks – she did at last unwillingly go to the bottom.

Another account described the great ship's end: 'Night came on – the swell ran high – three lower-deck ports on each side were open and in a few minutes the tremendous ruins of the largest ship in the world were buried in the deep. The waves passed over her, she gave a lurch and went down.' Before she sank, Lieutenant John Edwards of the *Prince* succeeded in getting a hawser across to the shattered leviathan, in the hope of taking her in tow. He reported:

We took the *Trinidad*, the largest ship in the world, in tow; all the other ships that could render assistance to the disabled were doing the same. Before four in the morn it blew so strong that we broke the hawsers twice, and from two such immense bodies as we were, found it difficult to secure her again; however, every exertion was made, and we got her again. By eight in the morning it blew a hurricane on the shore, and so close in that we could not weather the land either way. 'Tis impossible to describe the horrors the morning presented, nothing but signals of distress flying in every direction, guns firing, and so many large ships driving on shore without being able to render them the least assistance. After . . . four days without any prospect of saving the ship or the gale abating, the signal was made to destroy the prizes. We had no time before to remove the prisoners, and it now became a most dangerous task; no boats could lie alongside, we got under her stern, and the men dropped in by ropes; but what a sight when we came to remove the wounded, of which there were between three and four hundred. We had to tie the poor mangled wretches round their waists, or where we could, and lower them down into a tumbling boat, some without arms, others no legs, and lacerated all over in the most dreadful manner. About ten o'clock we had got all out, except for thirty-three or four, which I believe it was impossible to remove without instant death. The water was now at the pilot deck, the weather dark and boisterous, and taking in tons of water at every roll, when we quitted her, and supposed this superb ship could not remain afloat longer than ten minutes. Perhaps she sunk in less time, with the above unfortunate victims, never to rise again.

Manning one of the rescue boats was a seaman of the *Revenge*, who said afterwards:

On quitting the ship our boats were so overloaded in endeavouring to save all the lives we could, that it is a miracle they were not upset. A father and his son came down the ship's side to get on board one of our boats; the father had seated himself, but the men in the boat, thinking from the load and the boisterous weather that all their lives would be in peril, could not think of taking the boy. As the boat put off the lad, as though determined not to quit his father, sprang from the ship into the sea and caught hold of the gunwale of the boat, but his attempt was resisted, as it risked all their lives; and some of the men resorted to their cutlasses to cut his fingers off in order to disentangle the boat from his grasp. At the same time the feelings of the father were so worked upon that he was about to leap overboard and perish with his son. Britons could face an enemy but could not witness such a scene of self-devotion: as it were a simultaneous thought burst forth from the crew, which said, 'Let us save both father and son or die in the attempt!' The Almighty aided their design, they succeeded and brought both father and son safe on board our ship . . .

We were obliged to abandon our prize, taking away with

us all our men and as many of the prisoners as we could. On the last boat's load leaving the ship, the Spaniards who were left on board appeared on the gangway and ship's side, displaying their bags of dollars and doubloons and eagerly offering them as a reward for saving them from the expected and unavoidable wreck; but however well inclined we were, it was not in our power to rescue them, or it would have been effected without the proffered bribe.

A lieutenant of the *Ajax* also engaged in the rescue added:

Everything alive was taken out, down to the ship's cat. My boat was the last to leave. We had put off from the starboard quarter when a cat, the only living animal aboard, ran out on the muzzle of one of the lower-deck guns and by a plaintive mew seemed to beg for assistance: the boat returned and took her in.

Shortly before the *Achille* had detonated in the vast explosion that marked the end of the battle, British ships' companies had manned what few boats remained intact at that point to pick up survivors who had leapt into the sea to escape the fiercely burning vessel. Amongst them was a young woman, remembered by an officer of the *Revenge* who assisted with the rescue:

Towards the conclusion of the battle the French 74-gun ship *Achille*, after surrendering, caught fire on the booms. The poor fellows belonging to her, as the only chance of saving their lives, leaped overboard, having first stripped off their clothes, that they might be the better able to swim to any pieces of floating wreck or to the boats of the ships sent by those nearest at hand to their rescue. As the boats filled, they proceeded to the *Pickle* schooner, and, after discharging their freight into that vessel, returned for more. The schooner was soon crowded to excess, and, therefore, transferred the poor shivering wretches to any of the large ships near her. The *Revenge*, to which ship I belonged, received nearly a hundred of the number, some of whom had been picked up by our own boats. Many of them were badly wounded, and all naked. No time was lost for providing for the latter want, as the purser was ordered immediately to issue to each man a complete suit of clothes.

On the morning after the action I had charge of the deck, the other officers and crew being at breakfast, when another boat load of these poor prisoners of war came alongside, all of whom, with one exception, were in the costume of Adam. The exception I refer to was apparently a youth, but clothed in an old jacket and trousers, with a dingy handkerchief tied round the head, and exhibiting a face begrimed with smoke and dirt, without shoes, stockings, or shirt, and looking the picture of misery and despair. The appearance of this young person at once attracted my attention, and on asking some questions on the subject, I was answered that the prisoner was a woman. It was sufficient to know this, and I lost no time in introducing her to my messmates, as a female requiring their compassionate attention. The poor creature was almost famishing with hunger, having tasted nothing for four-and-twenty hours, consequently she required no persuasion to partake of the breakfast upon the table. I then gave her up my cabin, for by this time the bulkhead had been replaced, and made a collection of all the articles which could be procured to enable her to complete a more suitable wardrobe. One of the lieutenants gave her a piece of sprigged blue muslin, which he had obtained from a Spanish prize, and two new checked shirts were supplied by the purser; these, with a purser's blanket, and my ditty bag, which contained needles, thread, etc., being placed at her disposal, she, in a short time, appeared in a very different, and much more becoming, costume. Being a dressmaker, she had made herself a sort of a jacket, after the Flemish fashion, and the purser's shirts she had transformed into an outer petticoat; she had a silk handkerchief tastily tied over her head, and another thrown round her shoulders; white stockings and a pair of the chaplain's shoes were on her feet, and, altogether, our guest, which we unanimously voted her, appeared a very interesting young woman.

'Jeanette', which was the only name by which I ever knew her, thus related to me the circumstances. She said she was stationed during the action in the passage of the fore-magazine, to assist in handing up the powder, which employment lasted till the surrender of the ship. When the firing ceased, she ascended to the lower deck, and endeavoured to get up to the main deck, to search for her husband, but the ladders having been all removed, or shot away, she found this impracticable; and just at this time an alarm of fire spread through the ship, so that she could get no assistance. The fire originated upon the upper deck, and gradually burnt downwards. Her feelings upon this occasion cannot be described: but death from all quarters stared her in the face. The fire, which soon burnt fiercely, precluded the possibility of her escaping by moving from where she was, and no friendly counsellor was by with whom to advise. She remained wandering to and fro upon the lower deck, among the mangled corpses of the dying and the slain, until the guns from the main deck actually fell through the burnt planks. Her only refuge, then, was the sea, and the poor creature scrambled out of the gun-room port, and, by the help of the rudder chains, reached the back of the rudder, where she remained for some time, praying that the ship might blow up, and thus put a period to her misery. At length the lead which lined the rudder-trunk began to melt, and to fall upon her, and her only means of avoiding this was to leap overboard. Having, therefore, divested herself of her clothes, she soon found herself struggling with the waves, and providentially finding a piece of cork, she was enabled to escape from the burning mass. A man, shortly afterwards, swam near her, and, observing her distress, brought her a piece of plank, about six feet in length, which, being placed under her arms, supported her until a boat approached to her rescue. The time she was thus in the water she told me was about two hours, but probably the disagreeableness and peril of her situation made a much shorter space of time appear of that duration. The boat which picked her up, I have heard, was the *Belleisle*'s, but her sex was no sooner made known than the men, whose hearts were formed of the right stuff, quickly supplied her with the articles of attire in which she first made my acquaintance. One supplied her with trowsers, another stripped off his jacket, and threw it over her, and a third supplied her with a handkerchief. She was much burnt about the neck, shoulders, and legs, by the molten lead, and when she reached the *Pickle* was more dead than alive. A story so wonderful and pitiful could not fail to enlist, on her behalf, the best feelings of human nature, and it was, therefore, not praiseworthy, but only natural, that we extended towards her that humane attention which her situation demanded. I caused a canvas screen berth to be made for her, to hang outside the wardroom door, opposite to where the sentry was stationed, and I placed my cabin at her disposal for her dressing-room.

Although placed in a position of unlooked-for comfort, Jeanette was scarcely less miserable; the fate of her husband was unknown to her. She had not seen him since the commencement of the battle, and he was perhaps killed, or had perished in the conflagration. Still, the worst was unknown to her, and a possibility existed that he was yet alive. All her enquiries were, however, unattended with success.

Captain Moorsom of the *Revenge* added: 'We were not wanting in civility to the lady; I ordered her two pusser's [purser's] shirts to make a petticoat and most of the officers found something to clothe her; in a few hours, Jeanette was perfectly happy and hard at work making her petticoats.'

Jeanette became a legend throughout the British fleet but she was not the only one. Second Lieutenant Lawrence Halloran of the *Britannia*'s marines noted: 'Among the prisoners brought on board from one of the ships was a man in the costume and character of a Harlequin, pressed, we believe, off the stage the evening previous to the battle without having time to change.'

Midshipman Hercules Robinson of the *Euryalus*, which was also engaged in rescue, related: 'I helped to save a black pig, which swam over; and what a glorious supper of pork chops appeared instead of our usual refection of cheese, biscuit and salt junk [preserved meat].'

In the shattered *Intrépide*, wallowing in heavy seas, Lieutenant des Touches recorded:

In the half-darkness, while the tempest was still gathering

its forces, we had to pass through a leeward gun-port more than eighty wounded who were incapable of movement. With infinite trouble we did it, by means of a bed-frame and capstan bars. We were then taken in tow by an English frigate, which we followed, rolling from side to side and making water everywhere. At a certain point I noticed that the work of the pumps was slowing down, and I was told that the door of the storeroom had been forced and that everybody, French and English, had rushed there to get drunk. When I got to these men, reduced to the state of brutes, a keg of brandy had just been broken and the liquor was running along the deck and was lapping the base of a candle which had been stuck there. I only just had time to stamp out the flame, and in the darkness threatening voices were raised against me . . . With kicks and punches I made them get out of the storeroom, I barricaded the door, and reached an understanding with the English officer to avert the danger which seemed imminent . . .

I wished to stay on the *Intrépide* up to the last agonised minute of one of my friends, who had been judged too badly injured to be transferred. He was a sub-lieutenant called Poullain, with whom I was closely connected, and who had begged me not to leave him in the anguish of his last hour . . .

When I had heard the last sigh of my poor comrade, there were just three of us alive on the *Intrépide*: an artillery captain and a midshipman who had not wished to leave me . . . our situation grew worse every minute. Among these bodies and spilt blood, the silence was disturbed only by the sound of the sea, and a dull murmur made by the water in the hold as it rose and spread in the vessel. Night began to close in, and the vessel settled deeper in the water, making it easy to calculate that it would have disappeared before daybreak. Having nothing more to do, I let myself fall asleep but the artillery officer, become nervous, heaped wooden debris up on the deck and wanted to set fire to it, as he preferred a quick death to the slow agony which was being prepared for us. I saw his intention in time to oppose it absolutely. We found a lantern, which was fixed to the end of a rod, which I advised him to wave.

By a lucky chance, the *Orion* passed within hailing distance. We hailed her, and a boat took us off. Soon afterwards, the *Intrépide* disappeared beneath the waves.

A midshipman from the *Bellerophon* was with the prize-crew on board the Spanish *Monarca* and found that the danger was not only from foundering and trying to keep afloat by pumping but from a possible attempt by her crew to retake the ship:

Our second lieutenant, myself, and eight men, formed the party that took possession of the *Monarca*: we remained till the morning without further assistance, or we should most probably have saved her, though she had suffered much more than ourselves; we kept possession of her however for four days, in the most dreadful weather, when having rolled away all our masts, and being in danger of immediate sinking or running on shore, we were fortunately saved by the *Leviathan*, with all but about 150 prisoners, who were afraid of getting into the boats. I can assure you I felt not the least fear of death during the action, which I attribute to the general confidence of victory which I saw all around me; but in the prize, when I was in danger of, and had time to reflect upon the approach of death, either from the rising of the Spaniards upon so small a number as we were composed of, or what latterly appeared inevitable from the violence of the storm, I was most certainly afraid; and at one time, when the ship made three feet of water in ten minutes, when our people were almost all lying drunk upon deck, when the Spaniards, completely worn out with fatigue, would no longer work at the only chain pump left serviceable; when I saw the fear of death so strongly depicted on the countenances of all around me, I wrapped myself up in a Union Jack, and lay down upon the deck for a short time, quietly awaiting the approach of death; but the love of life soon after again roused me, and after great exertions on the part of the British and Spanish officers, who had joined together for the mutual preservation of their lives, we got the ship before the wind, determined to run her on shore: this was at midnight, but at daylight in the morning, the weather being more moderate, and having again gained upon the water, we hauled our wind, perceiving a three-decker dismasted, but with Spanish colours up, close to leeward of us: the *Leviathan*, the first British ship we had seen for the last thirty hours, seeing this, bore down, and firing a shot ahead of us, the *Rayo* struck without returning a gun.

The gallant *Redoutable* had been taken in tow by the British *Swiftsure* but by five o'clock on the evening of the 22nd it was clear that she was sinking. Attempts were made to rescue her crew but many were lying, wounded and immobile, below decks. Soon after ten o'clock that night she sank. Midshipman George Barker described the scene:

At 9 p.m., the prize master of the *Redoutable* hailed us and requested us to give him some assistance as the prize was in a most wretched situation as they were scarcely able to keep the ship above water though they employed all hands (prisoners not excepted) at the pumps. We immediately sent a hawser on board and took the ship in tow, at the same time sending a lieutenant and a party of seamen to assist the prize master; it was impossible to ascertain yet how many ships had struck to the British flag, the fleets were so much scattered, and it so soon became dark after the action.

On the 22nd it came on to blow a most violent gale of wind, but the prize in tow seemed to weather it tolerably well, notwithstanding her shattered state, till about 3 in the afternoon, when from the violence of the rolling in a heavy sea, she carried away the foremast, the only mast she had standing: we now hoisted out our boats and sent them on board to save if possible the people on board of her, although there was a tremendous sea running and we were fearful lest the boat would be swamped alongside the prize. They happily succeeded in bringing off the greater part of them from the wreck as well as our own lieutenant and party of the seamen we sent on board, with the lieutenant and two midshipmen with some of the seamen all belonging to the *Téméraire*.

If our situation was disagreeable from fatigue and

inclemency of the weather, what must not the unfortunate prisoners have suffered on board the *Redoutable*. Previous to the action she had 800 men, nearly 500 were killed and wounded in action, and many of the surviving 300 perished; what added to the horrors of the night was the inability of saving them all, as we could no longer entrust the lives of our men in the open boats at the mercy of a heavy sea and most violent gale of wind. At 10 p.m. the *Redoutable* went down, and the hawser by which we still kept her in tow (in order if the weather moderated and the prize be able to weather the night through, we might once more endeavour to save the remainder of her crew) was carried away with the violence of the shock, this was now the most dreadful scene I have ever witnessed, we could distinctly hear the cries of the unhappy people we could no longer assist.

Towards the morning the weather moderated, and we had the good fortune to save many that were floating past us on pieces of wreck; at 9 of the 23rd we discovered a large raft ahead, and shortly afterwards a second, many of the unfortunate people were seen clinging to the wreck, the merciless sea threatening almost instant destruction to them, the boats were immediately lowered down and we happily saved 36 people from the fury of the waves. When the boats came alongside many of these unfortunate men were unable to get up the ship's sides, as most of them were not only fainting from fatigue but were wounded in a most shocking manner, some expired in the boats before they could be brought alongside completely exhausted and worn out with struggling to preserve their lives the whole of the tempestuous night upon a few crazy planks exposed to over-inclemency of weather. If our seamen had conducted themselves as brave men during the action, now it was they showed themselves as humane and generous as they were brave, when these unfortunate prisoners came on board, you might have seen them clothing them as well as a seaman's scanty stock would permit of, though scanty yet hard earnt, and in defence of the king, his family and his country at large.

The worst horror of the hurricane was the fate of the

wounded in the surrendered ships, who could not be rescued. An injured French soldier, who was saved from the *Pluton*, remembered:

During these unhappy days and nights, occasional cannon shots here and there were all that could be heard. I was told that these were vessels that had lost their masts and, hurled ashore, were calling for help. But it was not possible to take them off. Attempts had been made; several rowing boats and dinghies that had been sent for this purpose had capsized or sunk. The poor wretches were condemned to perish. Very few men escaped the disaster. The wounded were shrieking . . . they dragged themselves along on those limbs that were not maimed, and sought to avoid the death that they found further on. All of this presented the most hideous and heart-breaking sight.

Enemy ships that had been taken in tow – the prospect of prize-money glittering in their captors' imaginations – often had to be abandoned, as Captain Codrington of the *Orion* recounted:

I towed a prize belonging to *Bellerophon* from close to Trafalgar in safety for three days, but having my topsails blown out of the boltropes, and one bumpkin carried away, with the foremast wounded, and only six miles from the lee shore near St Mary's in the worst hurricane I ever saw, I was obliged to quit her, to save my own ship, which I had little hopes of.

In the helpless *Belleisle*, Lieutenant Nicolas recorded the mounting danger:

About midnight a midshipman entered the wardroom, where most of our cots were swinging, to say that the captain wished the officers to come on deck, as it was probable we should be ashore very shortly. This awful intelligence was received with much concern, and we instantly started on our feet. Just at this crisis one of the 24-pounders out of the stern-port broke adrift from its lashings, and the

apprehension of our danger had taken such entire possession of our minds, that the crash appeared to announce the
approach of our destruction. With difficulty I got on deck.
The ship rolled in the trough of the sea in such a manner
that the water came in through the ports and over the
waist hammock-nettings, and the shot out of the racks
were thrown about the decks, upon which the men, tired
and exhausted, were lying. At one o'clock the roar of
the elements continued, and every roll of the sea seemed
to the affrighted imagination as the commencement of the
breakers . . .

The hours lagged tediously on, and death appeared in
each gust of the tempest. In the battle the chances were
equal, and it was possible for many to escape, but ship-
wreck in such a hurricane was certain destruction to all,
and the doubtful situation of the ship kept the mind in a
perpetual state of terror. In this horrible suspense each
stroke of the bell, as it proclaimed the hour, sounded as the
knell of our approaching destiny, for none could expect to
escape the impending danger. In silent anxiety we awaited
the fate which daylight would decide, and the thoughts
of home, kindred, friends, pressed round the heart and
aggravated our despair. Each brightening of the clouds,
which appeared as if to mock our misery, was hailed as the
long looked-for dawn, and sank our wearied hopes into
deeper despondency as the darkness again prevailed. How
numerous were the enquiries made to the sentry, 'How
goes the time?' and when the welcome order to strike two
bells (that is, five o'clock) was heard, it aroused our sinking
energies, and every eye was directed towards the shore.
In a few minutes 'Land on the lee bow! put the helm up!'
resounded through the ship, and all was again bustle and
confusion. When we got round, the breakers were distinctly seen about a mile to leeward, throwing the spray to
such a terrific height that even in our security we could not
behold them without shuddering. This was a period of
delight most assuredly, but intense dread had so long overpowered every other feeling, that our escape from destruction seemed like returning animation, producing a kind of
torpor which rendered us insensible to our miraculous

preservation, and it was not until the mind had recovered its wonted calmness, that our hearts were impressed with a due sense of the merciful protection we had experienced. As the day advanced the wind abated, and the enlivening rays of the sun well accorded with our happiness. The *Naiad*, having us in tow, spread all her canvas, steering a direct course for Gibraltar.

As the storm abated, the crippled ships and the surviving prizes were taken in tow. Captain Fremantle of the *Neptune* wrote to his wife:

I am at present towing the *Victory* and the admiral has just made the signal for me to go with her to Gibraltar, which is a satisfactory proof to my mind that he is perfectly satisfied with old *Neptune*, who behaves as well as I could wish. The loss of Nelson is a death blow to my future prospects here, he knew well how to appreciate abilities and zeal, and I am aware that I shall never cease to lament his loss whilst I live. We have ten men killed and 37 wounded, which is very trifling when compared to some other ships, however we alone have certainly the whole credit of taking the *Santissima Trinidad*, who struck to *us alone*. Adml. Villeneuve was with me on board the *Neptune* over two days, I found him a very pleasant and gentlemanlike man, the poor man was very low! Yesterday I put him on board the *Euryalus* with Admiral Collingwood, but I still have the pleasure of feeding and accommodating his captain and his 2 aides du camp and his adjutant general, who are true Frenchmen, but with whom I am much amused, I have also 450 poor Spaniards from the *Santissima Trinidad*, with a true Italian priest born at Malta, I have found also an excellent French cook and a true Spanish pug dog. This fatigue and employment has entirely drove away the bile and if poor Nelson had not been among the slain I should be most completely satisfied, would you believe that old Collingwood has now made the signal for me to go off Cape Espartel instead of Gibraltar, the poor man does not know his own mind 5 minutes together . . .

My cabin that was so elegant and neat is as dirty as

a pig stye and many parts of the bulkheads are thrown overboard, however I shall find amusement and indeed employment in having them fitted in some new way. These Frenchmen make me laugh at the gasconnade as well as at their accounts of Buonaparte, the Palais Royal, Paris, etc. The French captain drinks your health regularly every day at dinner. The poor man is married and laments his lot, one of the younger ones is desperately in love with a lady at Cadiz and Frenchmanlike carries her picture in his pocket.

In some French and Spanish ships, their surrendered companies, who always outnumbered the British prize-crews and could pick up pikes, tomahawks and cutlasses, tried and succeeded in retaking their ships. The *Algésiras*, which had surrendered to the *Tonnant*, had been boarded by Lieutenant Charles Bennett, two midshipmen and fifty seamen. But the ship was so shattered that she proved almost impossible to control and was blown towards the rocky shore. On the evening of the 22nd, as one of the French officers, Lieutenant Philibert, wrote in his diary:

At 5 o'clock, seeing in these circumstances the possibility of recapturing our ship and of taking her into Cadiz before night closed down, we took the bearing of Cadiz lighthouse, north-north-east distant about 5 leagues.

The English lieutenant, who up till then had only busied himself in clearing the deck and firing signals of distress, had allowed himself to be carried by the currents and by the wind towards the Trafalgar shoal, from which we were not half a league. Having observed to him that we should be lost with all hands, he had the work of rigging topgallant-masts on our stumps undertaken, and this was very soon done, our crew lending them a hand, and as soon as the topgallant-sail serving as a foresail was trimmed, the ship bore up and we got clear of the shoal.

At 5.30, the officers left alive and unwounded assembled and decided unanimously that as soon as it was night we should retake the ship. The resolution once taken, we no longer occupied ourselves with anything but the measures indispensable to ensure the carrying out of our design.

At 7 o'clock in the evening, everything being ready, we invited the English officers, three in number, to repair to the great cabin where M. Feuillet, Admiral Magon's secretary, who spoke the best English, informed them in the name of the executive that after the noble defence of our ship we had a right to expect that assistance from the English fleet which they themselves had vainly demanded; that feeling ourselves thereby released from the obligations that we had assumed when placing ourselves in their power, we had decided to retake our ship, but that they might expect to be treated with consideration on our part, provided that they did not compel us to employ force by a resistance after which they would still find themselves obliged to yield. Before complying with our wishes, M. Bennett, the prize-master, and the other officers displayed a great deal of resistance and the greatest firmness. We promised them their liberty on our arrival in a French or an Allied port.

At 7.15, we were in possession of the ship, having the satisfaction of not having shed a drop of blood. At this minute the rejoicing was general and shouts of '*Vive l'empereur!*' were heard on all sides, even from our brave and unfortunate wounded . . .

We no longer thought of anything save the means to assure the speedy arrival of the ship into Cadiz roads. All the officers, the midshipmen and chief petty-officers betook themselves wherever needful and in a short time we had succeeded in re-establishing order and calm on board the ship. After having disarmed the English, they were placed in the great cabin under a strong guard and their officers in a separate cabin.

In these difficult and painful circumstances our crew and our troops have merited well-earned praise; the behaviour of the latter was moreover the more meritorious in that they were not at all accustomed to the sea and that it was their first campaign.

At 7.30, we being south-south-west of Cadiz lighthouse, we filled and steered before the wind for some time, with two topgallant-sails rigged on our stumps; working to rig a mizen topgallant-sail on the stump of the mizen-mast; but several of our guns having broken loose in the heavy sea, we hauled to the wind again and lay-to in order to secure them, taking advantage of this interval to clinch a cable to the only bower-anchor [heavy main anchor] that we had left. At 11 o'clock, this work being finished, we bore away and stood for Cadiz, having no one on board to pilot us but a quarter-gunner who had put in there several times. Although the weather was gloomy, with squalls, a heavy sea, rain falling continually and the wind blowing a strong gale from the south-west, which put us in fear of perishing before we could reach any anchorage what-soever, we were fortunate enough to cast anchor to the north-east of Cadiz lighthouse at 2 o'clock in the morning. But at daylight we perceived that we were very near the Diamond Rock, an extremely critical position as it ex-posed us to the greatest danger in case we dragged. Some of our ships were anchored in the bay; all our frigates and despatch-craft were there. The *Bucentaure* was ashore on the rocks of Cadiz point and many boats were going to take off the crew.

The *Indomptable* and the *San Justo* which were anchored near me, offered to take me in tow as soon as they should get under way, but this last set sail before our anchor was weighed, an operation that was the more difficult in that it was hindered by the confusion on the lower deck, the injuries to the capstan, and the lack of a messenger [cap-able component of a capstan] . . .

At daybreak, the weather better, the sea very heavy, several boats from our ships came alongside and we learnt that several longboats which had been sent from the port to our assistance the evening before had been lost with all hands. Two ships anchored further ahead of us had gone on shore in the night, having dragged until they struck on the rocks. At 6.30, the *Neptune* sent us a longboat with a hawser and a stream-anchor [light spare anchor]. We bent on another hawser and laid out this anchor ahead of us; as soon as it was fast we heaved in our cable, but the tide ebbing, we very soon began bumping heavily again on the rocks; then the capstan was pauled [braked] and all the people were employed in such measures of lightening the ship as still remained; we shifted the guns in the after batteries forward; all our boats which were injured as a result of the engagement, were broken up and thrown overboard. We also cleared away the greater part of our spare spars which were in the same condition; all the casks in the water-tiers were started and the water pumped out; a large quantity of firewood was thrown overboard; in fine, we got clear again on this tide and at noon we were no longer bumping; the ship continuing to make the same amount of water and not seeming to have suffered.

All the morning we had fired signals for help; several Spanish boats and boats from the squadron had come to take off our wounded but the heavy seas did not allow of our sending off any but the least severely injured . . .

Oct. 24th–25th. Fairly fine weather, heavy sea, a fresh gale from the south-west to the south-south-west, heaving on our anchor and hawser. At 1.30 we received a bower-anchor and a cable which were brought us by a Spanish schooner. We told her to let go the anchor as much ahead of us as she could; to this end she laid out a hawser ahead of our stream-anchor, but at the moment that she began to haul on it the heavy seas and the wind stiffening a great deal made the hawser part, and she let go this anchor abeam of us on rocky bottom in such a way that it could no longer be of any assistance to us.

Our cable was so chafed that at 20 fathoms from the clinch there was only one strand remaining; it held during a part of the night. We made vain efforts to weigh our anchor, it was fast among the rocks. Time being precious, owing to the tide, in the situation in which we found ourselves, we decided to sacrifice our anchor and to cut the cable; continuing to heave on the stream-anchor.

At 2.45, we were at long stay, the tide was nearly at its height; a single stream-anchor was left us, fast on the edge of the Galera rocks, on which we had nearly perished the previous night; no other assistance coming to us, we enquired of the pilot whether he was willing to get under way and attempt to reach the anchorage, supposing that there was sufficient water over all the reefs for us to be able to get over without touching; he refused, saying that it was better to wait and to pass the night as we were. As soon as we had sent him back on shore, the weather lowering in the south-west and the wind stiffening in the same quarter, we foresaw a night even more fearful than the preceding one; upon these considerations we decided to get under way and after having taken every precaution necessary so as to get off shore, we tripped the stream-anchor – our only remaining resource – and with the aid of the boats we cast on the proper tack and the ship at once fetched headway; she steered perfectly under two topgallant-sails and her mizen topgallant-sail. From that minute we saw that we were saved and we owe it in a great measure to the sailing qualities of the ship. We passed over the Galera bank and came to an anchor with our stream-anchor in Cadiz roads; at 5.30, we let it go in 6½ fathom water, sand and mud bottom, and an officer at once went on board the Commodore to inform him and to request a bower-anchor as soon as possible, the weather appearing threatening. At 10 o'clock, it came on in squalls, rainy, blowing in gusts; at 11 o'clock, a violent squall made us drag; at once let go a fluke [light anchor] which we had left, to which we clinched a hawser, and fired shots for help.

Half an hour after midnight we bumped heavily; our rudder was unshipped and we lost it as we had no boats and our rudder-chains had been severed in the action. At daybreak, the wind a strong gale from the south-west, much rain, we no longer perceived the *Indomptable* which had gone on shore and was lost in the night.

At 10 o'clock a bark [a merchant ship] . . . let go a best bower-anchor well ahead of us, and as soon as we had the end of the cable inboard we heaved it in until there remained 50 fathom scope.

So the *Algésiras* arrived safely in Cadiz, one of ten French and Spanish ships, most of them badly damaged, to do so, with her former captors still on board as prisoners. The British prize-crew on board the Spanish *Neptuno*, one of Dumanoir's ships, which had surrendered, been taken in tow by the *Minotaur* and then, as the storm worsened, cast adrift, suffered likewise. A seaman named Thorpe, a member of the prize-crew, described their ordeal. On the morning of 23 October, the *Neptuno* was wallowing off Cadiz with the British in control, when 'We then saw a squadron inshore consisting of 5 sail of the line, 3 frigates and a brig, which proved to be the enemy.'

The night before, the senior French officer to have escaped to Cadiz from the battle, Captain Julien Cosmao-Kerjulien, had decided to take all seaworthy ships back to sea in an attempt to recapture those taken by the British. Early on the 23rd, he had sailed in the *Pluton*, although she had suffered heavy battle-damage, together with two French and two Spanish battleships, five frigates and two brigs, all French. It was a gallant gesture and this was the squadron that Thorpe had sighted. He continued:

Thus situated, we expected assistance from our own fleet, but looked in vain. At 10 o'clock, rigged a spar to the stump of the mainmast and another to the taffrail, set a topgallant upon each and got another to the foremast in lieu of a foresail. At 3 o'clock, cut our cable and stood towards our own fleet with all sail we could set, but the enemy was gaining upon us fast from Cadiz. We cleared away our stern chasers and the magazine – the prisoners observing this, rose upon our people and retook the ship, in doing which they met with little opposition – indeed it would have been madness to resist. A slight resistance was made by some men who narrowly escaped with their lives. They now wore ship and stood towards Cadiz. At 4 p.m. *Le Hortense* French frigate of 44 guns took us in tow and towed us to the harbour mouth where we brought up amongst some of their disabled ships and rode till 3 o'clock the following day when we parted from our anchors and not having another cable bent to bring her up, they let her drive ashore near St Martin's Bay.

Unable to gain the safety of the anchorage at Cadiz, the *Neptuno* crashed on to the rocks. Thorpe remembered:

At this time the confusion on board is inexpressible, it being dark, and ignorant what part of the coast we were cast upon. Expecting the ship every moment to go to pieces. The Spaniards, naturally dispirited, now showed every symptom of despair. They ran about in wild disorder nor made the least effort to extricate themselves from the danger that threatened them. At daylight our people conveyed three ropes on shore – one from the cat-head, one from the bowsprit and another from the foremast-head – by the assistance of which a number of men got safe on shore whilst others were employed constructing a raft for more expeditiously landing, as well as to convey such as were unwilling to risk themselves by the ropes. When the raft was completed, 20 men ventured on board and arrived safe on shore, but the raft was driven so far upon the rocks that it was found impossible to get it off again. Those on board seeing this sad disaster, far from giving way to despair, immediately set about making another, which certainly was our last resource, as we had not any more spars fit for that purpose. When finished we launched it overboard and 20 men embarked on board it who arrived safe, one Spaniard excepted who was washed off by the surf. We then made fast a rope to the raft on shore and there being one already fast from the ship, the people dragged it off to the ship. When 28 men embarked on board, all of whom arrived safe on shore, the raft was again dragged on board and 28 men embarked, one of whom was washed from the raft (a Spaniard) by the surf and perished. The raft was much damaged upon the rocks. It was again dragged off onto the ship, but fate had decreed that all who remained on board should perish. The raft, laden, shoved off from the ship side, but ere it gained the shore it upset and every soul perished. No further attempt could be made to save those unfortunate men who remained on board, all perished . . . our loss amounted to four killed by the falling of the masts and rigging, and drowned . . .

Though the sufferings of our people were great, yet no imputation of cruelty or even unkindness can be alleged to the Spaniards. Those who arrived safe on shore looked upon our men as their deliverers, and there were instances of gratitude and kindness that would do honour to any nation. It is with regret the Spaniard goes to war with the English whom he wishes always to consider his friends. It is from the unfortunate situation of affairs – on the Continent he is compelled to cut a part so foreign to his interest and contrary to the public wish.

Meanwhile, Cosmao-Kerjulien's sortie, taking advantage of a north-westerly wind, made for the shattered ships strewn across the sea to the south. In the *Euryalus*, Blackwood noted:

The remains of the French and Spanish fleet have rallied and are at this moment but a few miles from us – their object, of course, to recover some captured ships, or take some of the disabled English; but they will be disappointed, for I think and hope we shall have another touch at them ere long. We are now lying between them and our prizes with 11 complete line of battleships, besides more ready to come to us if we want them.

Unaware of their enemy's strength, the British prepared for action and that meant casting off the tow-ropes of prizes in order to manoeuvre. One of those cast adrift, Villeneuve's flagship, the *Bucentaure*, was thereupon driven ashore by the storm and wrecked. But Cosmao-Kerjulien was able to get tow-ropes across to the helpless *Santa Ana* and take her to Cadiz, while the frigate *Hortense* tried unsuccessfully to do the same for the *Neptuno*. However, Cosmao-Kerjulien's gains were outweighed by losses. Of the five sail of the line he had bravely led out of Cadiz, three were driven ashore by the hurricane and lost. So, of the seventeen prizes held by Collingwood before the storm, two had been retaken by the enemy, six were driven ashore and lost and five were scuttled, or burned, by the British because they could not be saved in the high wind and sea. Only four now remained to be towed towards Gibraltar. However, Dumanoir and his four fugitive battleships were still missing.

Meanwhile, in the *Bellerophon*, Lieutenant William Cumby encountered a young midshipman who had been wounded at Trafalgar:

Ten sail of the enemy's line came out of Cadiz in good

condition and made a demonstration of attacking some of our crippled ships and frigates, who had been driven near Cadiz in the gale. When the signal was made for battle and our drums had beat to quarters for the purpose, the first person that caught my eye on the quarterdeck was little Pearson dragging with difficulty one leg after the other: I said to him 'Pearson you had better go below, wounded as you are you will be better there.' He answered 'I had rather stay at my quarters sir if you please!' On which I replied 'You had much better go down, someone will be running against you and do you further mischief.' To this he exclaimed, the tears standing in his eyes, 'I hope sir you will not order me below: I should be very sorry to be below at a time like this.' I instantly said 'Indeed I will not order you down and if you live you'll be a second Nelson.'

The ordeal of the past few days was encapsulated by Midshipman James Robinson of the *Mars* in a letter to his father:

Never did ships experience such awful weather as we, without masts (they were shot away), were tossed about at the mercy of the winds and waves and, what was worse, the sailor's curse, the land close to us. We burned and sunk our prizes as fast as we possibly could. Many of our own people perished, who had been sent on board of them when the weather was moderate ... My dear father, I would have written sooner but could not as I had my right arm a little bruised. Indeed it almost appears to be like a dream that I, the boatswain and seven men were the only survivors out of 16 men on the *Mars*'s forecastle.

On 26 October, Admiral Collingwood finally completed his official despatch to William Marsden, the Secretary to the Admiralty, which he had begun on the night of the 21st. He had continued writing throughout the enemy's sortie from Cadiz, from time to time giving orders to be signalled from the *Euryalus*.

The despatch had to be sent to London as soon as possible. Collingwood had earlier told Blackwood that he would probably have the honour of carrying it and presenting it at the Admiralty but neither he, nor his frigate, could be spared for so many of the fleet were unserviceable through battle- and storm-damage. Instead Collingwood chose the little schooner *Pickle*, a despatch vessel designed for such work, which was commanded by Lieutenant John Lapenotiere. She was ordered alongside the frigate and, at six o'clock on the morning of 26 October, Lapenotiere wrote in his log:

Answered the signal 84 [to pass within hail]. Bore up and made sail towards the commander-in-chief. At 9, the commander went on board of the commander-in-chief. At 10, discharged all the prisoners into the *Revenge*. At noon, the boat returned. In boat and made sail for England. The commander-in-chief south, 2 miles. Fresh breezes and cloudy with a heavy swell from the westward.

P.M. – At ½ past 12, wore and made sail to the north-west quarter, and parted company with the commander-in-chief.

CHAPTER 11

Aftermath

In the fleet the *Pickle* left astern, the casualty returns were being collated. The British losses were remarkably low: 449 killed and 1,214 wounded. Nelson had, of course, been killed, as had Captains Duff of the *Mars* and Cooke of the *Bellerophon*. In the *Victory*, fifty-seven had died and 102 had been wounded. Among the dead was the newly promoted Lieutenant William Ram who had confided in his sister in the days before battle (p. 46). His legs had been torn off by flying splinters and, in a frenzy of despair, grief or pain, he had torn off the tourniquets and bled to death. Also killed in the *Victory* was Midshipman Robert Smith, who had written so movingly to his parents under the shadow of the imminent engagement (pp. 56–7).

French and Spanish losses were much higher, particularly when the total included those drowned in the storm. The French had lost 3,370 killed or drowned and 1,160 wounded; the Spanish, 1,038 killed or drowned and 2,545 wounded. These totals rose as reports came in from French and Spanish ships that had been captured, or had escaped, and news arrived of those who had died from their wounds.

The *Victory* had ridden out the hurricane and been taken in tow by Fremantle's *Neptune*. All on board were aware of the admiral's cabin where Nelson's body had been taken. Dr Beatty recorded:

There was no lead on board to make a coffin: a cask called a leaguer, which is of the largest size on shipboard, was therefore chosen for the reception of the body; which, after the hair had been cut off, was stripped of the clothes except the shirt, and put into it, and the cask was then filled with brandy. In the evening [22 October] after this melancholy task was accomplished, the gale came on with violence from the south-west, and continued that night and the succeeding day without any abatement. During this boisterous weather, Lord Nelson's body remained under the charge of a sentinel on the middle deck . . .

The cask was placed on its end, having a closed aperture at its top and another below; the object of which was, that as a frequent renewal of spirit was thought necessary, the old could thus be drawn off below and a fresh quantity introduced above, without moving the cask, or occasioning the least agitation of the body. On the 24th there was a disengagement of air from the body to such a degree, that the sentinel became alarmed on seeing the head of the cask raised: he therefore applied to the officers, who were under the necessity of having the cask spiled [vented] to give the air a discharge. After this, no considerable collection of air took place.

The *Neptune* and the *Victory* slowly made their way to Gibraltar, where the shattered *Belleisle* had already arrived. Lieutenant Nicolas surveyed the scene from her deck:

Disabled ships continued to arrive for several days, bringing with them the only four prizes rescued from the fury of the late gale. The anchorage became covered with ships. In the mole lay six dismasted hulls, whose battered sides, dismounted guns, and shattered ports, presented unequivocal evidence of the brilliant part they had taken in the gloriously contested battle: a little beyond, the more recently arrived lay at their anchors. At this proud moment no shout of exultation was heard, no joyous felicitations were exchanged, for the lowered flag which waved on the *Victory*'s mast, marked where the mourned hero lay, and cast a deepened shade over the triumphant scene. The exertion which was necessary to refit the ships did not, however, permit the mind to dwell on this melancholy subject.

After the *Victory* arrived at Gibraltar on 28 October, Nelson's body was taken ashore, the brandy drawn off from the leaguer and replaced with spirits of wine to preserve it for the long voyage home. The *Bellerophon* reached port on the same day and put her wounded ashore. Amongst them was Jack Spratt, hoping to survive his badly wounded leg and be promoted lieutenant. Having refused to submit to amputation, he risked gangrene and had endured an uncomfortable week:

I suffered great pain from the sudden jerking of the ship as she pitched to the heavy sea in the gale, having in tow a dismasted line of battle ship, the *Temmarare* [*sic*] bound for Gibraltar. I could hear as well as feel the broken ends of my marrow bones as they grated by derrangement whilst I lay in my cot under the half-deck, where I received every kind attention from my gallant capt. and the wardroom officers that I was capable of receiving, which left a lasting impression on my mind.

I was obliged to be left at Gibraltar Hospital, where a high fever came on me and in my delirium I fancied I was playing at football; suiting the action to the thought I dislocated the broken bone as often as the surgeon put it to rights. In that state they held a consultation and came to the determination of locking up my leg in a long box and thus kept it at rest for nine days to facilitate the formation of callus, this being done and an orderly soldier and an old woman placed alongside my bed to be relieved alternately day and night.

I must not omit to mention an occurrence which happened on the 6th day. My good old nurse was very fond of smoking tobacco, which was not allowed in the wards, but one night after all the patients had fallen fast asleep from the effects of opiates, she put her head inside the chimney-board close to my cradle and there indulged in the weed. But the sentinel soon after opening the door of the sick ward to see all was right so alarmed the good old woman that she put the pipe in her pocket without extinguishing it and fell fast asleep.

I providentially awoke and found the ward full of smoke and my poor nurse on fire. So out I bundled regardless of my locked-up leg and wrapped her round with my bed rug and succeeded in extinguishing this burning old hag, who was not aware of her alarming situation although her petticoat and pocket were on fire. I suffered severely from my exertion for many days.

During this interval my fever gradually diminished but

I suffered from a gnawing pain in my leg as if a mouse was nibbling the calf of my leg [and this] obliged me to make use of my dirk, which I constantly thrust into the box to relieve my pain. I thought at one time rock scorpions had made a nest in the dressing round my leg. The faculty wondered what irritated me and produced such strange fancies, sometimes taking it for a good omen of the bone uniting but on the ninth day all the faculty were present to witness the opening of the box: viz. Drs Gray, Thompson and M. Bouvier, who was soon let into the secret and, the dressing cleared, such a sight presented itself as they never beheld before: hundreds of large, red-headed maggots nearly an inch long were sticking into the calf of my precious limb, only the tip of their tails to be seen and I am sure their heads could not be far from the bone.

I fancy I see the French surgeon M. Bouvier's attitude this moment with his shoulders shrugged up to his very ears with his hands straight down with the fingers turned up backwards, looking alternately at the surgeons. The forceps were soon produced to extract them but failing as they broke short off, which made me feel more acutely their struggles.

A thought at length struck Bouvier and away he set off at full speed to his medicine chest and soon returned with a phial in his hand, the contents of which he poured into my honeycombed calf, which made me smart with pain but it had the desired effect, those maggots (I fancy I see them now) were produced by Spanish flies attracted by so many wounded after the Battle of Trafalgar, which beset the hospital, blackening the ceiling of the sick ward and depositing their eggs on and about the wounded. But I was the first on whom they established themselves. I well remember that if the sentry was absent a moment they would drop down on us in swarms for which reason he was obliged to have a large branch of evergreens to keep them off.

And now for the ninth day's wonder, the effect of locking up the shivered limb from so many days outbalanced the havoc of my flesh as a surprising strong callus had formed upon both ends of the bone that bid defiance to every derrangement ever since . . .

By the great skill and superior and good management of our good surgeon, now Sir William Burnett and Physician General of the Royal Navy, my leg was saved and although nearly three inches shorter than the other is much better than an artificial one.

In hospital, Spratt heard news of the French officer, Salmon, whose life he had saved:

Mr Salmon was most grateful for the act rendered him and was one of the officers who remained in *L'Aigle* when she was stranded in Cadiz Bay in the awful gale which followed the action but most of our officers and the crew we first put on board of her in charge were saved but became prisoners to the Spaniards. This Mr Salmon behaved most kindly to my messmate Mr Snowery and others after they were wrecked inshore and he after[wards] hoped he would not leave this world before he shook me by the hand. *L'Aigle* was stranded in Cadiz Bay.

For another of the *Bellerophon*'s wounded, it was to be a matter for charity ashore. The ship's officers signed a certificate requesting help from the Chatham Chest for William Gaffney, aged about thirty, for 'severe wounds on his arms, neck, breast and face by which latter he lost the sight of his left eye from the explosion of combustible matter thrown in at the ports by the enemy on the 21st October'.

Often the survival of the wounded came as a surprise. Such was the case of the seaman from the *Belleisle* who had been shot in the head, given up for dead and was about to be thrown overboard when he was seen to be breathing (p. 143). Landed at Gibraltar, he survived because, as one of his officers said, 'After being a week in hospital, the ball, which had entered the temple, came out of his mouth.'

Damage to the ships, too, had to be assessed. On passage to Gibraltar, Captain Hardy described the ravages inflicted on the *Victory*, which had suffered less than some other ships:

The hull is much damaged by shot in a number of different

places, particularly in the wales, strings and spirketting, and between wind and water. Several beams, knees, and riders, shot through and broke; the starboard cathead shot away; the rails and timbers of the head and stem cut by shot; several of the ports damaged, and port timbers cut off; the channels and chainplates damaged by shot and the falling of the mizen-mast; the principal part of the bulkheads, halfports, and portsashes thrown overboard in clearing the ship for action.

The mizen-mast shot away about 9 feet above the deck; the mainmast shot through and sprung; the main yard gone; the main topmast and cap shot in different places and reefed; the main topsail yard shot away; the foremast shot through in a number of different places . . . the fore yard shot away; the bowsprit jibboom and cap shot, and the spritsail and spritsail topsail yards, and flying jibboom gone; the fore and main tops damaged; the whole of the spare topmast yards, handmast, and fishes shot in different places . . .

The ship in bad weather makes 12 inches water in an hour.

The ships were uncomfortable enough even for the uninjured. The seamen's hammocks, which had been stowed in netting along the gunwales of the upper deck as protection against splinters and musketry during the action, were usually shot to pieces. The officers' quarters were wrecked when a ship had been raked through the stern windows and, as these were boarded up, they lived in semi-darkness. There was little surviving furniture – as Collingwood had complained (p. 141) – and it was recalled that the surgeon of the *Tonnant*, Forbes Chevers, found that he had only a

singular relic of the battle, which signally represented the fury of the fire of musketry from the enemy's tops. When the ship was cleared for action, the Windsor chairs forming part of the wardroom furniture were suspended by a rope passed from the main- to the mizen-mast. The chair which fell to Chevers' lot had had part of its legs shot away and another bullet had passed completely through its thick oaken seat.

Then the ships had to be repaired, at least enough to ensure their safe passage to a British dockyard. Reaction to the excitement of battle began to set in. Captain Fremantle of the *Neptune* felt both irritation and boredom, as he wrote to his wife:

We are here refitting, with all three masts under and strange to say I am not quite dissatisfied. The fact is that I know perfectly well that if we were to go home just now whilst so many ships are awaiting repair, we should be hurried out again immediately to the Channel fleet, if there is one thing more disagreeable than another in this world it is being there, and under Adml. Cornwallis, besides that I have other reasons that apply more particularly to the discipline of my ship, which you would not understand.

Eliot Harvey* goes with the next 5 ships, his head is turned, never having been in action before he thinks every ship was subdued by him, and he wears us all to death, with his incessant jargon, since my arrival here I have lived much on shore. The society is much the same as it ever was except that the governor is not so hospitable as Genl. O'Hara. I dined with Mrs Tyers the day before yesterday, she has got a sound brood of daughters coming forward. Three of the elder ones are married and in England. There are really some very pretty women on the Rock, but nobody that conveys the idea of fashion or fine manners. This action of ours will I hope bring me more than a thousand pounds. There is one advantage being here namely that one has a chance of getting some prize-money, which is never got in Channel service . . .

Harvey is unmoved and on the eve of departure! Whenever you meet him or Lady Louisa don't fail to expatiate on his merits and gallantry in the action . . .

I begin to be a little tired of this same Gibraltar.

It was now realised that eight French and Spanish prizes had been lost in the storm and two had been recaptured, leaving only the four ships – the Spanish *Bahama*, *San Ildefonso* and *San*

* i.e. Eliab Harvey, captain of the *Téméraire*.

Juan Nepomuceno, and the French *Swiftsure* – to be escorted to Gibraltar. But there was relief among the British at reaching port, although they brought their grief with them. As Richard Anderson, the navigating master of the *Prince*, put it: 'Thank God we are now safe at Gibraltar and are in hopes of being sent home. We have lost 8 or 9 of the prizes, which will be against our prize-money, but the greatest loss is the loss of Lord Nelson. We all cry for him.'

The loss of the prizes was a bitter blow and, for the British captains, dreams of buying a country estate faded. Some blamed Collingwood for failing to obey Nelson's order to anchor, although his reasons might have been obvious to any seaman. A few drew personal parallels between the admiral and the dead hero. Captain Codrington wrote to a friend at the Admiralty:

Collingwood certainly went into action in the finest style possible and is as brave a man as ever stepped on board a ship; I can also believe him to be a very good man in his way but he has none of the dignity an admiral should have and seems to lose all the great outline of a chief command in his attention to minutiae . . . At all events, there is no longer a Lord Nelson to serve with here . . . *Never* whilst I live shall I cease to regret his loss. *He* made the signal to prepare to anchor; and had Admiral Collingwood *acted upon that hint* we might have secured almost all our prizes.

French and Spanish prisoners were put ashore at Gibraltar – the latter to be repatriated through Algeciras – except those senior officers who were being taken to England. Amongst those leaving the *Revenge* was Jeanette, who had been rescued from the *Achille*. Her principal (but unnamed) guardian was sad to see her go:

For several days, I was so much busied in securing the ship's masts, and in looking after the ship in the gales which we had to encounter, that I had no time to attend to my *protégée*. It was on about the fourth day of her sojourn that she came to me in the greatest possible ecstasy and told me that she had found her husband, who was on board among the prisoners, and unhurt. She soon afterwards brought him to me, and in the most grateful terms and manner returned her thanks for the attentions she had received. After this, Jeanette declined coming to the ward-room, from the very proper feeling that her husband could not be admitted to the same privileges. On our arrival at Gibraltar, all our prisoners were landed by order of the port-admiral, Sir John Knight, at the Neutral Ground, but under a mistake, as the Spanish prisoners only should have been landed there. Her dress, though rather odd, was not unbecoming, and we all considered her a fine woman. On leaving the ship, most, if not all of us, gave her a dollar, and she expressed her thanks as well as she was able, and assured us that the name of our ship would always be remembered by her with the warmest gratitude.

Some of the British prize-crews had found themselves in Cadiz, the ships having been driven ashore or retaken by their original crews. But the perils of the storm had overridden enmity and the British had done what they could for the wounded on board and helped to get them ashore. Now they, in turn, were aided by their enemies. According to Captain Codrington, a British navigating master had been in the prize-crew on board the Spanish *Rayo* when that ship was lost in the storm off Cadiz:

The poor Spaniards behaved very creditably indeed: they not only sent boats for them (English and all) as soon as the weather moderated, with bread and water for their immediate relief; but when the boat in which the master of the ship was sent had got into Cadiz harbour, a carriage was backed into the water for him to step into from the boat, all sorts of cordials and confectionery were placed in the carriage for him, and clean linen, bed, etc., prepared for him at a lodging on shore: added to which the women and priests presented him with delicacies of all sorts as the carriage passed along the streets. In short, he says, and with very great truth, that had he been wrecked on any part of England he would never have received one-half the attention which he did from these poor Spaniards, whose friends we had just destroyed in such numbers.

Collingwood had already written to the governor of Cadiz, the Marquis Solana, offering the immediate return of wounded Spanish prisoners and had received a fulsome reply. Indeed, the Spanish were equally generous to the British in their hands as Collingwood noted:

All this part of Spain is in an uproar of praise and thankfulness to the English. Solana sent me a present of wine, and we have free intercourse with the shore. Judge of the footing we are on, when I tell you he offered me his hospitals, and pledged the Spanish honour for the care and cure of our wounded men. Our officers and men who were wrecked in some prize-ships were received like divinities, all the country on the beach to receive them; the priests and women distributing wine and bread and fruit amongst them. The soldiers turned out of their barracks to make room for them; whilst their allies the French were left to shift for themselves, with a guard over them to prevent their doing mischief . . . All the Spaniards speak of us in terms of adoration.

An Englishman who happened to be staying in Cadiz described the aftermath of the battle:

Ten days after the battle, they were still employed in bringing ashore the wounded; and spectacles were hourly displayed at the wharfs, and through the streets, sufficient to shock every heart not yet hardened to scenes of blood and human suffering. When, by the carelessness of the boatmen, and the surging of the sea, the boats struck against the stone piers, a horrid cry, which pierced the soul, arose from the mangled wretches on board. Many of the Spanish gentry assisted in bringing them ashore, with symptoms of much compassion; yet as they were finely dressed, it had something of the appearance of ostentation, if there could be ostentation at such a moment. It need not be doubted that an Englishman lent a willing hand to bear them up the steps to their litters; yet the slightest false step made them shriek out, and I even yet shudder at the remembrance of the sound. On the top of the pier the scene was affecting. The wounded were carried away to the hospitals in every shape of human misery, whilst crowds of Spaniards either assisted or looked on with signs of horror. Meanwhile, their companions, who had escaped unhurt, walked up and down with folded arms and downcast eyes, whilst women sat upon heaps of arms, broken furniture, and baggage, with their heads bent between their knees. I had no inclination to follow the litters of the wounded; yet I learned that every hospital in Cadiz was already full, and that convents and churches were forced to be appropriated to the reception of the remainder. If, leaving the harbour, I passed through the town to the Point, I still beheld the terrible effects of the battle. As far as the eye could reach, the sandy side of the isthmus bordering on the Atlantic was covered with masts and yards, the wrecks of ships, and here and there bodies of the dead . . .

Among others I noticed a topmast marked with the name of the *Swiftsure*, and the broad arrow of England, which only increased my anxiety to know how far the English had suffered, the Spaniards still continuing to affirm that they had lost their chief admiral, and half their fleet. While surrounded by these wrecks, I mounted on the cross-trees of a mast which had been thrown ashore, and casting my eyes over the ocean, beheld, at a great distance, several masts and portions of wreck still floating about. As the sea was now almost calm, with a slight swell, the effect produced by these objects had in it something of a sublime melancholy, and touched the soul with a remembrance of the sad vicissitudes of human affairs. The portions of floating wreck were visible from the ramparts; yet not a boat dared to venture out to examine or endeavour to tow them in, such were the apprehensions which still filled their minds, of the enemy.

Amongst the bodies washed up on the Spanish coast were many of the British dead who had been thrown overboard, including Lieutenant William Ram of the *Victory*.

Yet this was not quite the end of the Battle of Trafalgar. The entire Franco-Spanish fleet had been accounted for – captured, sunk, burned, run ashore or in Cadiz – except for the four ships of the van squadron under Admiral Dumanoir which had disappeared. At first it was thought that they, too, had escaped to Cadiz; then, that they had continued south and entered the Mediterranean. Dumanoir had, in fact, reached the Straits but was struck by another gale. Seeing sails to the east and assuming them to be Admiral Louis's squadron, which had been detached for replenishment before the battle, he turned west into the Atlantic, then north in the hope of bypassing the British fleet and reaching safety at Rochefort or Brest.

Unknown to all concerned, Dumanoir's flagship, the 80-gun *Formidable*, and the three 74s, the *Duguay-Trouin*, the *Mont-Blanc* and the *Scipion*, were following much the same course as the *Pickle*. On 2 November, British frigates cruising off Cape Finisterre, in search of a French squadron from Rochefort which had been attacking British shipping, sighted four large ships and reported their presence to the nearest British squadron: five battleships – one of eighty guns, the others 74s – commanded by Captain Sir Richard Strachan. He began to hunt for the unknown enemy and, next day, closed to within a dozen miles of them.

On that same day, the *Pickle*, which had just entered the English Channel, herself sighted a battleship. This proved to be the *Superb*, commanded by Nelson's friend Captain Richard Keats and the flagship of Vice-Admiral Sir John Duckworth, who was under orders to join Lord Nelson's Mediterranean fleet. Both ships hove to, and Lapenotiere, although desperate to reach London with his news, reluctantly obeyed the order to come aboard the big ship. What transpired was remembered by a twelve-year-old volunteer in the *Superb*, Edward Trelawny:

Young as I was, I shall never forget our falling in with the *Pickle* schooner after Trafalgar, carrying the first despatches of the battle and death of its hero. Her commander, burning with impatience to be the first to convey the news to England, was compelled to heave to and come on board us. Captain Keats received him on deck. Silence reigned throughout the ship; some great event was anticipated. The officers stood in groups, watching with intense anxiety the two commanders, who walked apart. 'Battle', 'Nelson', 'ships', were the only audible words which could be gathered from their conversation. I saw the blood rush into Keats's face; he stamped the deck, walked hurriedly, and spoke with passion. I marvelled, for I had never before seen him much moved; he had appeared cool, firm, and collected on all occasions, and it struck me that some awful event had taken place, or was at hand. The admiral [Duckworth] was still in his cabin, eager for news from the Nelson fleet. He was an irritable and violent man, and after a few minutes, swelling with wrath, he sent an order to Keats, who possibly heard it not, but staggered along the deck, struck to the heart by the news, and, for the first time in his life, forgot his respect to his superior in rank; muttering, as it seemed, curses on his fate that, by the admiral's delay [spending three days at Plymouth loading stores], he had not participated in the most glorious battle in naval history. Another messenger enforced him to descend in haste to the admiral, who was high in rage and impatience. Keats, for I followed him, on entering the admiral's cabin, said in a subdued voice, as if he were choking, 'A great battle has been fought, two days ago, off Trafalgar. The combined fleets of France and Spain are annihilated, and Nelson is no more!' He then murmured, 'Had we not been detained we should have been there.' Duckworth answered not, conscience-struck, but stalked the deck. He seemed ever to avoid the look of his captain, and turned to converse with the commander of the schooner, who replied in sulky brevity, 'Yes' or 'No'. Then, dismissing him, he ordered all sail to be set, and walked the quarterdeck alone. A death-like stillness pervaded the ship, broken at intervals by the low murmurs of the crew and officers, when 'battle' and 'Nelson' could alone be distinguished. Sorrow and discontent were painted on every face.

Next day, as the *Pickle*, crowding all sail, hurried towards England, Strachan caught Dumanoir. What happened was described by Midshipman Frederick Romney of the frigate *Aeolus* in a letter home:

My dear Mary,

I was in hopes of seeing you last time we were in; but the consequence of our being despatched immediately with the flying squadron, under the command of Sir Richard Strachan, put a stop to all those hopes: but never mind – fortune always favours the brave . . . Nothing occurred until the 2nd Nov., when retiring to our cots, who should join us but the little *Phoenix*, with three cheers; which was returned with high glee from the whole of the squadron. She gave us information of four sail of the line of the enemy having chased her the whole day. Not a moment was lost in making sail. We continued in chase until that happy and glorious day . . . when we came up with the *Monsieurs* – Everything favourable – the weather mild and serene: the first gun was fired by the *St Margaret*: a running fight was kept up for four hours; when the enemy, finding they could not escape, hove to for us. A general action then commenced – in truth we were in the warmest of it during the whole of their tacking; which they did with the intent of cutting off our frigates. This placed us in a critical position, and obliged us to run the gauntlet with the whole of them. Thank God! we had only three men badly wounded: our rigging was cut up very much – there we continued at it, hot and warm, pelting away for three hours and twenty-five minutes, before we made them haul their haughty flag down – a happy sight. They proved to be *Le Formidable*, the admiral's ship, *Le Scipion*, *Le Duguay-Trouin*, and *Le Mont-Blanc*; two 80 guns and two 74s,* which had made their escape from Nelson, fifteen days from Cadiz, all fine ships; they are dreadfully cut up. I am not certain, but I think they had between six and seven hundred killed and wounded. The old admiral is one of the wounded.

Our little squadron consisted of only four sail of the line, and four frigates – our killed and wounded is so small as not to be worth mentioning; but I have met with a sad accident: in the hurry of clearing for action they hove my sea chest overboard, with all my clothes in it, except eight dirty shirts which I had in my berth: not I alone, but three

* In fact, one of eighty guns and three 74s.

of my messmates shared the same fate: therefore I shall require assistance to new rig me, until I receive my prize-money. This will be a grand spoke in my favour when I pass my examination,* which will be the first Wednesday in next month, if we are in harbour . . . A friend on board has just informed me, if I ask leave to pass my examina-tion, the captain cannot with propriety refuse me; if he should, by applying to the Admiralty they will grant me leave of absence for a short time – then we shall spend some happy hours! I think I deserve to be on shore now, for during six years I have not been six weeks on shore. God bless you!

* For promotion to lieutenant.

CHAPTER 12

Home

At half-past nine on the morning of 4 November 1805, Lieutenant John Lapenotiere landed at Falmouth and immediately hired a light post-chaise, drawn by four horses, for the journey to London. Driving day and night, he travelled the 265 miles in thirty-seven hours, reaching London in thick fog and arriving at the Admiralty in Whitehall at one o'clock on the morning of 6 November. There the Secretary, William Marsden, had only just retired for the night and was quickly roused to receive the travel-weary lieutenant. Marsden recalled:

In accosting me, the officer used these impressive words, 'Sir, we have gained a great victory; but we have lost Lord Nelson!' The effect this produced, it is not to my purpose to describe, nor had I time to indulge in reflections, who was at that moment the only person informed of one of the greatest events recorded in our history, and which it was my duty to make known with the utmost promptitude. The First Lord had retired to rest, as had his domestics, and it was not till after some research that I could discover the room in which he slept. Drawing aside his curtain, with a candle in my hand, I awoke the old peer from a sound slumber; and to the credit of his nerves be it mentioned, that he showed no symptom of alarm or surprise, but calmly asked: 'What news, Mr M.?' We then discussed in few words, what was immediately to be done, and I sat up the remainder of the night, with such of the clerks as I could collect, in order to make the necessary communications.

The elderly Lord Barham decided that the Prime Minister must be told at once. The news was sent along Whitehall to Downing Street and the door of No. 10 and at three o'clock William Pitt was woken and told the news. Later, a friend recounted:

Pitt observed, that he had been called up at various hours in his eventful life by the arrival of news of various hues; but that whether good or bad he could always lay his head on his pillow and sink into sound sleep again. On *this occasion*, however, the great event announced brought with it so much to weep over, as well as to rejoice at, that he could not calm his thoughts, but at length got up, though it was three in the morning.

A messenger was despatched with the news to the king, which reached Windsor Castle at half-past six that morning before the royal family had woken. Lord Barham next wrote a formal letter to the widowed Lady Nelson, who was at Bath and could not receive the letter for several days:

Madam, it is with the utmost concern that, in the midst of victory, I have to inform your Ladyship of the death of your illustrious partner, Lord Viscount Nelson. After leading the British fleet into close action with the enemy and seeing their defeat, he fell by a musket ball entering his chest. It is the death he wished for and less to be regretted on his own account. But the public loss is irretrievable. I can only add that events of this kind do not happen by chance. I recommend therefore your Ladyship to His protection, who is alone able to save, or to destroy.

A letter was written to Emma Hamilton by the Comptroller of the Navy, Sir Andrew Snape Hammond, ending with the words, 'I can say no more. My heart is too full to attempt to give comfort to others.' A naval officer, Captain John Whitby, was chosen as messenger and left for Merton immediately. Later, Emma Hamilton remembered:

I had come to Merton, and, feeling rather unwell, I said I would stay in bed on account of a rash. Mrs Bolton [Nelson's sister] was sitting by my bedside when all of a sudden I said, 'I think I hear the Tower guns. Some victory perhaps in Germany . . .' 'Perhaps', said Mrs Bolton, 'it may be news from my brother.' 'Impossible, surely. There is not time.'

Soon afterwards she heard a carriage enter the drive:

I sent to enquire who was arrived. They brought me word, Mr Whitby, from the Admiralty. 'Show him in directly,' I said. He came in, and with a pale countenance and faint voice said, 'We have gained a great victory.' 'Never mind your victory,' I said. 'My letters – give me my letters.' Capt. Whitby was unable to speak – tears in his eyes and a deathly paleness over his face made me comprehend him. I believe I gave a scream and fell back, and for ten hours after I could neither speak nor shed a tear.

The news flew through London, grief overwhelming jubilation. The editor of the *Morning Chronicle*, James Perry, a friend of Nelson's, wrote: 'There was not a man who would not have given up his life to achieve such a victory. Not a man who would not have surrendered every part of the victory (except the honour of Britain) to save the life of Lord Nelson.'

Bells were rung, saluting guns fired and the news spread across the country by the mail coaches. That night candles were lit in the windows of town houses, sometimes illuminating prints of Nelson, or hastily painted transparencies. Everywhere the reaction was the same, even among the most sophisticated. Lady Harriet Cavendish, daughter of the Duke of Devonshire, wrote to her sister:

I am safe in supposing you have heard all the details of the great events that have roused even me from my usual apathy upon those subjects. Poor Lord Nelson. The universal gloom that I hear of from those who have been in Town is the strongest proof of the regret he so justly deserved to occasion as otherwise I suppose such a victory at such a moment is everything, both for our honour and safety, and could have driven us half wild.

On the day after the news broke in London, *The Times* reported:

The victory created none of those enthusiastic emotions in the public mind which the successes of our naval arms have in every former instance produced. There was not a man who did not think that the life of the Hero of the Nile was too great a price for the capture and destruction of twenty sail of French and Spanish men of war. No ebullitions of popular transport, no demonstrations of public joy, marked this great and important event. The honest and manly feeling of the people appeared as it should have done: they felt an inward satisfaction at the triumph of their favourite arms; they mourned with all the sincerity and poignancy of domestic grief their Hero slain.

In Portsmouth, a visiting Russian naval officer, Vice-Admiral Dimitri Seniavin, described how

the news was received at Portsmouth of the fight off Trafalgar. I cannot describe the joy about the victory and the sadness about the death of Nelson! Only someone who had seen the delight of the English in similar circumstances could describe it on this occasion. From early morning the broadsheets were carried along the streets, describing the battle and the death of Nelson; sadness and joy mingled on the face of everyone, and everywhere could be heard the exclamation: Immortal Nelson! The ships and the fortress were firing their guns all day, and at night the town was wonderfully illuminated. The better houses were decorated with transparent pictures. One showed Nelson at the moment when the shot penetrated his chest and he had fallen into the arms of those surrounding him. Another portrayed Britannia with sorrowful face accepting the crown of victory. At night the streets were crowded. The garrison stood to arms and the regimental bandsmen played the National Anthem: 'Britannia, Rule the Waves!'

In Norfolk, the artist and diarist Joseph Farington happened to be travelling near Nelson's birthplace when he heard the news:

November 7. At one o'clock the postmaster at Rougham sent his post boy with orders to stop while an extraordinary gazette was read. It announced an engagement off

Cadiz between the English fleet under Lord Nelson and the combined fleets of France and Spain under Admiral Villeneuve, etc., in which 19 French and Spanish ships were taken and one burnt. Admiral Villeneuve taken. This agreeable news was attended with the painful information of the death of Lord Nelson who was killed by a musket-ball. In the evening we got a paper containing a bulletin from the Admiralty with the substance of the above.

The news upset the Prince of Wales, whom Nelson had suspected of having had sexual designs on Emma Hamilton. 'The prince has this moment recd. an account of the death of poor Lord Nelson,' wrote Maria Fitzherbert, his secret, morganatic wife, on 6 November, 'which has affected him most extremely.' Next day, she feared that his 'sorrow might help to prevent his coming to dinner at the Pavilion', his fanciful palace at Brighton. Mrs Fitzherbert confided to a friend that 'she was all for Lady Nelson and against Lady Hamilton, who, she said, hero as he was, over power'd him and took possession of him quite by force'. But, she concluded, 'Poor creature! I am sorry for her now for I suppose she is in grief.'

Soon the whole country shared the mixed emotions of triumph and sorrow. A keeper of a turnpike gate was reported as telling a traveller, 'Sir, have you heard the bad news? We have taken twenty ships from the enemy, but Lord Nelson is killed.' When the news reached Ireland, Lady Castlereagh wrote:

Never was there an event so mournfully and so triumphantly important to England as the Battle of Trafalgar. The sentiment of lamenting the individual, more than the rejoicing in the victory, shows the humanity and affection of the people of England, but their good sense on reflection will dwell only on the conquest because no death at a future moment could have been more glorious and might have been less so. The public would never have sent him on another expedition, his health was not equal to another effort and he might have yielded to the more natural but less imposing efforts of more worldly honours! Whereas he now begins his immortal career, having nothing to achieve on earth and bequeathing to the English fleet a legacy which they alone are able to improve. Had I been his wife, or his mother, I would rather have wept him dead than see him languish on a less splendid day. In such a death there is no sting and in such a grave everlasting victory.

Surprisingly, perhaps, London newspapers even reached the fortresses in France where captured British naval officers were imprisoned, or allowed the freedom of a town while on parole. News of Trafalgar had been largely ignored by French newspapers on instructions from Paris, but an English newspaper reached Verdun in December and the paroled Lieutenant William Dillon wrote:

I happened to enter the Caron Club about 11 o'clock one day when one of the committee came in with the English newspapers containing the account of Nelson's victory over the combined fleets of France and Spain. Lord Yarmouth, Col. Abercromby and several others of my friends seized hold of me as if by one accord, and, lifting me on the table, desired me to read in a loud voice the official report of that splendid victory. The most perfect silence having been secured, I communicated the details of Collingwood's letter to the Admiralty. When I had finished it, three hearty spontaneous cheers were given by at least one hundred members present, and those who were not near the table closed up and requested me to read the account a second time, which I readily agreed to do. I was then requested by Lord Yarmouth to explain the manner in which that battle was fought, as they did not understand the nautical description of the disposal of the two fleets. I did so by placing a parcel of books that were lying on the table in the position of the adverse fleets. We separated then, but, going out to the street, we met a crowd of French gentlemen who were anxious to know the reason of all that cheering. I told them of our splendid victory, and they were sadly cast down on the occasion. My French friends overloaded me with questions. They allowed they could not contend with us upon the ocean. 'We do not doubt', they said, 'that you have triumphed. But that you should have taken and destroyed so many ships without your losing any is a case we cannot admit. Our seamen can fight as well as yours, and surely you do not mean to maintain that our shot has not sunk *some* of your ships?' My only reply was that they might see Lord Collingwood's official report for themselves, by which it was perfectly clear that they had lost twenty sail of the line: but not one on our side, either lost or taken, a British admiral not daring to send home a false report.

Later, Dillon met a French officer who had been released from captivity in England and was on leave:

He had been wounded at the Battle of Trafalgar . . . This gentleman's name was Prigny. He was Adm. Villeneuve's flag-captain [in fact, chief of staff], and I do not recollect at any period of my life having enjoyed a more interesting conversation than I did in that officer's company. I found in Capt. Prigny an amiable and well-informed officer who did not, at the meeting which took place between us, conceal any of the facts or principal incidents which occurred between the hostile fleets on that important occasion. His ship, the *Bucentaure*, was taken possession by the *Mars*, 74, commanded by my former captain, George Duff, who was killed on that glorious day. After a conversation that lasted until 2 o'clock in the morning, wherein the gallant Frenchman made the most satisfactory replies to all my questions, I at length, fearing that I had made too many, said in conclusion, 'I am truly sensible of your polite attention in conveying to me the interesting details which you have so frankly given.' 'Not in the least,' he replied. 'We did not gain the victory, and the truth will out in due time. Therefore it would be absurd to conceal the events as they really happened.' 'Well,' said I, 'one more question before we part. What was the act on the part of the British fleet that made the greatest impression on your mind during that battle?' 'The act that astonished me the most', he said, 'was when the action was over. It came on to blow a gale of wind, and the English immediately set to work to shorten sail and reef the topsails, with as much regularity and order as if their ships had not been fighting a dreadful battle. We were all amazement, wondering what the English seamen could be made of. All *our* seamen were either drunk or disabled, and we, the officers, could not get any work out of them. We never witnessed any such clever manoeuvres before, and I shall never forget them.

The tidings of victory and the death of Nelson spread further across Europe and were greeted with mixed grief and jubilation in Paris, which became an emotional mirror-image of London. But wherever Nelson was remembered there was sorrow; even in Naples, where he had supported the Bourbon monarchy and helped suppress the republican rebels so effectively and ruthlessly. The poet Samuel Taylor Coleridge was there when the news of Nelson's death arrived. He remembered:

When he died, it seemed as if no man was a stranger to another; for all were made acquaintances by the rights of a common anguish . . . The tidings arrived at Naples on the day that I returned to that city from Calabria; and never can I forget the sorrow and consternation that lay on every countenance. Even to this day there are times when I seem to see, as in a vision, separate groups and individual faces of the picture. Numbers stopped and shook hands with me because they had seen the tears on my cheek, and conjectured that I was an Englishman; and several, as they held my hand, burst, themselves, into tears.

Emma Hamilton was to say, 'I was very happy at Naples but all seems gone like a dream.' At first she was distracted with grief, and a friend, who visited her a week after she had heard the news of Nelson's death, recalled:

I found her in bed. She had the appearance of a person stunned and scarcely as yet able to comprehend the certainty of her loss. 'What shall I do?' and 'How can I exist?' were her first words . . . 'Days have passed on and I know not how they end or begin – nor how I am to bear my future existence.'

Meanwhile the *Victory*, with Nelson's body on board, was on her way home, accompanied by two of the ships that had fought hardest on 21 October, the *Belleisle* and the *Bellerophon*. At one point she was under tow but otherwise sailed under temporary jury-rig, leaking badly and barely seaworthy. She anchored at Spithead off Portsmouth on 4 December and delayed a week while arrangements for the reception of Nelson's body were made in London. Then, as Able Seaman John Brown recorded: 'We sailed from Spithead on the 10th with Lord Nelson on board as usual . . . whilst every ship we passed cheered the noble *Victory*.'

When the ship passed Brighton, she was sighted by the Prince of Wales. A friend of his noted:

It was a large party at the Pavilion last night and the prince was not well . . . but before Prinny went off he took a seat by me to tell me all this *bad* news had made him bilious and that he was further overset yesterday by seeing the ship with Lord Nelson's body on board.

Just before Christmas, the *Victory* entered the Thames estuary at the Nore – near Chatham, where she had been built half a century before and where Nelson had begun his naval career – and there she was met by the Admiralty yacht. On board the old flagship, Dr Beatty examined Nelson for the last time:

The remains were wrapped in cotton vestments, and rolled from head to foot with bandages of the same material, in the ancient mode of embalming. The body was then put into a leaden coffin, filled with brandy holding in solution camphor and myrrh. This coffin was enclosed in a wooden one, and placed in the after-part of his Lordship's cabin; where it remained till the 21st of December, when an order was received from the Admiralty for the removal of the body. The coffin that had been made from the mainmast of the French commander's ship *L'Orient*, and presented to his Lordship by his friend Captain Hallowell, after the Battle of the Nile, being then received on board, the leaden coffin was opened, and the body taken out; when it was found still in most excellent condition, and completely plastic. The features were somewhat tumid, from absorption of the spirit; but on using friction with a napkin, they resumed in a great degree their natural character. All the officers of the ship, and several of his Lordship's friends, as well as some of Captain Hardy's, who had come on board the *Victory* that day from the shore, were present at the time of the body's being removed from the leaden coffin; and witnessed its undecayed state after a lapse of two months since death, which excited the surprise of all who beheld it. This was the last time the mortal part of the lamented Hero was seen by human eyes; as the body, after being dressed in a shirt, stockings, uniform small-clothes and waistcoat, neckcloth, and nightcap, was then placed in the shell made from *L'Orient*'s mast, and covered with the shrouding. This was enclosed in a leaden coffin; which was soldered up immediately, and put into another wooden shell: in which manner it was sent out of the *Victory* into Commissioner Grey's yacht, which was hauled alongside for that purpose. In this vessel the revered remains were conveyed to Greenwich Hospital; attended by the Reverend Dr Scott, and Messrs Tyson [Nelson's former secretary] and [Captain John] Whitby.

Lord Nelson had often talked with Captain Hardy on the subject of his being killed in battle, which appeared indeed to be a favourite topic of conversation with him. He was always prepared to lay down his life in the service of his country; and whenever it should please Providence to remove him from this world, it was the most ambitious wish of his soul to die in the fight, and in the very hour of a great and signal victory. In this he was gratified: his end was glorious; and he died as he had lived, one of the greatest among men . . .

His Lordship had on several occasions told Captain Hardy, that if he should fall in battle in a foreign climate, he wished his body to be conveyed to England; and that if his country should think proper to inter him at the public expense, he wished to be buried in St Paul's, as well as that his monument should be erected there. He explained his reasons for preferring St Paul's to Westminster Abbey, which were rather curious: he said that he remembered hearing it stated as an old tradition when he was a boy, that

Westminster Abbey was built on a spot where once existed a deep morass; and he thought it likely that the lapse of time would reduce the ground on which it now stands to its primitive state of a swamp, without leaving a trace of the abbey. He added, that his actual observations confirmed the probability of this event.

As it was, the Home Secretary, Lord Hawkesbury, agreed with Nelson's choice and wrote to the king:

As Westminster Abbey is at this time so very crowded with monuments, and as it was thought proper to lodge the standards taken from your Majesty's enemies in the different naval victories in the last war in St Paul's, your Majesty will perhaps consider that cathedral as the fittest place for this melancholy ceremony, as well for the erection in future of such monuments as it may be determined to raise to the memory of those who have rendered considerable naval or military service to their country.

On 23 December, Nelson's coffin was hoisted aboard the Admiralty yacht. At that moment, his vice-admiral's flag, which had flown at the *Victory*'s foremast, was struck and hoisted again in the Admiralty yacht at half-mast. It was the beginning of the formal obsequies.

The body was taken up-river to Greenwich, where it lay in state for three days in the Painted Hall of the Royal Naval Hospital. The crowds were so huge that the governor of the hospital, Nelson's mentor Admiral Lord Hood, wrote urgently to Lord Hawkesbury:

The mob assembled here is so very numerous that it is absolutely necessary that your Lordship should apply for a very *strong* party of cavalry to line the street on each side from Deptford bridge to the entrance of the hospital . . . or it will not be possible for the procession to move from hence. The mob consisted yesterday of upwards of 30,000 and equally so today and more outrageous. Townsend and the other peace officers say they never saw anything like it before.

On 8 January, Nelson's body was carried up the Thames in the state barge of King Charles II, rowed by men from the *Victory*. It was put ashore at Westminster and brought to the Admiralty where it lay, accompanied by Alexander Scott, the faithful chaplain, in a small room off the entrance hall.

The funeral, at St Paul's Cathedral on 9 January 1806, was magnificent. The streets between Whitehall and the cathedral were lined with troops and the procession – including 160 carriages for mourners – was so long that when the head of it arrived at St Paul's the rear had not left the Admiralty. Nelson's coffin was borne in a black funeral car with a prow and stern like the *Victory*'s and black plumes nodding at the corners of the canopy above. A detachment of seamen from the *Victory* escorted the coffin, some bearing the ship's colours. One of the party wrote home before leaving Chatham, where the ship was berthed:

There is 300 of us pickt to go to Lord Nelson Funral [*sic*]. We are to wear blue jackets and white trowsers and a black scarf round our arms and hats besides gold medal for the Battle of Trafalgar valued £7 round our necks. That I shall take care of until I take it home and show it to you. We scarce have room to move, the ship is so full of nobility coming down from London to see the ship, looking at shot holes.

It was a cold, still morning and the streets were thronged with silent crowds. One of the spectators was Lady Bessborough, who had already said of the public reaction to Nelson's death:

Nothing ever equal'd the consternation this wretched news has given – I never remember anything to equal it. All sides, all parties, unite in one general lamentation; amongst quite the lowest classes the discontent is so great that it was fear'd there would be a riot and troops were sent for three days all round London.

Now, watching the procession, she observed:

I do not in general think that grand ceremonies and pro-cessions are the genius of the English nation, and therefore they usually fail; but in this instance I must say I never saw anything so magnificent or so affecting, and very well manag'd except now and then that fault which pervades everything that is done, high or low, military and civil, in our govt. – I mean delays and not being ready. Amongst many touching things the silence of that immense mob was not the least striking; they had been very noisy. I was in a house in Charing Cross, which look'd over a mass of heads. The moment the car appear'd which bore the body, you might have heard a pin fall, and without any order to do so, they all took off their hats. I cannot tell you the effect this simple action produc'd; it seem'd one general impulse of respect beyond anything that could have been said or contriv'd. Meanwhile the dead march was played in soft tones, and the pauses filled with cannon and the roll of muffled drums.

Nelson's entire family was present, except for his widow, Fanny. Emma Hamilton was absent, too. His elder brother, William, an ambitious clergyman who had reaped the principal harvest of honours, including an earldom and a generous grant and pension, led the family mourners. Amongst the relatives present was Nelson's young nephew, George Matcham, son of his favourite sister, Kate. He wrote in his diary:

Thursday Jan. 9th. Rose at 6. Put on our full dress, and went to Clarges St. Took up the Boltons. Drove to the earl's, where breakfast was laid out. Saw the two sons of Lord Walpole, gentlemanly looking. Were not received at all by the earl, nor introduced to anybody. Put on there the cloaks, etc. About half-past eight the mourning coaches came. Lords Merton and Nelson went in the first, drawn by six horses. My father, Mr Bolton, Tom and myself in the second, and Messrs Barney, Walpole and Fielding (son to the great Fielding) went in the third as relations. Went into St James's Park. Found there a vast number of car-riages, waited for some time. Saw the Duke of York at the head of his troops, a handsome man, but shorter than the rest of the royal family. He talked a good deal to the aides de camp. Saw Mr Naylar as herald, I thought his dress very ridiculous, his garment being covered with armorial bearings, etc. Saw all the captains and admirals much confused, not being able to find their carriages. From hence we moved by slow degrees and about one arrived at the Horse Guards, where the procession was joined by the Prince of Wales, and Duke of Clarence. The body was then put into the car, which represented the stern and prow of the *Victory*. (This description was taken from *The Times*.) The case modelled at the ends in imitation of the hull of the *Victory*, its head towards the horses was ornamented with a figure of Fame, the stern carved and painted in the naval style with the word 'Victory' in yellow raised letters on the lanthorn over the poop. The coffin with its head towards the stern with an English Jack pendant over the poop, and lowered half staff. There was a canopy over the whole supported by pillars in the form of palm trees and partly covered with black velvet richly fringed, immediately above which in the front was inscribed in gold the word NILE at one end, on one side the word TRAFALGAR and on the other side the motto of his arms *Palmam qui meruit ferat*. The car was drawn by six led horses.

When the coffin was brought out of the Admiralty there seemed to be a general silence, and everyone appeared to feel for the death of so noble and such a good man. Poor Mr Scott (with another gentleman) came to our carriage and requested the heralds to let him go in the same coach with us. We were happy to receive him. After he had shaken us all heartily by the hand, he said with tears in his eyes, 'Ah poor fellow! I remained with him as long as I could and then they turned me away.' The procession moved on slowly, the soldiers lining the streets, and the band playing the Dead March in *Saul*. At Temple Bar it was joined by the mayor and suite, who took their place after the Prince of Wales. As it passed the regiments of the Dukes of York and Sussex, they stood still, and ordered that no salute should be made. At St Paul's we got out, and walked in procession up the Passage. It was the most aweful sight I ever saw. All the bands played. The colours were all carried by the sailors and a canopy was held over the coffin, supported by admirals. When we arrived at the choir, the relations were placed at each side of the coffin, on which was the coronet placed on a cushion. The service was read by the Bishop of Lincoln, but he did little justice to the occasion as his tone was monotonous and heavy. The Bishop of Chichester read the first lesson. When the body was conveyed to the dome for interment, the Prince of Wales passed close by us. He was dressed in the Order of the Garter. Next him was the Duke of York, and he was followed by the Duke of Clarence, who shook my father by the hand, saying 'I am come to pay my last duties here, and I hope you and I shall never meet on such a like occasion.' The organ played a dirge meanwhile, the service went on, the body was lowered and the herald declaring the titles of the deceased broke the staves and threw them into the grave. There were 5 dukes, besides the royal family. Mr Fox, Mr Sheridan and Tierney were present. After waiting some time we got to Clarges St and went to Brompton about 8 with Mr Scott.

Another boy watching the procession from the window of a house on Ludgate Hill was the thirteen-year-old Frederick Marryat. Many years later, after a successful career as a naval officer and then as a popular novelist, he remembered: 'As the triumphal car disappeared from my aching eye, I felt that death could have no terrors if followed by such a funeral; and I determined that I would be buried in the same manner.'

A third boy, who was in the cathedral, remembered the moment when the coffin was lowered into the crypt: 'The place of interment was under the centre of the dome and I remember the solemn effect of the sinking of the coffin. I heard, or fancied I heard, the low wail of sailors who bore and encircled the remains of their admiral.'

Unrecognised, except by their dress, were those who had fought at Trafalgar and could briefly be spared from the continuing war at sea. Amongst those escorting the hearse were: Hardy, Pasco and Atkinson of the *Victory*; Blackwood of the *Euryalus*; Harvey of the *Téméraire*; Moorsom of the *Revenge*; Bayntun of the *Leviathan*; Laforey of the *Spartiate*. Carrying the colours of the *Victory* were forty-eight of her seamen. Also present, but recognised by few, were the defeated Admiral Villeneuve and his flag-captain, Magendie, prisoners on parole.

Those captains still at sea waited for letters from home describing the event. Jane Codrington wrote to her husband in the *Orion*:

I am safely returned from our dear Nelson's funeral . . . And now you will expect me to say a word of the awful scene: all the ceremonies and order of the procession, etc., you will see by the papers; and I shall only speak of it with reference to my opinions and feelings. I can fancy nothing but the scene of action you describe, more grand, more awful and more solemn. It was certainly as fine a national spectacle, keeping in mind the hero whose life it closed, as can possibly be seen. But how can I account for its having not had the *great* and powerful effect on my feelings which I expected? I thought, with everyone else, that it would be the most affecting scene; that I should see faintings and swoonings; and that I, who am not practised in those things, should not be far from it. It was magnificent; it was solemn and impressive to the utmost degree; and with every shade of feeling I have for you, your profession, and every dear little member of it, it was a thought most soothing and gratifying that all I saw was in honour of a naval hero; but I was not moved beyond *self-control*. The part that spoke to my heart most powerfully (and that I must acknowledge did touch me deeply) was when the sailors of the *Victory* brought in Nelson's colours; and this I attribute to its being the only thing that was *Nelson* – the rest was so much the HERALD'S OFFICE. I do not mean to find fault with this, because it was a necessary pomp to satisfy the nation; but I mean only to account for not having wept bitterly and severely the whole time. Had it been a *quiet*, private funeral of his revered remains, I am sure I could not have supported it. Expectation and *heart* were also worn out in so many long hours of waiting. Now that it is over and *well* over, I must tell you that my *wish* to be present would not have conquered my other feelings had I not fancied *you* would *like* my having been there, though you could not yourself attend (which I have lamented every moment of this day), and in acquiescence with your desire, 'that our hearts should in every, the most trifling circumstance, beat in unison'. I know with what devotion you would have attended your most admired hero and example . . .

Let us, therefore, not continue to lament a death so fine and well-timed for *himself*; but rather turn with hope and reanimating confidence to our future Nelsons, who, perhaps, want opportunity alone to equal him. Need I say that amongst these my fond enthusiasm sees *you*, my good man, not least worthy of inspiring that dear hope? Heaven grant your career as brilliant as his; and as prolonged and happy, as a grateful wife can wish to the best of husbands.

Nelson's men commemorated him in their own way. Soon after the funeral, one of the seamen who had taken part arrived at the Covent Garden Theatre. As the *Naval Chronicle* reported:

In the pit, at an early part of the evening, a sailor, apparently about thirty years of age, and of a very healthy appearance, with the blunt and honest manner of a real tar, bawled loudly for those aloft (meaning the galleries) *to stow their jabber* (or cease their noise); increasing thereby the confusion which prevailed. Jack, at length, raising himself on one of the seats, exclaimed – '*Messmates aloft – three hearty cheers for Nelson and the Nile!*' – Jack was obeyed; nor were the shouts confined to the galleries only.

Jack, from the attention paid to him, was now inclined to indulge himself further, and producing a medal, to which he fastened a black riband, he gave the audience to understand that 'it was a medal which had been struck to commemorate the Battle of the Nile; and which, as the brave Nelson was no more, and it bore his head, he offered it to their notice (pointing to the black riband) in mourning! Much applause followed; and the medal in mourning was conspicuously waved by the sailor many times during the remainder of the night.

Jack having repeatedly called to the musicians between the acts of the tragedy, for 'Rule, Britannia', without being attended to, at the conclusion of the play forced his way, through all impediments in the pit, to the orchestra, when he again waved his black riband with the medal affixed to it, and insisted upon his favourite tune, and with which he was at this time indulged.

Much applause followed; and Jack, as he twirled round his black riband, lost the medal, which found its way to the stage. A gentleman in one of the boxes beckoned to a performer whom he observed standing against one of the wings at the side of the stage, to take up and bring to him the medal which the sailor had lost, which was accordingly done, and Jack soon after was again in possession of his prize.

The honest sailor then, until the close of the entertainment, continued tranquil; when he suddenly clambered over the orchestra, and succeeded in taking possession of the stage! Shouts, accompanied with much laughter, now predominated in the house, and Jack made several ineffectual attempts to *speechify*. The audience, however, at length become silent, to listen to what he had to say, when he addressed them in the following words: '*Ladies and Gentlemen*, Shall I give you a *handspike* [slang for a hornpipe] or a song?'

A song! a song! was exclaimed by many at the same time in the gallery; but Jack being beckoned to by a performer from the right hand stage-door, he retired before he had performed the vocal part of the task he had voluntarily undertaken to attempt.

Nothing more was heard of the sailor until the final piece, 'Nelson's Glory', was nearly concluded; when Mr Incledon [Charles Incledon, an opera singer] stepped forward to the front of the stage, and spoke the following words: '*Ladies and Gentlemen*, One of the brave crew of the *Victory* begs your permission to appear before you on this occasion, that he may join in the chorus of "Rule, Britannia".'

This extraordinary request was instantly granted, with very loud reiterated applause; when the honest sailor, of whom we have been speaking, again appeared, and, *sans cérémonie*, seized the British flag, which one of the performers supported, and exultingly continued to wave it above the head of Incledon, till the song of 'Rule, Britannia' was concluded.

This made a wonderful impression on the minds of the spectators; and the final curtain at length dropped amidst the loudest plaudits, in which the ladies in the boxes, and, in fact, every individual present most heartily joined.

As Nelson passed from being the maker of news to historical, indeed legendary, giant, his memory was cherished by those who had known him. But it was also exploited in commemoration on an almost industrial scale. The Dean of St Paul's put the marble sarcophagus and the elaborate funeral car on display to paying visitors. The Revd Alexander Scott was horrified and protested, 'Would you believe it? They are showing at St Paul's my poor Lord Nelson for money – I mean his coffin – I would wish everyone to see it – all the world – but not for money. Let the doors of St Paul's be thrown open. What a country ours is! The highest generosity mixed with the lowest degree of meanness.'

The Dean of Westminster Abbey followed suit, showing a life-size waxwork of Nelson to attract visitors. Amongst the first was Lady Hamilton. She, like a theatrical leading lady without her leading man, almost seemed to enjoy the high tragedy. On arrival at the abbey, she asked a verger if she could touch the figure, saying, 'I am sure, when I tell you who I am, you will not refuse me.' 'Oh, madam,' he replied, 'who could refuse you?' and unlocked the glass case. Emma rearranged a lock of hair above the face and it was reported, 'She would have kissed the lips . . . but the guide assured her the colour was not dry.'

Emma held court at her rented town house in Clarges St, where she was visited by the wife of Benjamin Goldsmid, the financier friend from Merton, with their son, Lionel. He was to recall:

I was eight years old and was allowed to accompany my mother and those of the family who made up the party from our house. I was a great favourite of Lady Hamilton's and bathed in tears at times as she talked over his [Nelson's] virtues and exhibited the various gifts he had made her on different occasions. I was on the bed to aid in passing the rings, shawls, bracelets, etc. shown to the company of about 15 persons seated in a semicircle at the foot of the bed – and as she thought perhaps at moments of her truly lamented hero and friend, I came in for numerous kisses and her usual remark – thank you my funny boy – or child you must come every day. The very coat in which the dear old admiral was dressed in the fatal battle and received his death wound was on the outside of the bed – the hole where the bullet passed through stiffened with congealed blood. There was most certainly a very serio-comic performance throughout the visit.

There was immediate talk of a memorial to Nelson's memory. Collingwood had suggested the idea to his captains and it was eagerly taken up by Captain Codrington. Only three weeks after the battle, the log of the *Orion* recorded:

The officers and ship's company being assembled, the captain read the proposal of the admiral to them that two thousand pounds* should be deducted from the prize-money for the action on the 21st October, 1805, for the purpose of erecting a monument on Portsdown Hill [behind Portsmouth] to the memory of Lord Nelson, the late commander-in-chief, which the officers and ship's company all agreed to, and as much more if required.

On the return of the *Victory* to Chatham, she was sketched by several artists, amongst them J. M. W. Turner, who was planning an epic painting of the battle. Nelson had once suggested to the American painter Benjamin West that he might one day paint him in a picture echoing his *Death of Wolfe*. West now did so; young Thomas Goble, who had taken the place of Nelson's secretary when John Scott had been killed, and had been beside the admiral when he was hit, was sent by the Admiralty to West's studio as adviser.

Arrangements for the exchange of prisoners began quickly. Admiral Villeneuve was living on parole near Sonning in Berk-

* Here, in Codrington's writing, is inserted, 'The people thought it too little.'

shire as a guest in the country house of Viscount Sidmouth, who, as Henry Addington, had been the Prime Minister responsible for the interlude of the Peace of Amiens. The admiral enjoyed considerable freedom and entertained visitors, including the current Prime Minister, William Pitt, who was himself to die a fortnight after Nelson's funeral. In April 1806, Villeneuve was returned to France and, on the 22nd, while on the way to his home in the south, was found dead in a hotel at Rennes with six knife wounds in his chest. It was announced that he had committed suicide because – as a letter claimed to have been found near the body said – he had 'reached the point where life is a source of shame and death a duty'. But such were the circumstances that political murder was, and remains, suspected.

Two of Villeneuve's captains, Jean-Jacques Lucas of the *Redoutable* and Louis Antoine Infernet of the *Intrépide*, were also exchanged. They were hailed as heroes and received by the Emperor Napoleon. It was reported in the *Naval Chronicle* [6 May],

At the audience which took place yesterday at St Cloud, Captains Lucas and l'Infernet, who have lately arrived from England, were presented to his Majesty. Captain Lucas commanded the *Redoutable*, in the Battle of Trafalgar, and conducted himself in the most gallant manner; he attempted to board the *Victory*, Lord Nelson's ship. Captain Infernet also behaved in the bravest manner. After an unfortunate affair, it is gratifying to acknowledge such conduct. His Majesty said to the captains, Lucas and Infernet, 'If all my vessels had conducted themselves as well as those which you commanded, the victory would have been ours. I know that there are several who have not imitated your example, but I have ordered their conduct to be investigated. I have appointed you Commanders of the Legion of Honour. The captains of the vessels who, instead of boarding the enemy, kept out of cannon-shot, shall be prosecuted, and, if convicted, made a dreadful example of.'

That the Battle of Trafalgar had given Britain command of the sea, however many more battleships Napoleon might build,

soon became clear. Shortly before Christmas 1805, Collingwood, still on board his flagship, had written in a letter to his
wife: 'There are neither French, nor Spaniards, on the sea and
our cruisers find nothing but neutrals, who carry on all the trade
of the enemy . . . Was there ever so complete a break-up of an
enemy's fleet?'

Biographical Notes

Detailing the subsequent careers of
selected survivors of Trafalgar

BEATTY, WILLIAM (d. 1842), Lord Nelson's surgeon at Trafalgar, was appointed physician to the Greenwich Hospital for naval pensioners in 1806 and remained there until 1840. He obtained a medical degree from the University of St Andrews in 1817, in the following year was elected a fellow of the Royal Society and, in 1831, was knighted by King William IV, who had also been a friend of Nelson's.

BERRY, CAPTAIN SIR EDWARD (1768–1831), one of Nelson's original 'Band of Brothers' at the Battle of the Nile, commanded the *Agamemnon* at Trafalgar and then took his ship to the West Indies, where he fought in the action off St Domingo. In 1806 he was made a baronet but remained a captain and served in the Mediterranean before taking command of a royal yacht in 1813 until the end of war with France. He was finally promoted rear-admiral in 1821 but never again served at sea.

BLACKWOOD, CAPTAIN HENRY (1770–1832), captain of the frigate *Euryalus* at Trafalgar, was afterwards given command of the 80-gun *Ajax* and joined Admiral Collingwood in the Mediterranean. While taking part in Admiral Duckworth's abortive expedition against Constantinople in 1807, his ship was destroyed by fire, although he himself was rescued. He then commanded the *Warspite* of 74 guns and again served in the Mediterranean, where he commanded the inshore squadron. In 1814 he was appointed captain of the fleet and was then promoted rear-admiral and, in recognition of ceremonial duties at the visit of the allied sovereigns in that year, granted a baronetcy. In 1819 he was appointed KCB and made commander-in-chief in the East Indies, where he remained for three years. In 1825, he was promoted vice-admiral and, two years later, made commander-in-chief at the Nore. In 1832, he died suddenly in Scotland, having been married three times and leaving a large family.

CALDER, VICE-ADMIRAL SIR ROBERT (1745–1818), who fought the inconclusive action with Villeneuve before Trafalgar, was granted the court martial he wanted to clear his name. However, when this was convened in December 1805, it found him guilty of an error of judgement and he was severely reprimanded. This ended his active career, although he rose by automatic promotion to full admiral in 1810 and was made KCB in 1815. He was married but had no children.

CODRINGTON, CAPTAIN EDWARD (1770–1851), captain of the *Orion* at Trafalgar, took part in the ill-fated Walcheren landings and campaign of 1809 and served off the coast of Spain in the Peninsular War, then in the Mediterranean from 1810 to 1813. In the War of 1812, he was involved in operations leading to the burning of Washington in 1814 and the Battle of New Orleans early in the following year. He ended the Napoleonic wars as a rear-admiral with a knighthood.

In 1827, he was appointed commander-in-chief in the Mediterranean at the time Greece was struggling for independence from the Ottoman Empire. In October that year, he commanded a British, French and Russian 'peace-keeping' force with orders to deter the Ottoman fleet from attacking the Greek mainland. He was to avoid conflict and fire only in self-defence. However, he blockaded the main Ottoman fleet in Navarino Bay and, in his efforts to persuade the Turkish admiral to return to Constantinople and Alexandria, took his own fleet into the anchorage. They were fired upon – possibly by accident – and Codrington immediately returned fire. In a few hours the Ottoman fleet was destroyed. He was recalled to London and blamed for 'this untoward incident'. Having expected honours and rewards, he was hurt and angry at this reaction to what he saw as a great victory, in what proved to be the last fleet engagement fought under sail. He demanded an inquiry. Cleared of blame, he was appointed to command the Channel squadron from 1839 to 1842. His final appointment was as commander-in-chief at Plymouth. His son became an admiral.

COLLINGWOOD, VICE-ADMIRAL SIR CUTHBERT (1748–1810) succeeded Nelson as commander-in-chief in the Mediterranean until his death five years later. He was raised to the peerage but was never able to return home to see his beloved wife and two daughters. His command stretched from the Atlantic coast of Spain, which became of vital importance when the Peninsular War began in 1808, to the Dardanelles and the Levant.

After Trafalgar, the British suspected that Napoleon, realising he could never invade the British Isles, might again turn his attention eastward and, by political or military means, attempt to take over the ramshackle Ottoman Empire, which could be reached overland. The main British strategic effort was then deployed in the Mediterranean, with the principal base in Sicily. Collingwood's role thereafter became almost as much diplomatic as naval and he had to deal with the difficult and unreliable King Ferdinand and Queen Maria Carolina of the Two Sicilies. He also had to contend with adversaries in Napoleon's own family: his brother Joseph, king first of Naples and then of Spain, and his brother-in-law Joachim – formerly Marshal Murat – who succeeded Joseph as king in Naples.

Admiral Collingwood was regarded as the wisest statesman in the theatre and his decisions were never questioned. He fought his last action – a deft but minor affair – four years after Trafalgar off the north-east coast of Spain. He died at sea, probably from stomach cancer, on 6 March 1810, and was buried close to Nelson in St Paul's Cathedral.

DUMANOIR LE PELLEY, REAR-ADMIRAL PIERRE-ETIENNE (1770–1829) was intercepted and captured by Admiral Strachan after Trafalgar, and was, like the British Admiral Calder, suspected of failing to carry out orders. However, he was 'acquitted with honour' by an inquiry at Toulon in 1809 and returned to duty. In 1811, he was senior naval officer at Danzig on the Baltic and, when it was besieged by the Prussians, was wounded in the head. In 1814, he supported the Bourbons on the fall of Napoleon and was made a Chevalier of the Order of St Louis and a count. In 1815, at the time of the return of Napoleon, he was escorting a new French ambassador to Constantinople. He was promoted vice-admiral in 1819. He became a deputy for La Manche and died in Paris.

FREMANTLE, CAPTAIN THOMAS (1765–1819), who had fought with Nelson at Tenerife and commanded the *Neptune* at Trafalgar, was promoted rear-admiral in 1810 and sent to the Mediterranean. From 1812, he commanded in the Adriatic, capturing Fiume (Rijeka) and Trieste, and was knighted in 1815. He was appointed commander-in-chief in the Mediterranean in 1818, and died at Naples a year later. He was married to Betsey Wynne, author of the celebrated *Wynne Diaries*.

GRAVINA, VICE-ADMIRAL DON FREDERICO (d. 1806), senior Spanish officer at Trafalgar, was severely wounded and landed at Cadiz after the battle. He refused to have an arm amputated, gangrene set in, and before he died a few weeks later he was said to have declared, 'I die happy. I am going, I hope, to join Nelson.' Regarded as a national hero by his countrymen, his body was first interred at the Panteón Nacional in Madrid and then in the Panteón de Marinos Ilustres near Cadiz.

HARDY, CAPTAIN THOMAS (1769–1839), Nelson's flag-captain at Trafalgar, was created a baronet after the battle. However, his promotion was slow and it was not until 1819 that, as only a commodore, he was appointed commander-in-chief of the South America station at a time when the Spanish colonies were struggling for independence. He was promoted rear-admiral at the age of fifty-six in 1825, and five years later became First Sea Lord. In 1834, he was made governor of Greenwich Hospital for naval pensioners and, when he died five years later, was buried there.

HARGOOD, CAPTAIN WILLIAM (1762–1839), who commanded the battered *Belleisle* at Trafalgar, then took his ship to the West Indies and to American waters in the following year. On 14 September 1806, he intercepted the French 74 *Impétueux* off Chesapeake Bay, drove her ashore and burned her, the United States overlooking this breach of their neutrality. In 1808, he served off the coast of Portugal and Spain during the Peninsular War, and in the Adriatic. His friendship with his former shipmate, the Duke of Clarence (later King William IV), stood him in good stead: promoted rear-admiral in 1810 and vice-admiral in 1814, he was knighted in 1815. He was commander-in-chief at Plymouth from 1833 to 1836. He died at Bath three years later.

HARVEY, CAPTAIN ELIAB (1758–1830), who commanded the *Téméraire* at Trafalgar, was promoted rear-admiral in the same year. In 1809, he served under Admiral Lord Gambier in the partly unsuccessful battle in the Basque Roads; in the subsequent row over the conduct of the action in the House of Commons, instituted by Captain Lord Cochrane, he took the admiral's part. Indeed, so furiously did he denounce Cochrane that he was court-martialled and dismissed the service, although reinstated the following year. He was never actively employed again, although he rose automatically to full admiral in 1819 and was knighted.

INFERNET, CAPTAIN LOUIS ANTOINE (1756–1815), who was from Provençal peasant stock and went to sea as a cabin-boy, commanded the *Achille* with distinction at Trafalgar and was taken prisoner. Repatriated under an exchange in 1806, he was received as a hero by the Emperor Napoleon and awarded the Légion d'honneur. He was posted to Toulon and remained there until 1814. On the restoration of the monarchy, he was made a Chevalier of the Order of St Louis. He died at Toulon in 1815.

LUCAS, CAPTAIN JEAN-JACQUES (1764–1825), captain of the *Redoutable* at Trafalgar, was taken prisoner but exchanged for a British officer and repatriated in 1806. Received by the Emperor Napoleon, he was awarded the Légion d'honneur. In 1809, he commanded the *Regulus*, 74 guns, in the Basque Roads when the anchorage was attacked by the British. Although Admiral Gambier remained at a distance and hardly affected the outcome, Captain Lord Cochrane attacked at night with fireships. The *Regulus* fouled another ship and ran aground but, after her guns were jettisoned, she was refloated and took refuge in Rochefort. In 1810, Lucas commanded another 74, the *Nestor*, and in 1815 was promoted rear-admiral. He died at Brest ten years later.

SCOTT, ALEXANDER (1768–1840), chaplain of the *Victory* and Nelson's interpreter and intelligence adviser, received no official recognition after Trafalgar but was awarded a Doctorate of Divinity by Cambridge University. He became vicar of Southminster, Essex, then, in 1816, of Catterick, Yorkshire, where he collected a large library of foreign books. He also became chaplain to the Prince Regent. Scott married in 1807 and had two daughters.

SMITH, REAR-ADMIRAL SIR SIDNEY (1764–1840) did not arrive off Cadiz in time to pre-empt the battle with his rockets and torpedoes, but later joined Admiral Collingwood to command his inshore forces. Moved to the Mediterranean, he was seen as a reincarnation of Nelson by Queen Maria Carolina of the Two Sicilies and promised to help her regain southern Italy and

Naples. Sometimes disregarding official British policy, he carried out operations along the Italian coast, relieving the fortress of Gaeta, capturing Capri and, obeying orders, supporting the landing that led to the victory of Maida in 1806. The following year he took part in Admiral Duckworth's futile attempt to force the Ottoman sultan to reject French overtures and favour the British. In 1808, he rescued the Portuguese royal family from Lisbon before it was captured by the French and took them to Brazil. Returning to the Mediterranean, he became second-in-command to the commander-in-chief, Vice-Admiral Sir Edward Pellew. After the fall of Napoleon and his exile to Elba, Smith attended the Congress of Vienna without invitation. There he founded the Knights Liberators and Anti-Piratical Society with the aim of freeing Christian slaves held in North Africa, which led to the British attacks on Algiers in 1816 and 1824. In 1840, he died in Paris, where he was popular amongst his royalist and naval friends. He was buried in the cemetery of Père Lachaise.

SPRATT, MIDSHIPMAN JAMES (JACK) (b.1771), who was badly wounded when boarding *L'Aigle* from the *Defiance*, was promoted lieutenant but was, because of his injury, given command of the signal station at Teignmouth in Devon. There he invented the 'Homeograph' system of signalling by handkerchief, which he believed inspired the semaphore method. By 1813, he had recovered sufficiently to be appointed to the 74 *Albion*, and served in the North Atlantic. However, severe winter weather so badly affected his leg that he was invalided home and given command of the prison ship *Ganges* at Plymouth. Granted a pension in 1817, he was promoted commander in 1838. Retiring to Teignmouth, he had raised a family of nine children, two of his sons following him to sea. He is recorded in 1849 as being in robust old age.

VILLENEUVE, ADMIRAL (PIERRE) COMTE DE (1763–1806), commander-in-chief of the combined French and Spanish fleets at Trafalgar, was taken prisoner and landed in England on 29 November 1805. He joined other senior French officers held on parole near Reading under easy conditions, which allowed him social visits to London and to attend Nelson's funeral. He was released in April 1806, in exchange for four British captains and was put ashore at Morlaix in Brittany. He at once wrote to the Minister of Marine, Admiral Decrès, for instructions, saying that he would await his reply at his hotel in Rennes. He suggested that, before joining his family in Provence, he stop at Paris to present his own account of the battle to the emperor in person. He planned to demand a full inquiry into Trafalgar and to call Captain Lucas of the *Redoutable* as a witness. No reply from Decrès had arrived by 21 April, and next morning Villeneuve was found dead on his bed, a knife still in his heart. An apparent letter of farewell to his wife was found in the room and it was announced that he had committed suicide. Doubts about this were expressed at the time and have persisted. Assassination has long been suspected, particularly since his death followed the pattern of those of the royalist General Pichegru and the British naval intelligence officer Captain John Wright, in a Paris prison. The mystery has never been solved.

Bibliography

ORIGINAL MANUSCRIPT SOURCES

Harvard University Archives, USA: Hewson Papers.
Monmouth Museum, Gwent: Nelson MSS Collection.
National Maritime Museum, Greenwich, Documents Depart-
    ment: including AGC/C/7; AGC/M/9; M580/201; MS
    77/163; JON/7/44; MS 9850; M580/201; NA1/3/20.
Royal Naval Museum, Portsmouth, Documents Department:
    RNM MISC. 1994/128; 92/133.

PRINTED SOURCES

Adkins, Roy. *Trafalgar: The Biography of a Battle*, London,
    2004.
Bevan, A. Beckford and H. B. Wolryche-Whitmore (eds). *A
    Sailor of King George: The Journals of Captain Frederick
    Hoffman, R.N., 1793–1814*, London, 1901.
Blackwood, Sir Henry. *Nelson's Watchdog: The Life of Sir
    Henry Blackwood*, The 1805 Club, London, 1998.
Bourchier, Lady Jane (ed.). *Memoir of the Life of Sir Edward
    Codrington*, London, 1873.
Broadley, A. M. and R. G. Bartelot. *The Three Dorset Captains
    of Trafalgar*, London, 1906.
Browne, G. Latham. *The Public and Private Life of Horatio Vis-
    count Nelson*, London, 1891.
Clarke, James Stanier and John McArthur. *The Life and Ser-
    vices of Horatio Viscount Nelson* (2 vols), London, 1809.
Clowes, William Laird. *The Royal Navy: A History* (7 vols),
    London, 1900.
Coleman, Terry. *Nelson*, London, 2001.
Collingwood, G. L. Newnham. *The Public and Private Corre-
    spondence of Vice-Admiral Lord Collingwood*, London, 1828.
Corbett, Sir Julian S. *The Campaign of Trafalgar*, London, 1910.
Czisnik, Marianne. *Admiral Nelson's Tactics at the Battle of
    Trafalgar* (thesis, as yet unpublished), Edinburgh University,
    2004.
Desbrière, Edouard, trans. Constance Eastwick. *Trafalgar: The*

Naval Campaign of 1805 (2 vols), Oxford, 1933.

Fenwick, Kenneth. *H.M.S. Victory*, London, 1959.

Fraser, Edward. *The Enemy at Trafalgar*, London, 1906.

——. *The Sailors Whom Nelson Led*, London, 1913.

Fremantle, Anne (ed.). *The Wynne Diaries* (3 vols), London, 1935–40.

Gardiner, Robert (ed.). *The Campaign of Trafalgar, 1803–1805*, London, 1997.

Hargood, Lady and Joseph Allen (eds). *Memoirs of the Life and Services of Admiral Sir William Hargood*, London, 1846.

Hewitt, James (ed.). *Eyewitnesses to Nelson's Battles*, Reading, 1972.

Hibbert, Christopher. *Nelson: A Personal History*, London, 1994.

Hughes, Edward (ed.). *The Private Correspondence of Admiral Lord Collingwood*, London, 1957.

Huskisson, Thomas. *Eyewitness to Trafalgar*, Royston, 1985.

Jackson, T. Sturges (ed.). *Logs of the Great Sea Fights* (2 vols), London, 1900.

James, William. *The Naval History of Great Britain* (5 vols), London, 1822–4.

Keegan, John. *The Price of Admiralty*, London, 1988.

King, Dean and John B. Hattendorf (eds). *Every Man Will Do His Duty: An Anthology of First-Hand Accounts from the Age of Nelson*, London, 1997.

Lambert, Andrew. *Nelson: Britannia's God of War*, London, 2004.

Lavery, Brian. *Nelson's Fleet at Trafalgar*, London, 2004.

Legg, Stuart (ed.). *Trafalgar: An Eyewitness Account of a Great Battle*, New York, 1966.

Lewis, M. A. (ed.). *W. H. Dillon: A Narrative of My Professional Adventures* (2 vols), London, 1956.

Mackenzie, R. H. *The Trafalgar Roll: The Ships and the Officers*, London, 1913.

Macmillan's Magazine, vol. 81, 1900.

Mariner's Mirror, The, vol. 65, 1979.

Matcham, M. Eyre. *The Nelsons of Burnham Thorpe*, London, 1911.

Minto, Countess of (ed.). *The Life and Letters of Sir Gilbert Elliot, First Earl of Minto* (3 vols), London, 1874.

Murray, Captain A. *Memoirs of the Life and Services of Admiral Sir Philip C. H. C. Durham, G.C.B.*, London, 1846.

Naval Chronicle, The, 1803–6.

Nelson Dispatch, The, The Nelson Society, 1982–2003: vol. 1, pt. 4; vol. 5, pts 4, 6 and 8; vol. 6, pts 5 and 9; vol. 7, pts 4, 8, 9 and 12; vol. 8, pt 1.

Nelsoniana, The Nelson Society, Bedford, 1999.

Nicolas, Sir Harris. *The Dispatches and Letters of Vice-Admiral Lord Viscount Nelson* (7 vols), London, 1844–6.

Padfield, Peter. *Nelson's War,* London, 1976.

Pettigrew, Thomas. *Memoirs of the Life of Vice-Admiral Lord Viscount Nelson,* London, 1849.

Pocock, Tom. *Horatio Nelson,* London, 1987.

———. *The Terror Before Trafalgar,* London, 2001.

Pope, Dudley. *England Expects,* London, 1959.

———. *Life in Nelson's Navy,* London, 1981.

Proceedings of the Carmarthenshire Antiquarian Society, vol. 1, 1905.

Terraine, John and John Westwood. *Trafalgar,* London, 1976.

Thursfield, H. G. *Five Naval Journals, 1789–1817,* London, 1951.

Thursfield, J. R. *Nelson and Other Naval Studies,* London, 1909.

Trafalgar Chronicle, The, 1999–2000, The 1805 Club, London.

Vincent, Edgar. *Nelson: Love and Fame,* London, 2003.

Warner, Oliver. *Trafalgar,* London, 1959.

Wyndham-Quin, W. H. *Sir Charles Tyler, G.C.B., Admiral of the White,* London, 1912.

Index

PENGUIN ONLINE

read about your favourite authors

•

investigate over 12,000 titles

•

browse our online magazine

•

enter one of our literary quizzes

•

win some fantastic prizes in our competitions

•

e-mail us with your comments and book reviews

•

instantly order any Penguin book

'To be recommended without reservation ... a rich and rewarding online experience' *Internet Magazine*

www.penguin.com

READ MORE IN PENGUIN

In every corner of the world, on every subject under the sun, Penguin represents quality and variety – the very best in publishing today.

For complete information about books available from Penguin – including Puffins, Penguin Classics and Arkana – and how to order them, write to us at the appropriate address below. Please note that for copyright reasons the selection of books varies from country to country.

In the United Kingdom: Please write to *Dept. EP, Penguin Books Ltd, Bath Road, Harmondsworth, West Drayton, Middlesex UB7 0DA*

In the United States: Please write to *Consumer Services, Penguin Putnam Inc., 405 Murray Hill Parkway, East Rutherford, New Jersey 07073-2136.* VISA and MasterCard holders call 1-800-631-8571 to order Penguin titles

In Canada: Please write to *Penguin Books Canada Ltd, 10 Alcorn Avenue, Suite 300, Toronto, Ontario M4V 3B2*

In Australia: Please write to *Penguin Books Australia Ltd, 487 Maroondah Highway, Ringwood, Victoria 3134*

In New Zealand: Please write to *Penguin Books (NZ) Ltd, Private Bag 102902, North Shore Mail Centre, Auckland 10*

In India: Please write to *Penguin Books India Pvt Ltd, 11 Community Centre, Panchsheel Park, New Delhi 110017*

In the Netherlands: Please write to *Penguin Books Netherlands bv, Postbus 3507, NL-1001 AH Amsterdam*

In Germany: Please write to *Penguin Books Deutschland GmbH, Metzlerstrasse 26, 60594 Frankfurt am Main*

In Spain: Please write to *Penguin Books S. A., Bravo Murillo 19, 1°B, 28015 Madrid*

In Italy: Please write to *Penguin Italia s.r.l., Via Vittorio Emanuele 45/a, 20094 Corsico, Milano*

In France: Please write to *Penguin France, 12, Rue Prosper Ferradou, 31700 Blagnac*

In Japan: Please write to *Penguin Books Japan Ltd, Iidabashi KM-Bldg, 2-23-9 Koraku, Bunkyo-Ku, Tokyo 112-0004*

In South Africa: Please write to *Penguin Books South Africa (Pty) Ltd, P.O. Box 751093, Gardenview, 2047 Johannesburg*

Penguin Classics

THE GATHERING STORM
WINSTON CHURCHILL

THE SECOND WORLD WAR VOLUME I

'The sinister news broke upon the world like an explosion ... Nothing could now avert or delay the conflict'

Winston Churchill's six-volume history of the cataclysm that swept the world remains the definitive history of the Second World War. Lucid, dramatic, remarkable both for its breadth and sweep and for its sense of personal involvement, it is universally acknowledged as a magnificent reconstruction and is an enduring, compelling work that led to his being awarded the Nobel Prize for Literature. *The Gathering Storm* vividly describes the steps that led to War, a period that ended with Churchill as Prime Minister: the aftermath of the First World War, the rise of Adolf Hitler, British attempts at appeasement and the eventual outbreak of conflict on a global scale for the second time in thirty years.

In his introduction, John Keegan discusses Churchill's historical methods and the extraordinary achievement of *The Second World War*. This volume also includes appendices, an index, maps and diagrams.

'This is a story told while the sweat and shock of mortal combat are still upon the teller' *Evening Standard*

PENGUIN CLASSICS

THEIR FINEST HOUR
WINSTON CHURCHILL

THE SECOND WORLD WAR VOLUME II

'After the collapse of France the question which arose in the minds of all our friends and foes was: "Will Britain surrender too?"'

Winston Churchill's six-volume history of the cataclysm that swept the world remains the definitive history of the Second World War. Lucid, dramatic, remarkable both for its breadth and sweep and for its sense of personal involvement, it is universally acknowledged as a magnificent reconstruction and is an enduring, compelling work that led to his being awarded the Nobel Prize for Literature. *Their Finest Hour* enthrallingly recounts key events and battles from May to December 1940 as Britain stood isolated while Nazi Germany pursued its seemingly unconquerable war path: the fall of France, Dunkirk and the Battle of Britain, the horrors of the Blitz and Hitler's plans to invade and crush Russia, his sole ally in Europe.

In his introduction, John Keegan discusses Churchill's historical methods and the extraordinary achievement of *The Second World War*. This volume also includes appendices, an index, maps and diagrams.

'This astonishing document ranks among the great classics of history'
C. V. Wedgwood

PENGUIN CLASSICS

THE GRAND ALLIANCE
WINSTON CHURCHILL

THE SECOND WORLD WAR VOLUME II

'Madness is however an affliction which in war carries with it the advantage of SURPRISE'

Winston Churchill's six-volume history of the cataclysm that swept the world remains the definitive history of the Second World War. Lucid, dramatic, remarkable both for its breadth and sweep and for its sense of personal involvement, it is universally acknowledged as a magnificent reconstruction and is an enduring, compelling work that led to his being awarded the Nobel Prize for Literature. *The Grand Alliance* recounts the momentous events of 1941 surrounding America's entry into the War and Hitler's march on Russia: the continuing onslaught on British civilians during the Blitz, Japan's attack on Pearl Harbor and the alliance between Britain and America that shaped the outcome of the War.

In his introduction, John Keegan discusses Churchill's historical methods and the extraordinary achievement of *The Second World War*. This volume also includes appendices, an index, maps and diagrams.

'The events would have made the narrative great even if the writer had not had Churchill's gift of style' *The Times Literary Supplement*

PENGUIN CLASSICS

THE HINGE OF FATE
WINSTON CHURCHILL

THE SECOND WORLD WAR VOLUME IV

'Soon Great Britain and the United States would have the mastery of the oceans and the air. The hinge had turned'

Winston Churchill's six-volume history of the cataclysm that swept the world remains the definitive history of the Second World War. Lucid, dramatic, remarkable both for its breadth and sweep and for its sense of personal involvement, it is universally acknowledged as a magnificent reconstruction and is an enduring, compelling work that led to his being awarded the Nobel Prize for Literature. *The Hinge of Fate* describes how the tide of the war gradually turned for Britain and its allies from constant defeat to almost unbroken successes: Japan's successful assault on the Pacific, Britain's attempts to aid a beleaguered Russia and the defeat of Rommel at the Battle of Alamein.

In his introduction, John Keegan discusses Churchill's historical methods and the extraordinary achievement of *The Second World War*. This volume also includes appendices, an index, maps and diagrams.

'A masterly piece of historical writing ... complete with humour and wit'
New Yorker

PENGUIN CLASSICS

CLOSING THE RING
WINSTON CHURCHILL

THE SECOND WORLD WAR VOLUME V

'This fearful battle of the air, the like of which had never before been known, or even with any precision imagined'

Winston Churchill's six-volume history of the cataclysm that swept the world remains the definitive history of the Second World War. Lucid, dramatic, remarkable both for its breadth and sweep and for its sense of personal involvement, it is universally acknowledged as a magnificent reconstruction and is an enduring, compelling work that led to his being awarded the Nobel Prize for Literature. *Closing the Ring* chronicles the period between June 1943 and July 1944 as the Allies consolidated their gains towards a drive to victory: the fall of Mussolini, Hitler's 'secret weapon', the mounting air offensive on Germany, strategies to defeat Japan and the plans for D Day.

In his introduction, John Keegan discusses Churchill's historical methods and the extraordinary achievement of *The Second World War*. This volume also includes appendices, an index, maps and diagrams.

'Not since Julius Caesar has a principal actor in a great conflict also been its most influential chronicler' Andrew Roberts, *Evening Standard*

PENGUIN CLASSICS

TRIUMPH AND TRAGEDY
WINSTON CHURCHILL

THE SECOND WORLD WAR VOLUME VI

'Hitler made his final and supreme decision to stay in Berlin to the end … It remained for him to organise his own death amid the ruins'

Winston Churchill's six-volume history of the cataclysm that swept the world remains the definitive history of the Second World War. Lucid, dramatic, remarkable both for its breadth and sweep and for its sense of personal involvement, it is universally acknowledged as a magnificent reconstruction and is an enduring, compelling work that led to his being awarded the Nobel Prize for Literature. *Triumph and Tragedy* recounts the dramatic months as the War drew to a close: the Normandy landings, the liberation of Western Europe, the bombing of Hiroshima and Nagasaki, and the surrender of Germany and Japan.

In his introduction, John Keegan discusses Churchill's historical methods and the extraordinary achievement of *The Second World War*. This volume also includes appendices, an index, maps and diagrams.

'It is our immense good fortune that a man who presided over this crisis in history is able to turn the action he lived through into enduring literature'
The New York Times

PENGUIN CLASSICS

ON WAR CARL VON CLAUSEWITZ

'War is an act of violence intended to compel our opponent to our will'

Writing at the time of Napoleon's greatest campaigns, Prussian soldier and writer Carl von Clausewitz created this landmark treatise on the art of warfare, which presented war as part of a coherent system of political thought. In line with Napoleon's own military actions, Clausewitz illustrated the need to annihilate the enemy and to make a strong display of one's power in an 'absolute war' without compromise. But he was also careful to distinguish between war and politics, arguing that war could only be justified when debate was no longer adequate, and that, if undertaken, its aim should ultimately be to improve the wellbeing of the nation. Combining military theory and pratice, *On War* has had a profound influence on subsequent thinking on warfare.

This edition contains a detailed introduction examining Von Clausewitz's skill and reputation as a writer, philosopher and political thinker, as well as bibliography, notes and a glossary.

Edited with an introduction by Anatol Rapoport

PENGUIN CLASSICS

THE BOOK OF THE COURTIER
BALDESAR CASTIGLIONE

'The courtier has to imbue with grace his movements, his gestures, his way of doing things and in short, his every action'

In *The Book of the Courtier* (1528), Baldesar Castiglione, a diplomat and Papal Nuncio to Rome, sets out to define the essential virtues for those at Court. In a lively series of imaginary conversations between the real-life courtiers to the Duke of Urbino, his speakers discuss qualities of noble behaviour – chiefly discretion, decorum, nonchalance and gracefulness – as well as wider questions such as the duties of a good government and the true nature of love. Castiglione's narrative power and psychological perception make this guide both an entertaining comedy of manners and a revealing window onto the ideals and preoccupations of the Italian Renaissance at the moment of its greatest splendour.

George Bull's elegant translation captures the variety of tone in Castiglione's speakers, from comic interjections to elevated rhetoric. This edition includes an introduction examining Castiglione's career in the courts of Urbino and Mantua, a list of the historical characters he portrays and further reading.

Translated and with an introduction by George Bull

PENGUIN CLASSICS

THE CAMPAIGNS OF ALEXANDER   ARRIAN

'His passion was for glory only, and in that he was insatiable'

Although written over four hundred years after Alexander's death, Arrian's *Campaigns of Alexander* is the most reliable account of the man and his achievements we have. Arrian's own experience as a military commander gave him unique insights into the life of the world's greatest conqueror. He tells of Alexander's violent suppression of the Theban rebellion, his total defeat of Persia, and his campaigns through Egypt, India and Babylon – establishing new cities and destroying others in his path. While Alexander emerges from this record as an unparalleled and charismatic leader, Arrian succeeds brilliantly in creating an objective and fully rounded portrait of a man of boundless ambition, who was exposed to the temptations of power and worshipped as a god in his own lifetime.

Aubrey de Sélincourt's vivid translation is accompanied by J. R. Hamilton's introduction, which discusses Arrian's life and times, his synthesis of other classical sources and the composition of Alexander's army. The edition also includes maps, a list for further reading and a detailed index.

Translated by Aubrey de Sélincourt
Revised, with a new introduction and notes by J. R. Hamilton

PENGUIN CLASSICS

THE STORM
DANIEL DEFOE

'Horror and Confusion seiz'd upon all ... No Pen can describe it, no Tongue can express it, no Thought conceive it'

On the evening of 26 November 1703, a hurricane from the north Atlantic hammered into Britain: it remains the worst storm the nation has ever experienced. Eyewitnesses saw cows thrown into trees and windmills ablaze from the friction of their whirling sails – and some 8,000 people lost their lives. For Defoe, bankrupt and just released from prison for his 'seditious' writings, the storm struck during one of his bleakest moments. But it also furnished him with material for his first book, and in this powerful depiction of suffering and survival played out against a backdrop of natural devastation, we can trace the outlines of Defoe's later masterpieces, *A Journal of the Plague Year* and *Robinson Crusoe*.

This new Penguin Classics edition marks the 300th anniversary of the first publication of The Storm. It also includes two other pieces by Defoe inspired by that momentous night, an introduction, chronology, further reading, notes and maps.

'Astonishing ... a masterpiece of reportage' Sunday Telegraph

Edited with an introduction by Richard Hamblyn